TERRITORIES OF HISTORY

Romance Studies

TERRITORIES OF HISTORY

Humanism, Rhetoric, and the Historical Imagination in the Early Chronicles of Spanish America

SARAH H. BECKJORD

THE PENNSYLVANIA STATE UNIVERSITY PRESS
UNIVERSITY PARK, PENNSYLVANIA

Publication of this book has been supported by a grant from
The Spanish Ministry of Culture.

LIBRARY OF CONGRESS
CATALOGING-IN-PUBLICATION DATA

Beckjord, Sarah H.
Territories of history : humanism, rhetoric, and the historical imagination in the early
chronicles of Spanish America / Sarah H. Beckjord.
p.   cm. – (Penn State Studies in Romance Literatures)
Includes bibliographical references and index.
ISBN 978-0-271-03278-8 (cloth . alk. paper)
ISBN 978-0-271-03279-5 (pbk. : alk. paper)
1. Latin America—History—To 1600—Historiography.
2. Humanism—Latin America—History.
3. Humanism—Spain—History.
4. History in literature.
5. Narration (Rhetoric).
I. Title.
II. Series.

F1411.B43 2007
980—dc22
2007022491

This book can be viewed at
http://publications.libraries.psu.edu/eresources/978-0-271-03278-8

For Álvaro, Tomás, and Lucas

CONTENTS

ACKNOWLEDGMENTS

This project has benefited from the generosity of a number of individuals and institutions. I am grateful to the Department of Spanish and Portuguese and the Graduate School of Arts and Sciences at Columbia University for the training, fellowships, and opportunities granted to me during the years of my graduate studies, when this inquiry began. In particular, I feel fortunate to have participated in Columbia College's Literature Humanities program. The combination of teaching and discussion among faculty that took place there changed my work in more ways than I can explain. The Boston College Faculty Fellowship awarded to me in 2004 granted invaluable research and writing time that enabled me to expand the original scope of the book. A number of individuals have read all or part of the text in its different stages over the years. Félix Martínez Bonati, who directed the dissertation, offered crucial insight in defining the project and made valuable suggestions on the manuscript. I greatly appreciate the suggestions and comments from Michael Agnew, Patricia Grieve, Michael Schuessler, Herbert Klein, Gonzalo Sobejano, Flor María Rodríguez Arenas, Matilda Bruckner, Álvaro Aramburu, James Krippner, and the anonymous reader for Pennsylvania State University Press. I am thankful to Press Director Sandy Thatcher for his interest and for making the book possible. Kristin Peterson provided skilled assistance, and Stacey Lynn edited the manuscript with great care. The Office of the Provost at Boston College contributed funds for the preparation of the index. Verónica Cortínez, Ourida Mostefai, and Krystyna von Henneberg offered key encouragement at critical moments. Needless to say, the errors and omissions are all my own.

INTRODUCTION

MANY SCHOLARS HAVE HIGHLIGHTED the richness of early modern writings on the New World, pointing to the complexities of narrative postures taken by writers who were often both participants and commentators on the project of discovery and conquest that Claude Lévi-Strauss once called humanity's most "harrowing test."[1] Part of contemporary interest in the textual wealth of the sixteenth-century chronicles of the Spanish Indies stems not just from the vast territorial expanse and novelty of the subject matter for European readers, but also from the ways in which these often strangely shaped writings are connected to the origins of modern forms of anthropology, ethnography, social and natural science, and also to the beginnings of the modern novel and of the discourse on universal human rights.[2] In this sense, it has become a critical commonplace that early modern Spanish authors frequently blur boundaries between history, fiction, myth, science, and philosophy, and that their informative reports and chronicles dispatched to imperial authorities are often packaged together with illusions of Eden or Atlantis, rumors of Amazons, and the hyperbolic self-fashionings of those who would seek to transform eyewitness experience into private or political gain.[3]

Yet alongside the often-commented-upon inventive and hybrid aspects of the early Spanish accounts of America, one also finds in some of these works a largely unrecognized but nonetheless vigorous spirit of reflection, debate, and experimentation that seeks to delineate methods and narrative techniques appropriate for the writing of history. The broad reach of Spanish imperial expansion in the sixteenth century brought with it intense intellectual controversy that sought to grapple with urgent questions of justice and

---

1. Lévi-Strauss, *Tristes Tropiques,* 74.

2. Campbell, among others, has aptly described this phenomenon in her *Witness and the Other World* (166).

3. The continuing interest on the part of both historians and literary critics concerning the role of the imagination in these texts can be seen in the recent exchange between David Boruchoff, "The Poetry of History," and Franklin W. Knight, "On the Poetry of History."

rights, truth and falsehood, fact and "fiction." While narrative credibility has always been a concern in historiography, given history's particular claim to truth, the question of how to gauge textual reliability gains new relevance and urgency in works by authors such as Gonzalo Fernández de Oviedo (1478–1557), Bartolomé de Las Casas (1484–1566), and Bernal Díaz del Castillo (1495?–1584). Oviedo and Las Casas discuss explicitly the role of imagination and fabrication in history, for the most part as a way of attacking the reliability of rival historians. Although neither one of these authors translated his insights into a consistent method throughout his voluminous writings, one senses in their works a concerted effort to chart boundaries in historical discourse. This critical line of thinking, I suggest, in itself tells us much about these early writers, about the competing pulls of science and religion upon them, and the ways in which they sought to bring the conceptual tools of sixteenth-century humanism to bear on the New World. In retracing their debates over the nature of historical discourse and the forms appropriate to it, one glimpses ways in which colonial experience appears to have challenged these authors and even inspired them to change some of the assumptions with which they had begun their monumental projects. Their critical commentaries on the writing of history are a treasure trove of insight; one finds in them an instance of the sort of innovative and creative thinking that Walter Mignolo has highlighted as stemming from cultures in conflict at the frontiers of empire.[4] The importance of this fascinating trove of epistemological reflection and narratological consciousness derives from its ability to reveal conceptual fault lines, such as those in which superstition and magic are contrasted to more "rational" modes of analysis, as in the case of Oviedo, and those in which an inquisitorial rhetoric is harnessed to the critique of empire, as in the case of Las Casas. In the works of both of these authors, writing history becomes a contested site in which supernatural versus natural knowledge, and magic versus religion, are debated as signs of authorial reliability.[5] In addition, their discussions have striking parallels to recent debates concerning the status of narrative in historical discourse.

Why, one might ask, has this wealth of ideas at the very foundations of the Spanish-American intellectual and literary tradition not yet been sufficiently recuperated? The answer may be found in the checkered reception of the writings of colonial Latin America. Neither Oviedo's nor Las Casas's

4. Mignolo, *Local Histories*, 5, refers to this as "border thinking."

5. In a different context, Styers, in *Making Magic* (25–68), discusses the ways in which early modern writings on magic, witchcraft, and superstition are a reflection of a turning in Western culture toward modern forms of rationality.

major historical works were published in their entirety until the nineteenth century, and the early positivist readers tended to view their works as documentary sources whose data needed to be extracted and recomposed into more accurate accounts of events. Pioneering twentieth-century scholars such as Ramón Iglesia, Edmundo O'Gorman, and Irving Leonard sought to counteract this approach by reading colonial texts in a more holistic fashion so as to understand the philosophical and cultural codes that shape them.[6] Small but significant changes in critical emphasis, which coincided with the larger poststructuralist questioning of what constitutes "history," culminated in recent decades in a paradigmatic shift by which the histories of the Spanish West Indies were recuperated and studied for the most part by literary or cultural critics. While the postmodern critique of history's traditional claims to truth, accuracy, and reliability, and the resulting emphasis on the narrative aspects of the practice, have prompted a great deal of debate within the discipline of history, the increasing inclusion of historical texts as objects for literary study has in itself only more recently begun to receive in-depth critical consideration. If the insights that grew out of the intellectual climate of recent years have helped us to see the rich hybridity of colonial works, they may also have obscured an important undercurrent within the texts themselves that seeks to define the norms and boundaries of historical writing.

In reconstructing the rich tradition of historiographical reflection in sixteenth-century Spain and its colonies and arguing for its relevance to present concerns, I have drawn on several quite distinct scholarly tendencies. In its early stages, this project sought to investigate the expressions in New World historiography of debates long considered fundamental to the literary production of the Spanish Golden Age and was inspired by new historicist trends. By undertaking a literary study of historiography, my work was modeled on the rhetorical analyses of *crónicas de Indias* undertaken by scholars such as Margarita Zamora, Rolena Adorno, and Enrique Pupo-Walker, among others. And yet, my findings led me to adopt a methodological approach that, to my knowledge, has not been used in the context of the chronicles of the Spanish-American colonial period. The authors I found most illuminating for understanding the reflection on the writing of history in the context of the New World have explored, in one way or another, the usefulness of narrative theory to gain precision on distinctions between

---

6. Iglesia, *Cronistas*; O'Gorman, *Cuatro historiadores*; Leonard, *Books of the Brave;* see also Frankl, *El antijovio.*

historical and fictive narratives. They include scholars as diverse as Félix Martínez Bonati, Dorrit Cohn, Gérard Genette, and Anne Rigney. At the same time, my work has been inspired by an emerging body of scholarship on early modern epistemology and empiricism that seeks to examine the interplay of science and religion in the production of knowledge during the early modern period, perhaps most notably represented by the work of Lorraine Daston.[7] The formidable challenges presented to those who attempted to account for the history of the New World led them to far-reaching insights concerning the writing of history, and their critiques of humanist rhetorical models are often formulated in terms that evoke important political, religious, and scientific concerns.

The immediate context for Oviedo and Las Casas was the classical tradition as had been interpreted by Christian humanists. Aristotle, as is well known, wrote that history relates "the thing that has been," and poetry, "a kind of thing that might be, i.e., what is possible as being verisimilar or necessary," thus concluding that poetry is "something more philosophic and of graver import than history." For Aristotle, then, history is mere chronology, a narration of singular events without any universal signification ("what Alcibiades did or had done to him").[8] What Aristotle denied to history, the humanists of the sixteenth century delivered. This reversal is perhaps best illustrated by the image, common to the rhetorical or preceptive treatises of the period,[9] of the model inquirer—and his textual persona, the narrator—as a sage or wise man able to conjure up events and figures beyond his experience and to bring them to life in an exemplary narrative. History, for many humanists, becomes the supreme discipline, overshadowing—at least in theory—not just poetry but even moral philosophy. Indeed, it becomes a vehicle for teaching not just singular events but universal truths.

It is within the context of the humanists' high standards and expectations for historical narrative and the historian that the early chroniclers of the Indies inscribed their work and endeavored to grapple with the challenging material of the New World. Gonzalo Fernández de Oviedo in the *Historia general y natural de las Indias* (1535, 1557, 1851–55) and Bartolomé

---

7. Daston, "Historical Epistemology" and "Marvelous Facts," as well as Pomata and Siraisi, eds., *Historia: Empiricism and Erudition.*

8. Aristotle, *Poetics,* 2323, § 9.

9. By "preceptive," I mean the sort of treatises, commonly written by humanist scholars of this period, which sought to establish the "precepts" or rhetorical rules for writing history. I refer to them in Chapter 1.

de Las Casas in the *Historia de las Indias* (written 1527–60, pub. 1875–76) constantly measure their own histories (and those of others) against the daunting humanist norms, and yet manage to effect their own reversals, finding audacious narrative solutions to the monumental task of explaining the New World to the Old. Often, they frame their attempts to address the issue in terms of a conflict between history and "fiction," and also in terms of concerns that continue to preoccupy theorists of narrative and historians alike: the nature of the truth represented, the qualities and perceptive abilities of the narrator, and the credibility of the narrative both in relation to the evidence and to the manner in which it is written. They also frequently formulate their critiques of their rivals' works in terms that dismiss them as mere magical or superstitious practice.

In Chapter 1, "Historical Representation in the Spanish Humanist Context," I examine the ideas of Juan Luis Vives (1492–1540) as a paradigmatic expression of humanistic thinking on the writing of history in the early modern period. While Vives's contribution on the method and rhetoric for history has long been recognized, my analysis distances itself from earlier studies by focusing on the properly narrative framework he proposes. Writing in the 1530s, Vives endeavors in his *De ratione dicendi,* and in other texts in which he discusses the problem of history, to define the ideal qualities of the historian and of historical narration, and his treatise became a touchstone for later writers on the subject, both in Spain and elsewhere. His notion of an ideal historical narrative as seeking a mirrorlike objectivity congruent with the norms of probability and of Christian belief has its sources in Augustine and places a heavy burden on the historian. For Vives, the model inquirer is a humanist sage, a sort of "terrestrial divinity" who possesses almost supernatural powers to discern the meaning of events beyond his experience and to represent them as if directly perceived. In this sense, the humanist historian for Vives would seem to possess truly fantastic powers, which must logically derive either from divine inspiration or from the resources of the imagination. Vives links the notion of the historian's unnatural perception to his problematic requirements that historiography reflect a vision coherent both with the norms of probability and with the divine plan, as well as to his suggestion that history might escape what he views as the "fallen" condition of human language, that is, the tenuous reliability of everyday discourse. In these idealizing tendencies, as well as in Vives's interchangeable use of terms such as "lies," "fiction," and "lying histories," one finds the sort of imprecision that has bolstered the critical commonplace of a confusion between "history" and "story" in the sixteenth century. Vives's notions of the sweeping perceptive powers of the writer of history resurface in later *preceptistas* such as Luis Cabrera de Córdoba and Jerónimo de San José, and in the ironic presentation of humanist notions on history and the historian in Cervantes's *Don Quixote*.

In Chapter 2, "Conjecture and Credibility in the *Historia general y natural de las Indias* by Gonzalo Fernández de Oviedo," I explore a number of ways in which Oviedo both bows to and reformulates the humanist norms in his work. In particular, I show how his innovative method is bound up in a critique of the idea of the historian as a distant sage. The notion of the historian (and his textual analogue, the author-narrator) as able to conjure up an image of the past beyond his experience and present it as if directly perceived, which has such positive connotations in the preceptive tradition, takes on a strikingly negative dimension in Oviedo's work, and this author draws on the literature of reproof of superstitions to point to signs of an "unnatural" and therefore unreliable authorial perspective. Such a narrative stance employs a point of view that he associates not with the divine authority of the Christian sage, but with the more dubious conjectures of the armchair soothsayer. In asserting the importance of eyewitness experience in recording New World history, he arrives at the important view that reliability in historical narrative can be sought and measured by the author-narrator's adherence to his own natural perspective, that is, by his clearly separating his own words and views from those of others. Oviedo's stated refusal to mix his own words or perspective with those of the figures he seeks to represent has far-reaching consequences in terms of the structure (or lack thereof) of his work, as well as in the ambiguous notion of exemplarity it embodies. If the historian's authority is necessarily constrained to his natural range of vision, then he operates under considerable restrictions concerning what he can or cannot assert as known and certain about the agents and events he represents. Although Oviedo does not always stick to his stated method, the systematic use of distinct perspectives and styles in his work amounts to a—for the most part—methodically sustained experiment in historical representation. By the end of his voluminous account, Oviedo takes his own method one step further, urging his readers to become, in effect, model historians, and encouraging them to actively engage themselves in assessing the value of the testimony of others and to sharpen their wits and guard against the deceptions inherent in everyday discourse. One finds a similar sensibility—albeit one expressed in terms free of the religious concerns of the earlier polemic—in the contemporary critique of poststructuralism by scholars of narrative such as Martínez Bonati, Genette, Rigney, and Cohn (more on this later).

Chapter 3, "Vision and Voice: The *Historia de las Indias* by Bartolomé de Las Casas," looks at the efforts by this author to exploit and transform Oviedo's methodological assumptions and versions of events, turning them against their author, as well as some of the problematic consequences (in epistemological terms) that result from this approach for Las Casas's own adopted narrative point of view. Even as Las Casas adopts a prophetic tone that would seem to resuscitate the persona of the humanist historian, his polemics with Oviedo, while bitter, advance the understanding of boundaries in historical discourse. Amid the scathing criticisms that he often directs at his rivals, one senses an effort to gain lexical precision. In his critique of Oviedo's theory of the New World as the long-lost Atlantis or Hesperides, for example, one finds a consistent effort to separate the material of classical "myth" from that of colonial history. Unlike merely entertaining fictions, Las Casas further suggests, "lies" in history belong to a more insidious form of deception, one that hints at a discrepancy between external utterance and inner belief. Las Casas devotes much of his history to exposing the "heresies" of his rivals, and in this accusatory mode he presents himself as able to detect through textual evidence the inner betrayals of others. In keeping with his goal of writing an orthodox version of New World history, he portrays himself as a sort of inquisitorial prophet who is able to decipher a divine plan. His curious representation of himself (often in the same scene) as both eyewitness and third-person actor constitutes a return to earlier historiographical practices, even as it brings into focus important questions of textual reliability. The widely varying range of what the narrator can perceive in the *Historia de las Indias* lends his work a peculiar shape, one that tries not only to conform to the compelling model of the Augustinian philosophy of history, but also to answer Oviedo's competing narrative experiments. A study of the complex makeup of his narrative self points as well to significant distinctions on the problem of narrative reliability in historical versus fictional texts.

In Chapter 4, "History and Memory: Narrative Perspective in Bernal Díaz del Castillo's *Historia verdadera de la conquista de la Nueva España*" (1550–81, pub. 1632), I examine a work that, although written at the margins of both empire and humanist debates over the writing of history, presents similar narrative dilemmas. To a far greater degree than the histories of Oviedo or Las Casas, the *Historia verdadera* emits perplexing signals as to its own discursive character. The close study of the author's narrative techniques enable us to describe with some precision the textual codes that have permitted his work to so readily be read as "literary" or even "novelistic." In particular,

Bernal Díaz's various uses of the present tense are a distinct feature of his work that signal problems of narrative distance and perspective, permitting the author in places to achieve remarkable insights into the minds of others, a characteristic commonly associated with modern works of fiction. In this sense, we can pinpoint moments in which Bernal Díaz's narrative failures (in historiographic terms) constitute some of his most important literary achievements. At the same time, his treatment of character and his concern for addressing the narrative configurations of the existing historical tradition give evidence of a complex and properly historiographical project.

In focusing on debates over the "formal" and epistemological reflections of these sixteenth-century authors, I am not trying to suggest that they lacked doctrinary and political agendas, much less that their historical projects could be understood outside of the power struggles of the Spanish colonial enterprise in America. If I have not included a case from an indigenous perspective, it is not out of disinterest for those who wrote from a culturally different point of view, but rather because such an endeavor would substantially extend the reach of this project (and likely best be approached using a different theoretical basis). The writers I have included for study here all wrote roughly at the same time, participated in similar debates, and confronted similar narrative dilemmas, even as they found quite different solutions to their tasks. By limiting the study to a group of writers who shared some of the same predicaments as well as familiarity—great or minor—with the humanist program, I hope to show how the crisis in the humanist rhetorical model of history challenged authors as distinct in their training and background as Oviedo and Bernal Díaz.

This book intends to break new ground in two ways: by bringing to light a critical line of thinking on the part of early historians of the Indies, and by indicating the ways in which this line of thinking both anticipates and is clarified by more recent efforts to describe the logic and characteristics of historical writing as distinct from those of fiction. In recent decades, much of the literary study of historical texts has been inspired by the work of Hayden White and Roland Barthes, among others, concerning the role of narrative in historical writing. In its most extreme form, this approach has resulted in the reduction of history to rhetoric, as has been noted by Carlo Ginzburg, who also argues that the debate about truth that ensued from this approach is perhaps one of the most pressing intellectual issues of our times.[10] Although Barthes and

---

10. Ginzburg, *History, Rhetoric, and Proof,* 49.

White are usually associated with the "linguistic" turn in historical studies, the origin of this turn could be located much earlier, and Ginzburg himself has traced its philosophical lineage from the ancient sophists through the skepticism of Nietzsche.[11] In the Anglo-American context, Nancy Partner points to the more recent shift by practitioners of the New Criticism of the 1950s, consisting of a movement away from searching for the "authorial" intention of the literary text to focus instead on the "textual" intention. She suggests that Barthes and later White essentially would extend these insights, which, in the context of New Criticism had been applied for the most part to fictive or poetic texts, to historiography in their attempt to conceptualize textual intention as the locus of the meaning not just in fiction, but in history as well.[12]

White's works in particular have played a central role in the narrative turn in historical studies of the last three decades, and any attempt to sum them up runs some risk of oversimplification, as Richard Vann has noted. Vann points out that White's adoption of the essay form has meant that his positions are formulated in various ways throughout numerous texts, and that White himself has resisted requests for clarification on some of the evident ambiguities.[13] A case in point is the notable imprecision with which White consistently has equated the writing of history with that of fiction. In an early essay, titled "The Fictions of Factual Representation," which was included in *The Tropics of Discourse: Essays in Cultural Criticism* (1978), he writes: "*historical events* differ from *fictional events* in the ways that it has been conventional to characterize their differences since Aristotle," but goes on to argue that in their narrative dimensions, historical texts are essentially "fictions" that purport to represent historical facts.[14] In another essay included in this collection, "The Historical Text as Literary Artifact," he suggests that the same set of historical events could serve as a basis for a narrative configuration that could be either tragic or comic, and that the mode of representation chosen by the historian is "essentially a literary, that is to say, fiction-making, operation."[15] Thus, historical narratives are "verbal fictions, the contents of which are as much *invented as found* and the forms

11. Ibid., 1–25.

12. Partner, "Hayden White," 170–71, pointedly illustrates some of the "dislocations" that poststructuralism has brought to bear on the discipline of history.

13. Vann, "The Reception of Hayden White," 143–45.

14. White, "Fictions of Factual Representation," in *Tropics of Discourse*, 121 (emphasis in the original).

15. White, "Historical Text as Literary Artifact," in *Tropics of Discourse*, 84–85.

of which have more in common with their counterparts in literature than they have with those in the sciences."[16] Elsewhere in this essay, he equates the "fictive" aspects of historical discourse with ideology.[17] The ideological misuse of history is a concern to which White returns in "The Politics of Historical Representation," included in *The Content of the Form: Narrative Discourse and Historical Representation* (1987), where, in addressing critics who have accused him of promoting a "debilitating relativism," he seems to suggest that even factually inaccurate (and "morally offensive") versions of history may play a valid role in nationalistic or revisionist politics. Although in this regard he professes concern for the need to "discipline" the role of the imagination in history to keep it in line with the "rules" of evidence, he states that in his or her inventive faculty, the historian is taken over by "an operation exactly like that of the novelist" at the time of writing his or her text.[18] Although White somewhat tempers his use of terms such as *fiction* in later works, he continues to argue, in *Figural Realism* (1999), that literary and historical discourse "are more similar than different since both operate language in such a way that any clear distinction between their discursive form and their interpretive content remains impossible."[19] Variations in expression on this problem aside, White's basic tenets boil down to the idea that historiography is a kind of rhetorical discourse more concerned with political effectiveness and persuasion than with truth, and that like fiction, it presents a self-contained textual world. Further, one could say that White's own formulations of the problem—and many of the critical studies inspired by his model—are characterized by the prominence of the loose use of terms such as "fiction" and "rhetoric" in attempting to account for the role of narrative in historical writing.

If the broad effect of the narrative turn in contemporary criticism can generally be said to have led to a remarkable range of interdisciplinary work in the humanities in recent decades, the numerous and forceful critiques of White's views have not always crossed traditional disciplinary divides.[20] Several of these critiques have focused on White's lack of terminological

16. Ibid., 82 (emphasis in the original).

17. Ibid., 99.

18. White, "Politics of Historical Representation," in *Content of the Form,* 67–68 and 77–81. For a critique of the political implications of White's views in the Latin American context, see Mackenthun, "Epilogue," in *Metaphors of Dispossession,* 299–301.

19. White, *Figural Realism,* 6.

20. For a sampling of critiques of White's views, see, in addition to the articles by Partner and Vann cited above (and included in *History and Theory* 37, no. 2, an issue devoted to White's legacy), Zagorin, "Historiography and Postmodernism."

and conceptual precision. Ginzburg, for example, argues that the rhetorical approach in historical studies represented by White has engaged in a telling misunderstanding of the concept of "rhetoric." This critic devotes a good part of *History, Rhetoric, and Proof* to recovering what he sees as the foundational concept in Aristotle's *Rhetoric:* the notion that evidence and proof are the definitive ingredients in the discourse of history. Ginzburg argues in essence that proof and evidence are in Aristotle the building blocks for all rhetorical discourse, including history, but that this central concept has been frequently obscured by the notion of rhetoric as a purely persuasive or politically expedient discourse only tenuously connected to the notion of truth.[21] Likewise, literary theorists critical of White's views have pointed to the wide range of meanings associated with the word *fiction.* In *The Distinction of Fiction* Cohn notes the commonplace contemporary confusion in the use of the term *fiction* to mean widely different things, from "untruth" to "all literature" or "all narrative." She argues that this conflation of terms "is weighted with considerable ideological freight," and is a product of the contemporary critique of the intellectual grounding of traditional historical practice.[22]

So much has been written on this latest episode in the age-old quarrel between history and fiction that any attempt to summarize will fall short. What I would like to highlight here is the contribution of theorists who have argued that the concept of fictionality itself is crucial for understanding the nature of the boundaries between historical and fictive narrative. My own approach will highlight the ideas of Martínez Bonati, Cohn, and Rigney, whose diverse contributions in accounting for the kinds of imagination that go into historical writing have not, perhaps, been widely recognized. I share with them the idea that it is a mistake to equate the narrative or representational aspects of historical writing with the concept of fictionality. The notion that poetic or fictive discourse is distinct from other kinds of speech has, of course, ancient roots; in Aristotle it already appears under the clear-cut category of mimesis. In the context of twentieth-century debates, I will draw on Félix Martínez Bonati's philosophical account of the distinctive character of fiction, which was first published in 1960.[23] In this book, and in later essays on the subject, Martínez Bonati argues that fiction is logically and ontologically distinct from all other kinds of discourse. He posits

21. Ginzburg, "Aristotle and History, Once More," in *History, Rhetoric, and Proof,* 38–53.
22. Cohn, *Distinction of Fiction,* 9. See also Rigney, "Semantic Slides," 31–46.
23. Martínez Bonati, *Fictive Discourse.*

that the imaginary quality of the fictive narrator and fiction's freedom from referential constraints are the fundamental phenomena that distinguish fictive or poetic works from all other types of discourse. Both Rigney and Cohn expand on the implications of the concept of fictionality for understanding the workings of historical narrative. Cohn in particular draws on the work of Martínez Bonati to specify that, unlike the imaginary narrators of fiction, the writer of history tells his or her tale in his or her own voice, or at least takes responsibility for the account, and refers to events and individuals that by definition are assumed by both author and reader to have had an existence external to the text. In this sense, historical discourse is similar to other forms of nonfictional discourse and to many speech acts of everyday communication. This apparently simple distinction concerning voice has vast logical consequences for what the historian can assert as known and certain and, thus, for the range of his or her voice and vision and, in particular, for the portrayal of character or actors in history. Finally, Cohn echoes the sorts of concerns mentioned by Ginzburg in reminding us that unlike fictional narrative, which has been traditionally studied as having two levels (story and discourse), the territory of historiography is necessarily circumscribed by a third level largely irrelevant in the works of imagination: that of facts, evidence, sources, and their relationship to narrative.[24] By juxtaposing the views of these scholars to those of writers from the conflictive sixteenth-century colonial context, I hope not just to excavate and illuminate an early and valuable critical tradition in Hispanic intellectual history, but also to update discussions of colonial Spanish American historiography with regard to recent theoretical discussions. Finally, I will examine the usefulness of models that, to my knowledge, have not been applied to the context of early modern historiography.

While the rhetorical analysis of the chronicles of the Indies has led to an important body of critical work, one to which in many ways I am indebted, it is still a relatively new field whose assumptions and practices have yet to be fully examined. My approach in *Territories of History* is neither to take on the problem of distinctions between history and fiction in a theoretical fashion, nor to suggest that such boundaries are entirely fixed. My study, rather, consists of an analysis of key sixteenth-century historiographical accounts of the New World, which themselves problematize the relationship of history versus fiction. By juxtaposing the insights of our own era to the epistemological and

24. Cohn, *Distinction of Fiction*, 110–14.

narratological concerns that pervade these foundational texts of early modern Spanish colonialism, I highlight a common spirit of inquiry and, more generally, test the findings of recent critical efforts to characterize historiographical as opposed to fictional narrative. In their attempts at historiographical orthodoxy as well as in their innovative transgressions, the works under study here invite one to contemplate problems of boundaries in discourse. Given that the recovery of the *crónicas de Indias* as part of the "literary" Spanish American tradition has coincided with, or perhaps even anticipated, the larger poststructuralist questioning of what constitutes "history," it is important to find such vigorous reflection, debate, and borderline experimentation within these foundational works themselves. In *Myth and Archive: A Theory of Latin American Narrative,* Roberto González Echevarría has argued that the "relationships that narrative establishes with non-literary forms of discourse are much more productive and determining than those it has with its own tradition."[25] If this is indeed the case, it is all the more urgent to understand the particularly narrative characteristics of these "non-literary" forms, as well as the imaginative ways in which they become integrated in the literary heritage. In this regard, the analytical tools that help to underscore discursive boundaries may also assist in describing the manners in which the material of history becomes transformed both into fiction and into a literary tradition.

25. González Echevarría, *Myth and Archive,* xvi.

1

HISTORICAL REPRESENTATION IN THE
SPANISH HUMANIST CONTEXT: JUAN LUIS VIVES

Si la brevedad de la vida y la misma razón permitiera que un hombre viviera muchos
siglos y anduviesse muchas provincias y considerasse lo que ay en todas y en qué
consiste la fuerza y poder y lo que se avia seguido en bien o en mal de cada cosa, caso
o negocio de cada príncipe o particular en hecho y consejo, ¿quién no diría ser gran
consejero? ¿Quién su parecer no tendría por oráculo en las determinaciones y respuestas
consultado? Lo que niega la naturaleza, da la historia, pues los que la saben parece que
han vivido muchos siglos, visto todas las regiones, hallándose en todos los públicos
consejos y presentes a todo lo acaecido, notándolo y juzgándolo con cuidado.
—CABRERA DE CÓRDOBA

[If the brevity of life and reason itself permitted a man to live many centuries and to travel
through many provinces, considering all that is in them, and in what their strength and
power consists, and what had been accomplished well or badly in the affairs, negotiations,
deeds, and counsel of each prince or citizen, who would not consider him to be a great
advisor? Who would not take his advice, determinations, and answers as if an oracle?
What nature denies mankind, history grants him, because those who know history appear
to have lived through many centuries, seen all the regions, found themselves in all the
public councils and present at all events, noting and judging them carefully.]

IN THIS PASSAGE OF HIS TREATISE on writing history (*De historia: Para entenderla y escribirla*, 1611),[1] the humanist Luis Cabrera de Córdoba (1559–1623)[2]
praises the discipline of history in the highest terms. Historical knowledge,
he states, fosters a type of clairvoyance otherwise denied humans and grants
a perspective that ostensibly enables one to overcome the natural limitations of individual experience and memory. The attentive reader of history,
he suggests, makes for a wise advisor because his knowledge extends as if he
had lived through centuries, traveled through vast regions, and witnessed

---

1. Cabrera de Córdoba, *De historia*, 40–41. All translations are my own.
2. An active diplomat and erudite historian, Cabrera de Córdoba participated in missions for
Philip II to Italy and Flanders in the 1580s, and helped to organize the armada against the British
in 1588. After the king's death, he devoted himself to writing. In addition to *De historia*, Cabrera
published part 1 of *Historia de Felipe II* in 1619. For biographical and bibliographical information,
see Montero Díaz, "La doctrina de la historia," which contextualizes the author's work with regard
to other major Golden Age treatments on the writing of history, from Vives to Jerónimo de San
José.

notable debates and events. In Cabrera's view, the reading of history would appear to impart not just the illusion of a direct perception of the past, but the ability to prophesy the future: "El que mira la historia de los antiguos tiempos atentamente, y lo que enseñan guarda, tiene luz para las cosas futuras, pues una misma manera de mundo es toda" ("He who looks carefully at and learns from ancient history, has insight on the future, because the world is of one nature").[3] The constancy of human nature through the ages means that history, by recording experience and providing models of conduct to either emulate or avoid, gives insight that can be extrapolated to the future. Cabrera de Córdoba's vision of history as cyclical or predictable, borrowed from Thucydides,[4] takes on practical applications with important discursive consequences: the reading of history imparts to mere mortals a kind of supernatural vision of past and future.

By suggesting that the perspective gained from reading history is unnatural, that it grants a view beyond that available in everyday life, Cabrera de Córdoba was recasting a number of traditions that imagined not the reader, but the writer of history—and his textual persona, the narrator—as a clairvoyant visionary able to decipher the past and to act as oracle for the future. In *The City of God*, Augustine had characterized the sacred historian as part inquirer and part prophet, thus alluding to the epistemological concerns that inevitably emerge in the act of writing history. According to Augustine, secular historians record versions of events that are always partial and incompatible with other accounts. Non-Christians are thus at a loss in judging credibility in such histories: "The very disagreement of historians among themselves affords us an opportunity to choose for credence those whose contentions are not at variance with the divinely inspired history to which we adhere. Very different is the plight of the ungodly city's citizens. . . . When these people study the books of [men of authority] . . . they do not know what or whom to believe. We, on the other hand, have the support of divine authority in the history of our religion."[5] While pagan accounts are as limited as the point of view of those who write them, and thus full of disagreements and contradictions, Christian historiography,

---

3. Cabrera de Córdoba, *De historia*, 11.

4. The cyclical idea of history, common to the Greek tradition, is exemplified by Thucydides' observation in *History* (48) that human nature dictates that past events "will at some time or another and in much the same ways, be repeated in the future." See also Polybius's similar view in book 12 of the *Histories*, as quoted by Barnes, *History of Historical Writing*, 33–34, and Mazzarino, *The End of the Ancient World*, 17–31.

5. Augustine, *City of God*, 408, book 18, chap. 40.

for Augustine, is sanctioned by divine authority and marked by coherent biblical patterns of Fall and Redemption. Thus sacred historians "wrote parts of their works in their capacity as careful historians, and other parts in their capacity as divinely inspired prophets, and the distinction was so clear to the writers themselves that they understood that the former parts should be attributed to themselves while the others should be attributed to God speaking through them. Thus the human parts would be a matter of the fullness of historical knowledge, while the inspired parts would have the full force of revelation."[6] The notion of the historian as wise prophet or inspired seer is evident in other medieval traditions, which, drawing on Hebrew, Arabic, and Eastern sources, as well as Classical ones, doubted, like Augustine, the reliability of human historical records and sought to gain more certain information by studying the heavens. Many an astrologer- or cosmographer-historian ventured to overcome the natural limitations of mortal perspectives by seeking more accurate chronologies (and even predicting important events) based on the conjunctions of the stars.[7] One should not minimize the diversity of medieval historiographical practices, many of which, as Beryl Smalley notes, followed Isidore's injunction to rely on eyewitness accounts as the most truthful material for history.[8] Fernán Pérez de Guzmán, for example, emphasizes in the prologue to his *Generaciones y semblanzas* the need for the historian to be either present at notable events, or to rely on trustworthy witnesses.[9] And yet, as R. W. Southern writes, the biblical, pagan, Christian, and astrological conceptions of prophecy in history all together made a "formidable array" of sciences expressing a cohesive "relationship between time and eternity, between the mind of God and the minds of men, between the pattern of past events and the future, which most people found compellingly persuasive."[10]

6. Ibid., 406, book 18, chap. 38. On the idea of history and prophecy in Augustine, see Markus, *Saeculum*, 187–96, 231–32; and Press, *Development of the Idea of History*, 112–19.

7. For an overview of the connections between history and astrology, see Campion, *Great Year;* Smoller, *History, Prophecy, and the Stars*, 61–89; Koselleck, *Futures Past*, 9–10; and Mazzarino, *The End of the Ancient World*, 28. Frances Yates, in *Art of Memory*, and Mary Carruthers, in *Book of Memory*, offer many insights on the topic as well.

8. Smalley, in *Historians in the Middle Ages* (22–25), provides a succinct summary of medieval historiographical trends. See also Southern, "Aspects of the European Tradition of Historical Writing." Black, in "New Laws" (151–55), notes the privileging of eyewitness testimony in medieval hagiography.

9. Pérez de Guzmán, *Generaciones y semblanzas*, 2.

10. Southern, "History as Prophecy," 172.

Following Augustine and the Christian tradition of history as the earthly fulfillment of a divine plan, much of the sixteenth- and seventeenth-century rhetorical or preceptive literature from Spain on the art of writing history focuses on the range of the historian's vision as a sign of his reliability.[11] The more immediate roots of Cabrera de Córdoba's efforts to describe in a systematic fashion the theory, method, and discursive norms of history can be found in the works of Juan Luis Vives (1492–1540). Cabrera's shift away from the notion that the author of history required supernatural perceptive abilities, suggesting instead that it is the reader who increases his awareness through the careful study of historical texts, tells us much about the intense debates over the problem of writing of history that emerged in sixteenth-century Spain and its colonies. Writing in the 1530s, Vives had alluded to the seemingly fantastic feat achieved by historical narrative, as well as its practical applications in terms of teaching prudence: "Experiences that are foreign to us are learned by the knowledge of the past preserved in memory, which we call history. History makes it possible for us to see past events as if they were no less present to us than those occurring right now, so that we can exploit them as if they were our own."[12] We can discern here the idea, so dear to the Italian humanists, of rhetorical eloquence as essential to creating prose able both to "live on and to move the will of others."[13] But for Vives, as we shall see, the historical imagination enacts a gesture that is not just extraordinary but seemingly divine in attempting to recuperate the truth about the past in an objective fashion, and thus to re-create for the reader the illusion of a firsthand view of bygones not witnessed. Indeed, in the writings of Vives the notion of the privileged or unnatural perspective of the historian is problematic, because this author is concerned less with communication with higher powers than with establishing practical guidelines for reading and writing history within a humanist program.[14] In Vives's

11. By "preceptive literature" I mean the rhetorical treatises written to convey or teach the norms or maxims of writing history. Montero Díaz, "La doctrina de la historia," lists and studies the major humanists writing in Spain on the subject in the sixteenth and seventeenth centuries, including Vives, Paez de Castro, Fox Morcillo, and Cabrera, among others.

12. "Experimenta aliena ex cognitione prioris memoriae discuntur, quae historia nuncupatur; eaque efficit, ut praeteritis non minus videamos interfuisse, quam praesentibus, illisque perinde uti posse ac nostris." Vives, *De disciplinis,* book 5, chap. 1, in *Opera,* 6:388. I quote for the most part from Mayans's edition of the *Opera omnia.* Unless otherwise noted, translations from Latin to English are my own in collaboration with Álvaro Aramburu.

13. Struever, *Language of History,* 61; see also Cochrane, *Historians,* 479–93; and Black's review of the theory of historical writing in the Italian humanist tradition in "The New Laws."

14. Terms such as *humanist* and *humanism* have been the source of debate. I follow Kristeller's sensible and erudite guidelines on the sixteenth-century use of *humanist* as referring to the

description of the theory and practice of historical writing, one finds the interesting paradox of the unnatural, fantastic narrative stance of the narrator of history posited as a sign of the reliability or objectivity of the narrative, a point to which I will return later.

The "Case" for History in the Spanish Humanist Tradition

Perhaps one should not be overly perplexed by the paradoxes in preceptive works such as those of Vives. Victor Frankl has shown that it is common to find essentially incompatible points of view juxtaposed in Spanish rhetorical treatments of history from the sixteenth and seventeenth centuries, and suggests that this is in fact a characteristic common to the "mannerist" aesthetic of the period.[15] The main views on the criteria of historical truth that coexisted (and often overlapped) uneasily at the time are borrowed, according to Frankl, from different ages and correspond to different spiritual attitudes, which he categorizes as: the authority of eyewitness experience, cultivated by the historians of Classical antiquity and reinterpreted in the Renaissance; the idea of the (inspired) historian as decipherer of an occult spiritual verity, characteristic of Renaissance individualism; an archaic, pre-Renaissance taste for chivalric codes, such as the notion of *fama;* and medieval thinking in the tradition of Augustine, renovated by the Counter-Reformation, which emphasized history's role as evidence of God's will on earth.[16] Other scholars of sixteenth-century historiography emphasize different aspects of the cross-mixing of divergent points of view on the subject, and even alternative ones, as in the case of the connection between astrology and history. The range of conflicting ideas about the nature of historical truth current at that time, often within a single work, would appear to point to something of an intellectual crisis.[17]

"professor or teacher or scholar" of the humanities, that is, grammar, rhetoric, history, poetry, and moral philosophy. The humanities were "a cultural and educational program which emphasized and developed an important but limited area of studies . . . and was concerned essentially neither with the classics nor with philosophy, but might roughly be described as literature." Kristeller, *Renaissance Thought,* 9–10.

15. Frankl, *El antijovio,* 52.

16. Ibid., 37–39.

17. As Ortega y Gasset wrote in "Esquema de las crisis" (76): "La confusión va aneja a toda época de crisis. Porque, en definitiva, eso que se llama 'crisis' no es sino el tránsito que el hombre hace de vivir prendido a unas cosas y apoyado en ellas, a vivir prendido y apoyado en otras." Gilbert, in *Machiavelli and Guicciardini,* analyzes the "crisis" in humanist historiography as a tension between traditional rhetorical norms and a new political orientation in the discipline. For a more general "cultural map" of the period, see Kristeller, *Renaissance Thought.*

The signs of crisis are perhaps highlighted by the fact that, amid the often contradictory mix of Classical and Christian views on the nature of history, there was, nonetheless, general agreement among preceptors of the discipline that historical narrative should be both truthful and exemplary, a superior type of discourse.[18] The "legislators of history," as José Godoy Alcántara called the authors of rhetorical discourse on the subject, commonly expressed in philosophical terms the notion of the superiority of history over poetry due to its ability to communicate truth, and moralists and rhetoricians frequently made their point by comparing the virtues of history to the vices of fiction.[19] The problem of establishing boundaries between historical and fictional discourse was not only addressed in the rhetorical and philosophical treatises, but confronted in the historical narratives such as those of Oviedo and Las Casas, and represented and exploited in imaginative works of the time as well. Often, efforts to distinguish history from fiction turn on concerns that continue to preoccupy students of narrative today: the nature of the "truth" represented (whether literal or allegorical), the qualities and perceptive abilities of the narrator (whether a direct witness or a judge of reports, possessing a vision that is wise and inspired, or limited in scope), and the credibility of the narrative both in relation to the "facts" (as regards their verisimilitude and consistency with the divine plan) and to the literary or narrative style in which it is written.

While the "case" against fiction in Golden-Age Spain has been much studied and the heated controversies on the subject well anthologized, the other side of the argument, pertaining to the writing of history, has been perhaps less well appreciated.[20] The relative merits of history and fiction are

18. A full survey of the *ars historiae* that proliferated in Spain in the sixteenth century is beyond the scope of this project. See in particular Montero Díaz, "La doctrina de la historia"; Godoy Alcántara, "Discurso"; Menéndez y Pelayo, *Historia de las ideas*, 1:673–81; Frankl, *El antijovio*, 82–295; Lewis, "Humanist Historiography," 68–101; Mignolo, "Metatexto"; and Cortijo Ocaña, "Introducción." On the idea of the superiority of historiographical discourse, see Nelson, *Fact or Fiction*, 53; Kohut, in "Retórica," reviews the theme in the writings of Vives, Fox Morcillo, and Llull.

19. For a similar, earlier trend in the Italian Cinquecento, see Weinberg, *History of Literary Criticism*, 1:13–16; for Spanish writers on the subject, see Kohut, "Retórica."

20. Ife, in *Reading and Fiction* (12), notes that: "Attacks on imaginative literature in sixteenth-century Spain have been much anthologized but not always well understood. Undoubtedly one of the major barriers to understanding has been the very virulence of the terms in which they are expressed, and the tendency to dismiss the arguments as overstated and narrow-minded, particularly when so many of the criticisms come from churchmen." He further identifies (1–37) the Platonic roots of the moral and metaphysical criticisms of fiction, and surveys their implications for narrative experiments in fictional works of the period. Forcione, in *Cervantes, Aristotle* (3–87), examines the Aristotelian components of the debate, as does Riley, in *Cervantes' Theory* (1–26). For studies, sources, and compilations of sixteenth-century attacks on fiction in Spain, see (among others)

constantly weighed in the preceptive discussions, and one might assume that if the criticisms of imaginative literature were commonplace at the time, so would have been the defenses of history. In the writings of Vives, for example, the invectives against "lying" fictions are paralleled by an effort to describe the norms and characteristics of "truthful" historical narration. If fiction is found to be faulty because it is manifestly "untrue" and immoral, can history be demonstrably accurate and exemplary? Vives suggests that ideally it can, and in his discussion one finds important insights on the power of narrative, the nature of the experience of reading, how to evaluate truth in narrative, and how to achieve credibility when writing. The case for history put forth by Vives was more complex than has been noted and resonated not just in the rhetorical or preceptive works and the historiography of the period, but also, and in a way that has perhaps not been sufficiently recognized, in fictional works that sought to exploit or thematize some of the paradoxes that emerged from the preceptive discussions.[21]

In reading treatises on the writing of history in this period, one finds that the preoccupation with how to record the "truth" is a site of epistemological ambiguity. Beneath the surface of the reassuring commonplaces about historical discourse as a treasure trove of experience, brimming with true stories of important deeds by great men, one can detect in preceptive treatises such as those of Vives a sense of anxiety concerning even the basic assumptions of the discipline. The characterization of the model historian (and his narrative persona) as visionary with unnatural or magical powers is just one way in which such uncertainties were expressed by even the most enthusiastic defenders of historical narration. The kind of incompatibility in the criteria for truth described by Frankl was accompanied by a crisis in the idea of exemplarity in history, as Anthony Hampton has argued.[22]

Menéndez y Pelayo, *Orígenes de la novela,* in *Obras completas,* 13:440–46, 463–65; Bataillon *Érasme et l'Espagne,* 1:651–71; Thomas, *Spanish and Portuguese Romances,* 147–79. On the similar quarrel in the Italian context, see Weinberg, *A History of Literary Criticism.* Nelson, in *Fact or Fiction* (38–55), while somewhat more attentive to the norms of historical narration than other critics who have addressed the topic, nonetheless draws most of his examples from the realm of fiction in a wide range of European sources.

21. Historians such as Montero Díaz, in "La doctrina de la historia" (xv–xvi), and Lewis, in "Humanist Historiography," have suggested that the preceptive works had little effect on the writing of the histories of the Conquest. Although it is clear that treatises on history such as that of Vives were not used as models to be followed slavishly, the works of authors as diverse as Oviedo, Las Casas, and Bernal Díaz reflect an awareness of the critical issues that emerged in the quarrel between history and fiction, and so of views such as those of Vives, as will be shown in the following chapters.

22. Hampton, *Writing from History,* 30.

As I hope to show, the quarrel between history and fiction in sixteenth- and early seventeenth-century Spain contributed to a rich vein of reflection on historical writing and, more specifically, on the characteristics of the historical narrator and the conditions for and signs of credibility or reliability in historical narrative.

In general, one can agree with Kristeller that the humanist treatises deserve attention not only for their opinions concerning pressing issues of the time, but for the "elegance and clarity of their style and their vivid personal and historical flavor as well as through their well selected and mellowed classical wisdom."[23] Part of the interest in the treatises that deal specifically with the idea of history and its writing, in addition to their relevance to the debate over boundaries in discourse and the image they convey of the perspective appropriate to the historical narrator, lies in the fact that there was no single classical source for the art of history.[24] While critics of fiction found philosophical ammunition in Plato's works, and defenders of poetry in Aristotle, those concerned with history had no foundational text. The insights as to the method and the narrative perspective appropriate to history evident in the accounts of the great historians of Greece and Rome more often than not advocated profoundly different approaches. Cicero had remarked that, although "open to view," the precepts of history had yet to be spelled out. The brief indications in *De oratore* (as in Quintilian's *Institutio oratoria*) left much room for elaboration.[25] In their efforts to fill this gap, sixteenth-century writers on the problem of history were trying to make what they viewed as a singularly modern contribution to an ancient discipline. Vives's attempt to account for a systematic view of history and historical narrative appears to have been undertaken in the spirit of this larger project.[26]

23. Kristeller, *Renaissance Thought*, 18.

24. Gilbert, *Machiavelli and Guicciardini*, 205.

25. Menéndez y Pelayo, in *Historia de las ideas* (1:673), notes that Renaissance *preceptistas* were "much freer" in writing about history than those who addressed poetics "porque tenían menor cúmulo de preceptos que acatar religiosamente." Cicero, whose observations are central to Vives's exposition, notes in *De oratore* (II.xv, 62–64): "nowhere do I find [the art of history] supplied with any independent directions from the rhetoricians; indeed its rules lie open to view."

26. In the preface to *De tradendis disciplinis*, Vives, ever aware of questions of credibility in discourse, not to mention rhetorical conventions of modesty, writes: "I have often been ashamed at what I have ventured to undertake . . . in thinking that I should dare to attack authors consecrated by their standing through the centuries." Vives, *On Education*, 8 (Watson's translation). He quotes Seneca's view that the ancient authors should be guides, not masters, and suggests, by way of method, that close study of the original texts and careful observation of nature will lead to worthwhile discoveries: "Truth stands open to all. It has not as yet been fully occupied. Much truth has been left for future generations to discover" (ibid., 9). In this sense, Vives participates in the broader tendency of Renaissance rhetors to distinguish themselves from both medieval and classical precursors.

Rather than survey all of the numerous treatises in the rich vein of historical reflection in sixteenth- and seventeenth-century Spain, I will limit the discussion to the works of Vives in the hope of giving his ideas on the discursive properties of history a fuller treatment than would be possible in a more panoramic view.[27] Vives's comprehensive discussion merits in-depth consideration for a variety of reasons, but mainly because he summarizes the preceptive *topoi* on the question, giving them an original twist, because his thoughts on the matter became something of a pillar for later *preceptistas,* and because his ideas were relatively well known and accessible to the sixteenth-century reading public. While a number of scholars have studied the distinctiveness of Vives's views on history, I depart from earlier treatments by focusing on the properly narrative aspects of these views and the problems they present in terms of narrative perspective in history, as well as by examining some of the broader implications of Vives's apparent skepticism concerning language as a medium for conveying truth.[28] Drawing on the critical methods of humanism, the insights from Italian Renaissance historiography, and the use of perspective in the pictorial arts, Vives imagines the possibility of an objective narrative of historical events, and suggests some guidelines for achieving this as well as for distinguishing truth from lies in narrative.[29] His interpretation of the Augustinian notion of the historian as part researcher and part prophet, while in some ways a site of self-contradiction, is one that is richly suggestive, because it encapsulates problems concerning the writing of history that continue to interest scholars today.

27. Montero Díaz, in "La doctrina de la historia" (xvi), writes: "Fue España, durante esa época, el país en que más libre y ampliamente se meditó sobre la problemática general de la historia"; cf. Godoy Alcántara, "Discurso"; Menéndez y Pelayo, *Historia de las ideas,* vol. 1; Frankl, *El antijovio;* Mignolo, "Metatexto"; and Kohut, "Retórica." For a less generous view of the importance and originality of Vives and his followers, see Lewis, "Humanist Historiography," 68–101. On the preceptive works in the Italian tradition, see Cochrane, *Historians and Historiography,* 479–93; and Black, "New Laws."

28. A number of scholars have pointed to the distinctiveness of Vives's views on history: Sánchez Alonso, *Historia,* 1:361–63; Bonilla, *Luis Vives* 2:305–28; Usón Sesé, "El concepto de la historia"; Cuccorese, "Juan Luis Vives"; and Frankl, *El antijovio.* My discussion of the works of Vives is particularly indebted to Frankl, who notes (121–37) that Vives is innovative on a number of counts: the idea of the different levels of "truth" in history, the emphasis on exact chronology for achieving "truth" in narrative, and the conviction that careful study of primary sources could lead to singular and valuable results. On the availability of Vives's works after 1532, see Noreña, *Bibliography,* iv–vi.

29. Although aware of the astrological views of history current at the time, Vives bases his discussion on those of Augustine and the humanists. For an indication of Vives's views on astrology, see his "Genethliacon Iesuchristi" (1518), in *Opera* (7:3–17), a devotional work in which the first-person narrator tells of visiting the Nativity scene in a dream and offering to tell the horoscope of the newborn. Mary disabuses the narrator of his "errors" with a Christian version of the celestial powers at work at the time of the birth of Christ.

Vives and the Paradox of the Historian as *Vate*

Vives's discussion of the concept and writing of history (and its relationship to fiction) ranges over a number of works, most notably *De disciplinis* (Bruges, 1531), which includes *De causis corruptarum artium* and *De tradendis disciplinis,* and *De ratione dicendi* (Bruges, 1532). Vives also wrote numerous other passages, treatises, and dialogues relevant to more general questions concerning language, truth, and probability in narrative.[30] His reflections on the subject are thus contained within works that have a much broader scope, and yet one can perceive in his writings an effort to put forth a systematic theory of history and its methods.[31] Throughout the discussion, Vives constantly contrasts his vision of the potential virtues of the historian's discipline to what he views as the corrosive defects in the existing historiographical record. The vehemence with which he describes the flaws in Classical historiography and Christian hagiography—often similar in tone to his better-known criticisms of fiction—somewhat overshadows his constructive discussions of the topic in *De tradendis disciplinis* and in *De ratione dicendi.*

At the core of Vives's consideration of historical writing there seems to lie a concern for designing a pedagogical program adequate for preparing students and citizens for the political, religious, and historical challenges of his day. Faced with a scarcity of historical texts that live up to his exalted notion of the discipline, and with what he perceives as pernicious competition from seductive "light" literature, Vives paradoxically ends up by suggesting that historians adopt techniques akin to those of fiction so as to make history "alive" and meaningful. His proposal brings up important questions related to the concepts of probability and verisimilitude and merits detailed discussion because it becomes a source for critical debates concerning the writing of history, such as those found in the chronicles of the Indies. At the same time, Vives's discussion exemplifies the sort of blurring of boundaries considered to be characteristic of this period.[32]

---

30. In book 2, chaps. 4–6, of *De causis corruptarum artium* (1531), Vives discusses the causes that have corrupted historiography and the other liberal arts; and in book 5, chaps. 1–4, of *De tradendis disciplinis* (1531), he advocates teaching history as a central part of the humanist curriculum. In "De vita et moribus eruditi" (1531), in *Opera* (6:416–37), he describes the qualities and training of the humanist scholar, including the historian. He lays out the constructive norms and requirements for proper historical narration in his rhetorical treatise *De ratione dicendi* (1532), particularly book 3. His ideas on probability are outlined throughout the latter, as well as in *Instrumento probabilitas*, in *Opera* (3:82–120).

31. Montero Díaz, "La doctrina de la historia," xxii.

32. Nelson, *Fact or Fiction,* 49.

Vives frames his discussion as both critique of past historiographical practices and a prescription for the future map of the discipline. In book 2, chapter 5 of his *De causis corruptarum artium,* he seeks to establish the "just" boundaries of history by positing "truth" as its definitive foundation (the basis on which to demarcate its limits from other types of discourse) and teaching as its final goal. In particular, the proximity of historical narrative to poetic fiction and to legal rhetoric leads Vives to map the territory of history as distinct from these types of discourse in content and intent, if not always in form. He reviews earlier efforts to define the term, some of which emphasized the need for the historian to have witnessed the events he records, and others of which defined the historian as inquirer into a distant past beyond his experience. He presents the Greek tradition as one in which poetic fiction irreversibly encroached upon history's terrain. Early Greek poets (Vives does not name them here, although later he mentions Homer, Hesiod, and others) are lambasted for having misunderstood their "proper" function (to preserve the past for didactic purposes) and exploiting instead history's potential as entertainment: "[They] mixed truth with falsehood and even deformed the truths, when they believed that in this way they would possess greater charm or command greater admiration. To this effect, they abused figures of speech, metaphors, allegories, ambiguities, and similarities between things or names. Of a man named Taurus, they said he was *a real bull;* . . . of a long lance, they said it *reached the sky.*"[33] For Vives, poetic language and tropes inherently distort the memory of the past. While poets "lied" purposely to captivate and entertain their audiences, other authors did so unintentionally by perpetuating errors in names and places. The use of incompatible calendar systems resulted in hopelessly confused chronology. Some based their work on unreliable sources such as rumors, personal letters, and funeral orations, leaving a legacy of figural language and factual errors to subsequent generations. In Vives's harsh assessment, neither research nor revelation would be sufficient to reverse the poetic distortions of historical fact endemic to the early Greek poetic tradition. Later Greek authors mistook praise as the main goal of history. Herodotus and Diodorus Siculus, Vives suggests, sought to compete with Homer and Hesiod, but, lacking the

---

33. "Veris miscuerunt falsa, et ipsa eadem vera alio detorserunt, ubi plus putarent habitura vel gratiae vel admirationis: abusi sunt ad eam rem loquendi figuris, metaphoris, allegoris, amphibologiis, similitudinibus rerum, aut nominum: ut hominem cui esset nomen *Tauro,* taurum *bovem* esse proderent . . . *longam* hastam, *caelum tangere.*" Vives, *Causis,* book 2, chap. 5, in *Opera,* 6:102 (emphasis in original).

poets' prodigious epic material, they created a "marvelous" vision of reality. Other ancient historians, blinded by patriotism, tended to exalt the achievements of their own nations while minimizing those of others: "There were some who with praises tried to magnify their own deeds and to lower with hostile reproaches those of others as much as possible. Neither attitude is proper to the historian, who should leave each event in its own natural dimension. Among the writers of Greek histories, you will find that, as the saying goes, *an Indian elephant is made out of a mosquito.*"[34] Gross disproportions, lack of balance, and partial views are the manifest signs of the poetic exaggerations and lies that infiltrated the ancient historical record.[35]

Likewise, in his view, Christian hagiography has been plagued by hyperbole. Although modern historians fare better than the ancients in this account, they have erred not simply in defending the reputation of their countries (the job, he tells us, "not of a historian, but a lawyer"),[36] but in selecting their topics, choosing to record trivial events, such as banquets, hunting expeditions, and love intrigues. Vives chastises authors such as Jean Froissart (1337–1410), Enguerrand de Monstrelet (1390–1453), Philippe de Commynes (1445–1509), and Diego de Valera (1412–88)[37] for omitting the most exemplary and useful elements in history. He is remarkably specific about what should not be included: overly insignificant details—the sort treasured by historians today—have no place here (they might well distract from the moralizing and exemplary synthesis), and neither do narratives of revenge and war—the traditional fare of history—because they elicit a perverse pleasure from the reader and encourage future generations to imitate the bloody savagery of the past.[38] History's role in educating the soul means that topics of peace and examples of reason, moderation, and Christian piety should predominate. He reprimands modern historians as well on stylistic questions, reproaching them for failing to intersperse their

---

34. "Quidam, et sua laudibus in majus auxerunt, et aliena inimica insectatione quantum ipsis licuit depresserunt, quorum neutrum est historici, sed singula suae magnitudini ac naturae relinquere: invenias apud scriptores rerum Graecorum *ex culice*, quod ajunt, *factum elephantum Indicum.*" Vives, *Causis*, book 2, chap. 6, in *Opera* 6:106 (emphasis in original).

35. He cites Sallust on the elegant inaccuracy of Athenian historians, and more specifically, of Plutarch's *Parallel Lives*, which, Vives suggests, unfairly sought to equate the rising greatness of the Romans with the dwindling achievements of the Greeks. See Bonilla, *Luis Vives*, 306–7, and Cuccorese, "Juan Luis Vives," on Vives's severe evaluation of Greek historians.

36. Vives, *Causis*, book 2, chap. 6, in *Opera*, 6:108.

37. For overviews of the works of the French authors, see Barnes, *A History of Historical Writing*, 76–77; on Valera, see Carbia, *Crónica oficial*, 59–60.

38. Vives expands on this topic, so relevant to the recording of the history of the Indies, in *De concordia et discordia humani generis*, in *Opera* (5:193–403).

own commentary and opinion into the narration of events. To exercise judgment is an essential requirement, in his view: objective narration and moral gloss are complementary facets of true history if it is to foster prudence. Last but not least, he criticizes their works as so unreadable as to be irrelevant. While those writing in Latin have "a base and extremely dirty style, or better, no style at all," those who write in the vernacular do so with a style that is "uniformly monotonous and grey, with no salt, grace, or refinement, so that only with difficulty can the work capture the reader's attention for more than half an hour."[39] Vives's metaphor of books as nourishment is important because it hints at a much larger concern. Reading or listening to stories, he suggests, is a basic human need, one that people will fulfill at any cost. The lack of appealing historical prose leads readers to consume chivalric romances, such as the "manifestly lying" Amadís or Lancelot cycles that grant their readers no knowledge beyond an "inane" pleasure.[40] Although Vives's tirade against the dangers of chivalric romance today seems quaint and excessively moralizing, we can perhaps sympathize with the spirit in which it is offered if we consider in our own time some of the more escapist forms of popular diversion and their impact on the attention span and critical thinking skills of consumers of these forms of entertainment. One can well imagine that Vives's concern for grounding an educational program on history (rather than on evasive fictional works) stems from a desire to develop a pedagogy able to match the crises of his time, which included violent strife in the context of religious divisions and of Spanish imperialist expansion, moral issues of which he was painfully aware. Further, Vives's insistence on the excesses and omissions of previous historians (only a handful of historians—Thucydides, Livy, Tacitus, and a few others—merit rereading, in his view) points to something of a sea change in the perception of the status of history among the disciplines. Vives's imagined ideal of an objective and exemplary narrative, distinct from both the classical and medieval models, indicates the central position accorded history within his educational program, as well as a deep concern for the discursive strategies appropriate to transmitting it. His grim description of the history of historiography is thus

39. "A nostri in illo suo Latino sermone, stilo sunt sordidissimo, ac spurcissimo, seu nullo potius . . . si vernaculis scribunt linguis, unus est totius orationis color fusucs, et dilutus; unus habitus, sine sale, sine ulla gratia, et cultu, tenere ut lectorem dimidium horae vix possit." Vives, *Causis,* book 2, chap. 6, in *Opera,* 6:109.

40. Vives, *Opera,* 6:109. See his critique of chivalric romance in *Institutio feminae christianae,* chap. 5.

closely linked to his discussion in *De tradendis disciplinis* of the importance of history and how to go about studying it, as well as to his guidelines for proper historical writing in *De ratione dicendi*.

In book 5 of *De tradendis disciplinis,* he argues that the pleasure and utility to be derived from history are connected to the innate human drive to inquire about things that lie beyond individual experience. Vives suggests that the unique function of narrative rests in its ability to communicate the experiences of others. Narrative about strange or momentous events would appear to be so naturally compelling, that once readers or listeners are drawn in, they drop everything so as to learn the outcome of the story. In a fascinating passage in book 2 of *De ratione dicendi,* he elaborates on this phenomenon, attributing it to the psychological sensation of listening to or reading stories:

> We are moved by the events that befall others as by our own; and we put ourselves in the place of others . . . that is why the description of the fortunes and troubles of others, as in histories, affects our spirit. Moreover, in other accounts that we know are fictitious, we rejoice, laugh, cry, hope, fear, hate, sympathize, or become indignant or angry, and even more so if events are displayed as if before the eyes so that you think it is not a narrative, but a scene made real, so that we are no longer just moved by the feelings of others, but by their very misfortunes, as if they had befallen ourselves or one of our own. In this way we are pained by the adversities and miseries of others, even when those who had to bear them were not pained by them.[41]

In the act of reading or listening, the figures and actions evoked in the text would appear to become re-created as a scene or spectacle in the mind of the reader. Vivid narrative commands belief, especially when the reader or listener knows it to be imaginary. While all narratives elicit an emotional response, fiction does so more powerfully because it would appear to bring

---

41. "Movemur eadem ratione alienis casibus tamquam nostris, et nos in eorum vicem succedimus . . . ergo descriptiones alienorum malorum aut bonorum, ut in historiis, concutiunt nostros animos, et alioqui in iis quae esse fabulosa scimus, exhilaramur, ridemus, damus lacrimas, speramus, metuimus, odimus, indignamur, favemus, irascimur, idque tanto magis si velut ob oculos ponantur, ut non narrari credas, sed agi, ut iam non moveant nos affectus alieni, sed casus ipsi, tamquam si nobis aut nostris contigissent: ergo res adversas et miserables dolemus, etiam si hi non doluerint qui sunt perpessi." Vives, *De ratione dicendi,* book 2, chap.14, in *Opera,* 2:166.

things to life. By presenting events as if perceived ("a scene made real"), fictive narrative prompts the reader to identify with imaginary characters, and even to experience imaginary pain. It is the possibility of this intense psychological identification with, or vicarious experience of, the fate and emotions of others that makes narrative such an important concern for Vives. In an early anticipation of Coleridge's notion of the suspension of disbelief, Vives notes that fictional accounts paradoxically appear to command credibility in a way that works of history do not.[42] Indeed, as we shall see, in a somewhat stunning reversal, he appears to advocate that particular histories be written in such a way as to convey the experience of fiction, or at least that they harness some of the power of purely imaginary narrative to represent "true" and exemplary events and figures. In this sense, although he considers history to be distinct from fiction in content and intent, the historian may borrow from the techniques of fiction to foster exemplarity and indeed may be required to do so, not just to remain alive and meaningful to readers, but to reach any audience at all.

Ife has noted the way in which Vives's and other moralists' critiques of fiction have their source in Plato's *Republic,* where Socrates raises moral and metaphysical objections to the use of fiction (in this case, epic poetry) in the early education of leaders in the ideal state.[43] Plato, it is true, does not address the problem of historical accuracy or inaccuracy in the Homeric poems (he suggests that the truth about the past cannot be known, and that the basic procedure of "lying poets" is to invent). His main objections refer rather to the implausibility and sacrilegious character of the portrayal of the divinities and heroes as proof of the falsehood or unreality of the entire narrative, and to the inappropriateness of epic for the moral instruction of future leaders. Not only do the epics provide bad examples of gods and heroes governed by petty quarrels and base emotions, but the poetry of the narrative affects the reader or listener more profoundly than does everyday language. Might not the most pitiable scenes of the *Iliad,* he suggests, discourage citizens from engaging in battle for fear of pain, slavery, and death?[44] In what could be considered an answer to Plato, Vives responds to these concerns in arguing for the superiority (in pedagogical terms) not of philosophy, but of true history as a kind of narrative that, unlike the "lying fictions" of poets, is

42. His point here is similar to that which, in recent decades, Félix Martínez Bonati has formulated with greater precision as the ironical credibility achieved by the basic narrator of fiction. See, for instance, his *Fictive Discourse,* 28–36.

43. Ife, *Reading and Fiction,* 24–48.

44. See Plato, *Republic,* 382 and 598–600.

both veridical and able to channel the powerful psychological experience of narrative to virtuous or morally useful ends.[45]

Unlike old wives' tales or the "mendacious" kind of fictions described above, true history, Vives writes, fosters the teaching of prudence. Prudence, which enables one to channel one's passions sagaciously and to better the soul, has two sources: judgment and experience. Judgment is an innate, natural faculty that can be "polished" (but not learned) by studying the canonical ancient and Christian authors, as well as rhetoric and probability. Individual experience comes from one's character and actions over the course of a lifetime. But one can also gain access, he suggests, to the experience of others through reading or listening to history. The act of reading history brings alive the characters of the past to be contemplated and assimilated into the reader's own experience (and thus, it is important that it be well written). In teaching prudence, history fosters the ability to judge and synthesize information drawn from both study or reading and experience, and to apply these elements in a practical fashion, to act, in a sense, in anticipation of the future: "so that prudence is akin to a sort of divination, according to the old adage: whomsoever conjectures accurately should be regarded as the most discerning seer."[46] Significantly, Vives here links the notion of the soothsayer, or *vate,* not to the poet but to the writer of history, inasmuch as the historian possesses prudence and imparts it to the reader. History appears to have taken over in Vives's model the central place accorded memory in many medieval rhetorical systems, as described by Mary Carruthers: "Memory was . . . an integral part of the virtue of prudence, that which makes moral judgment possible. Training the memory was much more than a matter of providing oneself with the means to compose and converse intelligently when books were not readily at hand, for it was in trained memory that one built character, judgment, citizenship, and piety."[47] Although Vives urges careful attention to Christian topics and

---

45. For a discussion of the problem of poetry in Plato's *Republic,* see Vives's dialogue *Veritas Fucata* (1522), in which Truth and Falsehood negotiate a truce, legislating the role of each in poetry, as well as Nelson's comments on this text in *Fact or Fiction,* 45–48.

46. "Ut genus sit quoddam divinationis prudentia, quemadmodum prisca sententia declaratur: *Bene qui conjecerit, hunc vatem perhibeto optimum.*" Vives, *De tradendis disciplinis,* book 5, chap. 1. Vives distinguishes between two kinds of prudence, that of the flesh and that of the soul. The former is condemned by the Scriptures and called by Paul "stupidity." In terms of the preferred prudence of the soul, he writes: "cui non sunt idonei natura stupidi, aut stolidi, nec inepti, et pueriles conjectores; quandoquidem prudentiae pars optima, in conjecturis sita est, quas de rebus sequentibus, e conjunctis, et transactis, sumimus." Vives, *De tradendis disciplinis,* book 5, chap. 1, in *Opera,* 6:387.

47. Carruthers, *Book of Memory,* 9. In *De anima et vita,* book 2, chap. 2, Vives speaks of memory as a faculty of the soul that is particularly sparked by visual images and by feelings.

outlook, he envisions history less as prophecy or revelation of God's will than as an aid to refining human judgment and to directing the will properly. As the institutionalized form of memory, history plays a crucial role in cultivating prudence in the moral citizen.

If Vives imagines the historian as a wise man and optimal teacher of citizens, he often ascribes feminine characteristics to historical narrative, thus illustrating his use of the sort of mixed metaphor that Rebhorn finds common to rhetorical discourses of the period.[48] For history to be the "wet nurse" of prudence in the individual, it must record true events and experiences. As the "mother" of all the other arts, history must lay a solid and reliable foundation for the study of medicine, moral philosophy, law, and theology. As the crucial link between past and future, history is a "generative" force necessary for social and intellectual continuity: the art most essential to understanding mankind's place in the world. Within the humanist program, the study of history takes precedence over (or becomes inextricably linked to) moral philosophy. In qualifying historical narrative as chaste (motherly, nurselike), as opposed to its "licentious" fictional counterparts, Vives alludes to a *topos* and advocates a program of reading to entertain and instruct in practical matters without overwhelming the senses and encouraging immoral vicarious experience.[49] Vives completes this section of *De tradendis disciplinis* by proposing an order for the study of history as well as a list of "false" histories that should be avoided.

In *De ratione dicendi*, Vives expands on the points made earlier from the perspective of writing history. He proposes guidelines to be applied to any kind of history—whether sacred or human. He distinguishes description (of fixed things) from narration (of things or events as they move in time), and categorizes narrative types according to their intended end or goal, which can be either to teach or explain, to persuade, or to capture the reader's or listener's attention, although he notes that these goals are often mixed. Narrative that aims to teach or explain must be "true"; that which aims to persuade must be probable or at least well feigned, while narrative intended for entertainment or holding the audience's attention has greater freedom.[50]

As narrative that aims to explain or teach what is not known, historiography must endeavor to represent the "truth"—in both particular and universal

---

48. Rebhorn, *Emperor of Men's Minds*, 12.

49. On the Greek myth of Mnemosyne (Remembrance) as mother of the Muses, see Arendt, "Concept of History," 43. On the chastity of history versus the seductiveness of fiction, see the ideas of Giovanni Pontano (1426–1503) (as quoted by Frankl, *El antijovio*, 178) and Weinberg, *History of Literary Criticism*, 1:14; also Gilmore, *Humanists*, 48.

50. Vives, *De ratione dicendi*, in *Opera*, 2:204.

terms—with exactitude. Although in writing history numerous approaches can be taken (to narrate the private life of one individual or many, the public actions of one individual or many, the life of one or numerous nations), Vives emphasizes framing the subject in such a way as to highlight what is exemplary. The requirement of truth, he concedes, will vary to some extent depending on the kind of historical narrative. The representation of the "simple and integral" truth, which corresponds to the strictest sense of the term, is required in documents such as pacts, alliances, and other public decrees, as well as in religious texts, where each and every word must be able to sustain critical examination. In other narratives that deal with "particular events," however, it is sufficient for the historian to define his subject based on the "substantial" truth or general meaning of events, that is, what is exemplary or morally useful, and to include dramatic representations of speeches so that his work will be both entertaining and instructive. While Vives has little to say about the narratives of decrees and pacts, in those of the "substantial" truth he finds it more difficult to dispense with the discursive elements that resemble those of fiction.

Vives's main criterion for historical narration is that it should apprehend the "image" (*imago, pictura, speculum*) of the past in a faithful manner, and yet he is quite vague as to how to achieve this. He does not discuss the treatment of sources or textual authorities, whether ancient or modern. He frequently invokes metaphors from the visual arts to emphasize the notion that historical prose should create the illusion of a precise narrative replica of events: "Since it is necessary [that history] be the mirror of time, if the historian says something false, the mirror will be false and will reflect what it has not received. But neither will it be a true image if it is greater or lesser than reality, that is, if the historian deliberately degrades or elevates reality."[51] Much like a painter trained in perspective and anatomy, the ideal historian should shape the events in his narrative in such a way as to preserve their proper proportions and to create the illusion of a direct perception of events: "History is like a painting, image, or mirror of past events. Just as the events of the past are told, so are those of the future."[52] In alluding to the notion of history as visual spectacle, Vives was drawing in part on classical conceptions, which represented historiography as analogous to visual

---

51. "Nam ut oportet esse speculum temporum, si falsum dicat falsum erit speculum, reddetque quod non acceperit; sed neque erit vera imago, si maior sit quam res, vel minor, id est si res deprimat consulto, vel attollat." Vives, *De ratione dicendi*, book 3 chap. 3, in *Opera*. For a similar formulation, see his *Causis*, book 2, chap. 6.

52. "Est enim velut pictura, et imago, atque speculum rerum praeteritum; ac quemadmodum res narrantur transactae, ita etiam ventura." Vives, *De ratione dicendi*, book 3, chap. 3.

representation in that in it the past is displayed as coexisting simultaneously with the present.[53] There is here a form of what Koselleck has called "naive realism" *avant la lettre*,[54] a hope that historiography might achieve in narrative the kind of precision that Renaissance techniques had brought to the visual arts. But historical representation for Vives is more than a mirror of time, a transparent reflection of truth: it must also illuminate events by commenting on their significance. The outlook and abilities of the historian, then, are crucial, and it is here that the analogies to pictorial perspective become problematic. Judging from the Greek root for history, *istorein* (to see), events should be presented as if directly perceived by an eyewitness.[55] The use of visual metaphors would seem to suggest the importance of direct observation, and yet there is no mention of actual witnessing as a prerequisite for the conscientious chronicler. The vantage point of Vives's ideal historical narrator is not limited, like that of an eyewitness, but rather encompasses a double perspective, both a panoramic and an inside view: "So as to foster prudence, causes, plans, and results are to be explained, as well as anything hidden or secret in the affair, for these things teach prudence more than the events that have been seen by all. As for the rest, just as we said that for description it is most convenient that the whole scene be put under the eyes, likewise in history it is most convenient that the totality of events should be displayed as if observed from a high place."[56] The historian should narrate as if he had been present, like a supernatural witness who both sees from a distance and also possesses inside knowledge concerning the "occult" meanings of events. In Vives's formulation, the sense of accurate figural or pictorial perspective is combined with a concern for revealing the profound meanings of events, less as prophecy (in the Augustinian sense) than as an aid for prudence. The well-trained and wise historian, in Vives's view, need not have actually been an eyewitness himself (this would provide only a partial

53. For the importance of history as "visual spectacle" in Livy and the classical rhetorical tradition, see Feldherr, *Spectacle and Society*, 4–5; Quintilian, *Institutio oratoria*, book 4, chap. 2.

54. Koselleck, *Futures Past,* 132–33, uses this term to refer to the *topos* of historiography as a "mirror" of events since antiquity.

55. "History is the explanation of an event, originally from the term *istorein,* which means to see, since he who has seen the events is also the one who relates them." ("Historia, explicatio est rei gestae quae ab *isorein* [*sic*] trahit applicationem, quod est videre, quia aliquis eam viderit, qui et narrarit." Vives, *De ratione dicendi,* book 3, chap. 3, in *Opera,* 2:205.

56. "Quocirca ad prudentiam explicentur causae, et consilia, et eventus, et si quid sit occultum et arcanum in negotio, nam illa magis prudentiam instituunt, quam gesta omnibus exposita; ceterum quemadmodum ad describendum diximus commodissimum esse si quis rem totam oculis subiiceret, ita ad historiam si tamquam ex alto omnia spectarit quomodo gerantur." Vives, *De ratione dicendi,* book 3, chap. 3, in *Opera,* 2:207.

understanding of events), but rather should re-create this narrative perspective imaginatively from his investigations. This ideal of presenting the past as if directly perceived by the narrator (but not necessarily witnessed by the "real" author) in historical narrative becomes a negative modality in the discussions of Oviedo and Las Casas, as we will see in the following chapters.

The most concrete advice Vives offers about actually achieving the goal of objectivity concerns reproducing an accurate chronology, which takes precedence over geographical concerns and also constitutes one of the chief narrative resources of historical discourse in holding the interest of the reader. By narrating events in the sequence in which they occurred, Vives suggests, the historian may postpone telling their outcome without resorting to the seductions he finds characteristic of entertaining or "licentious" narrative. But, more important, to visualize the precise sequence of events is to understand their causality: an exact chronology is the key to unlock the truth of history. Chronology reflects "natural order," the precise and necessary sequence of actual occurrences through time. If the narrative replicates this order of events faithfully, it will exhibit an internal coherence or logic that according to Vives, mirrors that of the real world. In contrast, "artistic" order—characteristic of epic poetry—permits deviations from natural chronological order to reflect aesthetic priorities or designs and, if used in historical narrative, will stand out as illogical or contrived in the same way that false arguments, lies, and exaggerations in language tend to manifest themselves as improbable or out of proportion. If historical truth is what is most "congruent" with nature, it can be approached through the instrument of probability, which turns out to be another central and problematic aspect of Vives's concept of history.

Vives deals with probability in *De ratione dicendi* and, more extensively, in his treatise on probability. As the method of applying what is known to discover what is uncertain, probability is necessary for all of the arts.[57] In granting mankind reason, Vives suggests, God imbued humanity with an innate ability to perceive the natural logic of the world through the senses and, thus, to grasp an inkling of the divine order of things. Sensory perceptions should be the first and best guides for understanding objects; careful observations of exteriors, causes, and effects will lead to insights as to hidden meanings. Next, the inquirer should resort to experts (the first being sacred

---

57. For an insightful discussion of the Aristotelian idea of probability in fictional and nonfictional discourse, as well as Renaissance reinterpretations, see Newsom, *A Likely Story,* 19–33 and 61–73.

authorities, the second, wise human opinion). In separating truth from falsehood, one looks for apparent contradictions, traces of deliberate intent to deceive, or evidence of unruly passion.

Probability, Vives suggests, is relevant to both narratives of true events and of fictional ones; conceptually it is close to verisimilitude, or the set of norms that apply to the realm of fictional narrative. Inevitably, in his view, art is an imitation of reality. On the one hand, "lies" contained in fictional narratives tend to make themselves manifest by contradicting what is natural and probable, by conflicting with one's innate understanding of how the world works; on the other, it is impossible for a fiction—no matter how outlandish—to be totally alienated from a recognizable representation of reality.[58] Although training in probable reasoning is an aid in distinguishing truth from falsehood in factual narrative, it is not a foolproof method; indeed judgments based on probability can be deceptive.[59] In narrating a true event that appears to exceed probability, such as a miracle, the author should present it in such a way as to make sense of it, adjusting the truth of the facts to the logical expectations of the reader so that it is *both* truthful and verisimilar. In his treatise on probability, he recommends using tags such as "I believe" when narrating or stating opinions about events that are in doubt and including an alternative perspective to correct a dubious or partial one, on the assumption that the confrontation of incomplete views or perspectives may hint at a fuller truth.[60]

Although history and fiction differ in terms of content and intent, and in the presence of disturbances in natural order, complex histories (those that have "color," such as the works of Sallust, Livy, and Thucydides) would appear nonetheless to employ imaginative narrative and discursive devices

58. "One cannot intentionally invent a narrative that is so absurd that it has no connection to the nature of things. This indicates to what extent our mind cannot even understand or rationalize completely against nature." ("Nec fingi dedita opera tam absurda potest narratio, quin quasi filum aliquod et colorem retineat naturae rerum; adeo contra naturam omnino mens nostra nec intelligere quidem valet, aut ratiocinari.") Vives, *De ratione dicendi*, book 3, chap. 7, in *Opera*, 2:218.

59. "Sometimes certain falsehoods appear to be more probable than certain truths, an error that stems not from the things themselves, but from our mistaken judgment. That is why narrative should be not just truthful (this would doubtless be enough for reality), but it should also appear verisimilar in relation to us." ("Sed aliquando falsa quaedam quibusdam veris fiunt probabiliora, quod non ex rebus ipsis nascitur, sed ex nobis prave judicantibus, ideoque non vere modo narandum est, quod rei quidem sufficeret, sed verisimiliter propter nos.") Vives, *De ratione dicendi*, book 3, chap. 4, in *Opera*, 2:213.

60. As Vives writes in *De instrumento probabilitas*, in *Opera*, 3:85: "The occasional error of the senses is corrected by another" ("sed quod uno tempore erratum est sensibus, alio corrigitur quod abo uno homine, sarcitur ab alio").

akin to those of fiction. Toward the end of his section on historiography, Vives brings his argument full circle, quoting Quintilian that history is in fact like a prose poem.[61] Ever concerned about reaching the reader, Vives recommends that historians include "agreeable diversions," digressions from strict chronology of events, such as invented speeches—whether in direct or indirect discourse—so as to stress important points. Whatever other elements (such as dialogues or digressions) are mixed with historical narration should not distort its substantial features. To write history in the form of a personal letter, he suggests, is to detract from its truth value. A reliable account requires not the limited first-person voice, but a distanced and impersonal narrative point of view.

An irreproachable history would highlight and interpret events in light of Christian values.[62] In this regard, the presence of the historian's voice as moral guide fulfills a crucial function in the text. As Vives explains in his criticisms of modern historians in *De causis corruptarum artium,* it is not enough just to record events in an exact fashion. For history to teach prudence, the moral commentary of the author must illuminate the narrative, judiciously recommending exemplary acts and condemning reprehensible ones. Thus, while the ideal historical narrator should represent events as if directly witnessed (even if the real author-historian has not done so), the judgment exercised upon them should be the historian's own. Vives suggests that when it is not "plausible" for an author to state his opinion directly through the narrator, he may resort to figurative language or to present his view in the voice of another character.

Vives does not address the characteristics and training to be required of the historian in particular—he writes instead about the training of the Christian wise man in *De vita et moribus eruditi.*[63] An imitator of Christ, the man of letters should be of devout and dedicated character. He should keep in mind the limitations of human knowledge and understanding in view of the wisdom of God. In his *De concordia et discordia humani generis,* however, Vives characterizes the mind of the wise man as a "felicitous terrestrial divinity."[64] It is thus perhaps significant to find in Vives's ideal of an objective narrative of history (a mirror of reality) a fantasy that would seem to

---

61. Quintilian, *Institutio oratoria,* book 10, chap. 1.

62. For Frankl, this is the salient aspect of Vives's philosophy of history, as he explains in *El antijovio,* 121–37.

63. Vives, *De vita et moribus eruditi,* in *Opera,* 6:416–37.

64. "Tamquam terrestre quoddam numen felicissimum." Vives, *De concordia et discordia humani generis,* book 4, chap. 9, in *Opera,* 5:369, as quoted in Brading, "The Two Cities."

imply a narrator whose perception is not limited to ordinary perspective, a distant humanist free of human constraints and failings.[65] And, in this regard, it is perhaps ironic—given Vives's animosity toward the Greek poets—to find in his model inquirer a figure that would seem to recall both the Homeric bard and Augustine's researcher-prophet. In effect, Vives appears to imagine the ideal historical narrator as something like a divinely inspired *vate,* an image that, as I will show in the following chapters, takes on highly negative connotations in the works of Oviedo and Las Casas.

Vives's historiographical ideal would also seem to run against his broader view of language and its limited ability to communicate truth, or to put it another way, the connection between words or narrative and the world depicted. Indeed, the idea of congruence or integrity that is so central to his doctrine of history is complicated by the idea he expresses elsewhere that all human endeavors—including the practice of the liberal arts and language itself—have been tainted by the pattern of original sin.[66] In a sense, fully objective, transparent discourse would have been possible only in Paradise. Before the Fall, Vives suggests, there was no cause for misunderstanding and no need for lying: "At that time of clear consciousnesses, each person would have easily said what he wanted, and the hearer would have understood him clearly. In this state of probity and simplicity of spirits, the speaker could have manifested directly what he felt, and the hearer would have had confidence in one whom he did not suspect of lying. But now with the introduction of darkness in the spirit through sin, a simple explanation is no longer sufficient."[67] East of Eden, language is slippery, subject to misunderstanding and dissimulation. As a result, there is a need to determine "truth" based on argument, proof, and probability. Thus, to achieve an objective or transparent "image" of events would appear to imply a gesture that recuperates something like the original integrity of language, seemingly reversing the corruption inherent in human discourse since the Fall. Indeed, for Vives it is not just fiction that "lies." The ideal historian, it would appear, aspires to recover something like prelapsarian discourse, the transparency

65. On the theme of the limits of human understanding and the illusion of wisdom in the works of Vives, see his *Praelectio in Sapientem.*

66. For the ways in which medieval authors used the Fall in connection with theories of language and practical linguistic problems, see Eric Jager, *The Tempter's Voice.*

67. "In claritate illa ingeniorum et quisque facile esset quaecunque voluisset elocutus, et audiens liquido intellexisset, tum in tanta animorum probitate ac simplicitate et dicens recta exprompsisset quae sentiebat, et audiens habuisset fidem ei quem suspicatus non esset mentiri. Nunc vero tenebris animo inductis per delictum, sola explication non sufficit." Vives, *De ratione dicendi,* book 2, chap. 11, in *Opera,* 2:156.

of language before the Fall. In this sense, Vives's view of history is part of a more general Christian philosophy of the human condition. He appears to advocate as a practical possibility within an educational program something that he recognizes elsewhere to be an unreachable ideal—and it is precisely this ideal quality of history that seems to interest him most. His concern for accurate and exemplary recording of facts did not lead him to undertake a long historical narrative, although a number of his works deal with historical subjects.[68] He offers no practical advice—in terms of dealing with sources—for how to achieve this godlike view of the past, although in his devotional work "Genethliacon Iesuchristi,"[69] he alludes to a conflict over the method appropriate to sacred history in which revelation is judged superior to astrology. Other than Vives's historical overviews of the liberal arts, his works dealing with history tend to be either very short or to adopt literary forms that he himself considered inappropriate for "true" history, such as the dialogue or the personal letter.

In reviewing Vives's contribution on the writing of history, I have tried to show the way in which the "case" for history elicited a rich discussion concerning distinctions between historical and fictional discourse and problems of narrative perspective and reliability in Spain in the sixteenth century. Vives highlights points that not only resonated in the intellectual circles of sixteenth- and seventeenth-century Spain and its colonies, but that have continued to resurface in recent discussions of the problem. On the one hand, in suggesting that the fictive quality of works of the imagination command credibility in ways that "true" ones do not, Vives hints at something like Coleridge's notion of the suspension of disbelief as the fundamental experience of fiction, reformulated by Félix Martínez Bonati as the ironic credibility or validity accorded to the discourse of the fictional narrator as the basic "rule" in the experience of fiction. For this critic, the unqualified credibility that is granted to the narrator of fiction stems from the reader's ironic awareness that the discourse is artifice, and this awareness

---

68. Bonilla, in *Luis Vives* (314–28), lists the following works as dealing with historical topics: *De causis corruptarum artium; De tradendis disciplinis; De initiis sectes et laudibus Philosophiae* (1518); "De Gothis et quomodo ab iisden capta Roma" (1522), intended as a prologue for *Comentaria in XXII libros de Civitate Dei Augustini* (1522); "In Suetoniam quaedam," in which he reconstructs the beginning paragraphs of that author's *Life of Ceasar; De Europae Disidiis et bello Turcico dialogus* (1526); *De Francisco Gallorum rege a Caesare capto* (1525). I would add Vives's "Genethliacon Iesuchristi," which takes the form of a devotional dream narrative and explores the conflict between soothsaying and revelation in sacred history.

69. Vives, "Genethliacon Iesuchristi," in *Opera,* 7:3–17.

is unique to the experience of fiction.[70] On the other, Vives's suggestion that historians need to harness some of the more captivating techniques of fiction if they are to gain readers and fulfill their exemplary and instructive function is the sort of observation that bolsters the critical commonplace of a blurring of discursive boundaries during this period.[71] All in all, Vives's requirements for historiographical representation, based on a critical reading of the tradition and a hope for a future record of human events that would be both objective and redemptive, add up to an ambitious proposal, one that is as intriguing as it is impractical. His exacting standards and scrutiny of the textual signs of truth and falsehood, while perhaps a product of an era preoccupied with questions of dissimulation and deception,[72] bring into focus problems concerning representation and reliability that continue to interest theorists of narrative today. In particular, his view of credibility in narrative as involving a complex relationship between events (things), the narrative that captures them, and the reader's reception of their meaning is apt. In other ways, his doctrine of and norms for writing history perhaps elicit more questions than answers, such as the equation of fiction with pretense or lies, the idea of historical narrative as both mirror and illumination of events, and the narrative stance of the historian as necessarily re-creating the points of view of a direct witness and of an absent commentator. In any case, he appears to have tapped in to a very rich vein of discussion and debate on the subject. Vives, one suspects, might have approved of the energy, if perhaps not always the divisive tone, behind this debate.[73] The difficulties and paradoxes raised by Vives resurface continually not just in the preceptive tradition in Spain in authors such as Pedro de Rhúa, Sebastián Fox Morcillo, Cabrera de Córdoba, and Jerónimo de San José, but in the writing of the early historiography of the Indies as well.

70. Martínez Bonati, in *Fictive Discourse* (34–36), describes the phenomenon of the unreliable narrator as a variation of this model.

71. For a recent expression of this topical subject, see Boruchoff, "Poetry of History."

72. For a discussion of the sources and examples from Spain of doctrines authorizing dissimulation as it pertained to religious belief and the prevalence of the doctrine of "mental reservation" in a wider philosophical, legal, and intellectual context in sixteenth-century Spain, see Zagorin, *Ways of Lying,* 1–62 and 153–85. See also the entries for "lying," "dissimulation," and "mental reservation" in *The Catholic Encyclopedia,* ed. Herbermann et al.

73. To recall his reflections on the ancients and the moderns in the prologue of *De disciplinis:* "I would not desire that anyone should yield his opinion to mine. I do not wish to be the founder of a sect, or to persuade anyone to swear by my conclusions. If you think, friends, that I seem to offer right judgments, see well to it that you give your adherence to them because they are true, not because they are mine." *On Education,* 9 (Watson's translation).

Soon after the publication of *De disciplinis* and *De ratione dicendi* in the 1530s, Spain would witness what Frankl has called the birth of a new historiographical type. This history of "opposition" or "refutation," which Frankl associates with the histories of writers such as Bernal Díaz and Jiménez de Quesada, was

> destinada no sólo a retener un trozo de realidad, sino también a refutar otra descripción de la misma realidad, y escrita, por consiguiente, no sólo en vista de la imagen del hecho en cuanto tal, sino también con miras a otra interpretación del mismo, hasta tal punto, que toda la exposición histórica aparece orientada en la exposición del adversario.

> [destined not just to retain a slice of reality, but also to refute another description of the same reality, and therefore written not just in view of the image of the event as such, but also with an eye to another interpretation of the event, to the point where the whole historical exposition appears to receive its orientation from the exposition of the adversary.][74]

On the one hand, questions of the authority of the historian had become paramount, with many writers claiming credibility based on experience, not training.[75] On the other, despite all the assurances in rhetorical treatises of the superiority and exemplarity of historical writing, in practice "true" histories that fell into disfavor with the crown appear to have been far more likely to be subject to real censorship (book burning, bans on publication) than were the infamous books of chivalry.[76]

It was within the framework of the high standards and expectations for historical narrative and the historian elaborated by Vives and others that the early chroniclers inscribed their efforts to record the Spanish conquest and colonization of the Indies. Gonzalo Fernández de Oviedo in the *Historia general y natural de las Indias* and Bartolomé de Las Casas in the *Historia de las Indias* constantly measure their own histories (and those of others) against the daunting humanist norms and yet manage to effect their own reversals,

74. Frankl, *El antijovio*, 96.

75. See, for example, Frankl, *El antijovio*, 82–101; Zamora, "Language and Authority"; Adorno, "Discursive Encounter."

76. For a hypothesis concerning the suppression of historical and ethnographic texts, see Adorno, "Literary Production."

finding audacious narrative solutions to the monumental task of explaining the New World to the Old. Often, they frame their attempts to address the issue in terms of a conflict between history and "fiction," and in terms of concerns that preoccupied Vives: the nature of the truth represented, the qualities and perceptive abilities of the narrator, and the credibility of the narrative both in relation to evidence and to the manner in which it is written. Although in many ways Oviedo bows to the rhetorical norms of writing history, he also reformulates them by critiquing the idea of the historian as a distant wise man or *sabio*. The notion of the historical narrator as able to conjure up an image of the past beyond his experience and present it as if directly perceived takes on a strikingly negative dimension in his history. Oviedo draws on the literature of reproof of superstitions to point to signs of an "unnatural" and therefore unreliable authorial perspective on the part of his rivals. In turn, Bartolomé de Las Casas exploits and transforms Oviedo's insights and versions of events, turning them against their author. Even as Las Casas adopts a prophetic tone that would seem to resuscitate the optic of the wise historian, his polemics with Oviedo, while bitter, contribute to productive insights concerning boundaries in historical discourse. In the chapters that follow, I will try to do justice to the wealth of insights that emerged in the early historiography of the Indies.

2

CONJECTURE AND CREDIBILITY IN THE *HISTORIA GENERAL Y NATURAL DE LAS INDIAS* BY GONZALO FERNÁNDEZ DE OVIEDO

THE KINDS OF HOPES for and anxieties about the writing of history expressed by Vives are reflected, albeit indirectly, in the early historical narratives of the discovery and conquest of the New World. Although one finds few explicit references to the preceptive authors or works in these accounts, historians Gonzalo Fernández de Oviedo y Valdés and Bartolomé de Las Casas display in their histories a thorough knowledge of the rhetorical commonplaces concerning the writing of history as well as a shared concern for the narrative and discursive norms of the discipline. Indeed, one can perceive in these early histories of America efforts to come to practical terms with the broad outlines of the humanists' theory and method of history, as well as vehement debates over what constitutes reliable or credible narration.

In the *Historia general y natural de las Indias* (1535, 1547, 1557, 1851–55),[1] Fernández de Oviedo draws on the central points of the historiographical precepts as a way to assert his own authority, and, indeed, to propose a method capable of fulfilling the humanist hope for a history that would be both objective and redemptive. In constructing his narrative, Oviedo employs the humanist framework while reformulating its terms, as much to attack the versions of others as to put forth his own vision and narrative strategies for writing history. Narrative reliability becomes a thematic as well as formal concern for this writer, who criticizes earlier accounts of the discovery and conquest, such as those of Peter Martyr d'Anghera and Lucio Marineo Sículo, as not just inaccurate, but even made up or deliberately distorted, and argues for his own method and discursive practices as being superior and more objective. In the process, Oviedo alludes to what he sees as the discursive signs of "fiction" or fabrication. Without trying to reduce this complex and multifaceted work to a single methodological inspiration (this would be a misleading approach), I hope instead to highlight the ways

---

1. All quotations from the *Historia general y natural (HGN)* are taken from Pérez de Tudela Bueso's edition and are cited parenthetically in the text by volume and page number, followed by book and chapter where necessary. English translations are my own.

in which Oviedo responded to the humanists' exalted idea of the role of history and also to their critical methods for reading sources, while lending practical insights on the question of reliability in historical narrative. Oviedo's reflection on the boundaries of history in itself tells us much about his work, revealing the competing pulls of science and religion upon him and pointing to a contested site in which natural versus supernatural knowledge is posited as a sign of authorial reliability.

While the humanist categories are, I believe, fundamental to understanding what Oviedo was attempting to do in his history, I will also refer in places to a terminology that is external to this sixteenth-century context. In seeking to identify the textual signs of fabrication in the works of his opponents, and at the same time to establish his own historiographic method as credible, Oviedo anticipates in a rudimentary fashion some of the insights of recent critics who seek to specify in narratological terms signposts of historiographical as opposed to fictional discourse.[2] In and of themselves, foundational sixteenth-century histories of the New World such as those of Oviedo and Las Casas are a fitting place to examine these signposts. On the one hand, these authors thrived on antagonism and yearned for clear-cut indices that would distinguish truthful from "lying" or fictional discourse; on the other, their works reflect a keen awareness, common also to the recent critical discussion, about the range of vision and capabilities appropriate to the "reliable" historical narrator, as well as concerning the distinctive problems of portraying "characters" in history. While the insights of contemporary narrative theory are not likely to account for all distinctions between fictional and historical narrative (any more than were, for that matter, the rhetorical precepts of the humanists in this direction), at least they can assist in describing with greater precision the kinds of narrative strategies that emerged from the clash between the humanist ideals for history and the practice of writing the history of the New World. Finally, a clearer understanding of the ways in which historiographical discursive practices differ from those of fiction might also shed light on some of the critical imprecisions that occur when these boundaries are not taken into account by contemporary critics.[3]

2. See, in particular, the works of Martínez Bonati, Genette, Rigney, and Cohn.

3. For an uncritical use of the notion of "fiction" in history, see, for example, Beatriz Pastor, *Armature of Conquest,* 47 and 64–79, where the author characterizes the early writings on the Indies to be "fictionalizations" of the facts. Mignolo, "Cartas, crónicas"; Zamora, "Historicity and Literariness"; and González Echevarría, "Humanismo," all point to problems in the twentieth-century reception of the *crónicas* as "fiction." On the continuing relevance of this debate, see Boruchoff, "The Poetry of History," and Knight, "On the Poetry of History."

Life and Works

Born in Madrid in 1478, Oviedo at age thirteen joined the courtly entourage of Prince don Juan as a *mozo de cámara* (not a page, a function reserved for nobles).[4] After the prince's premature death in 1497, Oviedo traveled as a soldier and courtier in various parts of Italy, where he would later return with Gonzalo Fernández de Córdoba as secretary on an ill-fated expedition in 1512. With a royal appointment of notary public (*escribano general*) and several other official salaried commissions (e.g., *veedor de fundiciones de oro*), he traveled to the New World (Santa Marta) in 1514, participating in Pedrarias Dávila's expedition to the Darién (today Panama). Faced with the notoriously violent exploitation of natives that occurred on this expedition—and the loss of many Castilian settlers to famine and disease—Oviedo found means to return to Spain in late 1515. He would remain until 1520 lobbying at court, first against Pedrarias Dávila, of whom he was openly critical, and later against Las Casas. In 1519 he published a chivalric romance, *Libro del muy esforzado e invencible caballero de fortuna, propiamente llamado don Claribalte* (Valencia). Back in the Indies in 1520–23, he traded in pearls and acted as lieutenant governor (*teniente de gobernador*) of the Darién. He published *Sumario de la natural historia de las Indias* (Toledo, 1526), which he dedicated to Charles V and in which he collected his impressions of the population and natural resources of the Indies together with narratives of his own experiences in the Caribbean and on the mainland. After obtaining the title of *cronista real* in 1532,[5] Oviedo held the post of *alcaide de la fortaleza* (governor of the fortress) of Santo Domingo and continued to write his historical and other works until his death in 1557.

His major work, *Historia general y natural de las Indias,* was written over a number of decades and only about one third of it was published

---

4. The basic contemporary biography is by Pérez de Tudela Bueso in "Vida y escritos," with important contributions by Otte in "Aspiraciones"; by Gerbi, on the years in Italy, in *Nature in the New World;* and by Castillero, on the years in the Darien, in "Gonzalo Fernández de Oviedo." In "Panegírico" (48), Bolaños summarizes what he calls a critical "diálogo de sordos," clearing up points of confusion in Oviedo's biographical profile. Speculation about his origins (de la Peña y Cámara, in "Contribuciones," theorizes that he might have been of illegitimate birth and gives circumstantial evidence to support the *converso* hypothesis; Pérez de Tudela Bueso, in "Vida y escritos," alleges possible political motivations related to the Beltraneja controversy) appear to have been put to rest by Uría Ríu, who in "Nuevos datos" documents that Oviedo's father was Miguel de Sobrepeña, an old Christian from Asturias.

5. On Oviedo's title of *cronista,* granted by Charles V in 1532, and the characteristics of such a commission, see Carbia, *Crónica oficial,* 76–77.

in his lifetime.[6] The first part (Seville, 1535) included books 1–19, plus chapters 1–10 of book 20 ("Infortunios y naufragios"), which the author later expanded and moved to the end of the entire work as book 50. Oviedo subsequently continued the research and compilation of his history, adding considerable information. A second edition of part 1, titled *Crónica de las Indias* and bound in many copies with Francisco de Xerez's *Conquista del Perú*, was printed in 1547. An edition of parts 2 and 3 was in the process of being printed in 1557 but was interrupted by Oviedo's death and reached only part 2, book 20, chapter 35. The full work (parts 1–3) as we know it today, which incorporates additions to part 1 not included in the 1547 edition, was not published until the 1850s under the direction of José Amador de los Ríos. This edition became the basis for another with modernized spelling, an index, and new introduction by Pérez de Tudela Bueso in 1957. To date, there is no critical edition that shows the author's successive revisions of the first part.[7]

A number of scholars have recognized the value of Oviedo's insights on the writing of history, and I am especially indebted to the work of Antonello Gerbi, Stephanie Merrim, Kathleen Myers, Álvaro Bolaños, and Anthony Pagden on the *cronista*'s historiographic strategies and their links to humanist philological debates. My own work marks a new direction by examining Oviedo's stance on questions related to narrative voice and perspective, and by situating his insights on the problem of narrative reliability in history in the context of the literature of the reproof of superstitions of his day. Further, I argue that the importance of his reflections is clarified when read in light of twentieth-century efforts by theorists of narrative to grapple with discursive borderlines. More than just a general awareness of humanist concerns, one can detect in Oviedo's *Historia general y natural* a critical reading of the norms for narrating history and, in particular, the idea of the historian's (and the figure of the narrator's) distance and perspective on events as a sign of his reliability; the use of narrative perspectivism (that is, the juxtaposition of divergent accounts and narrative styles) as a technique for representing conflicting points of view; the idea of textual and narrative coherence as an

6. For early editions and existing manuscripts, see Turner, *Gonzalo Fernández de Oviedo* (7–13), to which Jesús Carillo's recent "Introduction" to *Oviedo on Columbus* adds precision and detail.

7. Although no careful study has been done to date of the differences between the first two editions of Oviedo's text, Turner, in *Gonzalo Fernández de Oviedo* (7–8), suggests that the one from 1547 is "substantially identical" to that of 1535. Myers, in "Imitación," has begun to study selected textual revisions in successive editions, finding that Oviedo's later revisions tend to privilege in some places ancient authorities over eyewitnesses. See also Carillo's valuable description of the editions and manuscripts in *Oviedo on Columbus* (25–30).

indicator of truth; and the problem of exemplarity in history. In this regard, one can perceive conflicting impulses concerning the humanist program in the *Historia general y natural*.[8] Oviedo's critical attitude would appear to stem in part from the practical experience and insights of this early chronicler of the New World and to reflect what Pagden has aptly described as a "tension between an appeal to authorial experience and the demands of the canon."[9] But in part, Oviedo's ideas and methods also respond to ambiguities and tensions inherent in the demands of the canon. One can discern in this work both a formal and a thematic questioning that would seem to unravel the kind of narrative program advocated by the humanists even as it affirms a new basis for historiographical reliability.

The Historian at Work: "Esta pluma, o escritor vuestro"

Fernández de Oviedo clearly shares the humanist call for a new kind of historian and method, distinct from both ancient and modern models, in this case, to record the vastness of the natural and human history of the New World. The task, he notes in the *proemio* of the first book of his history, is of such a magnitude as to make it virtually impossible:

> ¿Cuál ingenio mortal sabrá comprender tanta diversidad de lenguas, de hábitos, de costumbres en los hombres destas Indias? ¿Tanta variedad de animales, así domésticos como salvajes y fieros? ¿Tanta multitud innarrable de árboles, copiosos de diversos géneros de frutas, y otros estériles, así de aquellos que los indios cultivan, como de los que la natura de su propio oficio produce, sin ayuda de manos mortales? ¿Cuántas plantas y hiervas útiles y provechosas al hombre? ¿Cuántas otras innumerables que a él no son conocidas, e con tantas diferencias de rosas e flores e olorosa fragancia?

8. Whether Oviedo was self-taught, as Pérez Tudela Bueso would have it ("Vida y escritos," xix), or received the "education of a prince," as Manuel Ballesteros Gaibrois (*Gonzalo Fernández*, 45) suggests, most scholars agree that he was an earnest disciple of humanism. Gerbi's *Nature in the New World* remains the most complete work on the subject, although in stressing the Italian over the Spanish influences, this author somewhat overstates his case. Oviedo was, according to Gerbi, Spanish "by birth, language and office . . . but an early sixteenth-century Italian in his mentality, his scientific curiosity, and his lofty concept of his office of historian, and finally in his subtle humor" (139). On Oviedo's connections with humanists in the court of Charles V, see O'Gorman, "Prólogo," and Bataillon, who in *L'Erasme* (665) notes that Oviedo's histories were cited by Erasmists in Spain as an exemplary alternative to works of the imagination. For an overview of Spanish Erasmism, see Abellán, *El erasmismo*.

9. Pagden, *European Encounters*, 56.

[What mortal mind can comprehend such a diversity of languages, habits, and customs among the peoples of the Indies? Such a variety of animals, both domestic and wild and savage? Such an unnarratable number of trees, some copious with different kinds of fruits, and others sterile; some cultivated by the Indians, and others that nature alone produces without help from mortal hands? How many plants and herbs that are useful and beneficial to man? How many innumerable others unknown to him, and with as many differences of roses, and flowers and fragrant smells?] (*HGN,* 1:8)

This often-quoted passage can be taken in part as an example of Oviedo's panegyric style, praising as it does the "inexpressibility" of his topic. The marvels of the New World (and of the emperor's holdings) easily eclipse those of antiquity, and the magnitude of the task of recording them calls for our (modest) author to outdo both ancients and moderns. One sees here the *cronista*'s preference, in the first part of the history, for recording natural phenomena over human events.[10] Throughout the passage he underscores the limitations of any mortal comprehension or rendering of such a splendid creation. The series of interrogatives emphasizing the "innumerable" items to be cataloged in this encyclopedic project (followed, in the next paragraph, by a parallel series of exclamations: "¡Cuántos valles!" etc.), underline the notion that to record the fullness of New World history necessarily lies beyond an individual perspective and points to a very real concern about the qualifications required of the historian and the type of discourse appropriate to his topic. Yet it is not just the marvels of nature that he finds "unnarratable,"[11] but also, as we will see, the human deeds unfolding in the New World, the chronicling of which, he suggests, is most difficult to undertake with accuracy.

Oviedo problematizes the humanist concern for credibility in narrative right from the start. The subject matter of the Indies is not only unfamiliar, Oviedo suggests, but seemingly incredible in terms of scale: the inexperienced reader has no idea of what to expect. Even nature in the Indies appears to act in a fashion that is "unnatural" by Old World standards. The fertility and abundance of the New World defies expectations, receiving and nurturing

---

10. On the structural differences between the first part, where the natural phenomena and human actions alternate, and the second, where human actions predominate, see Bolaños, "Crónica de Indias," 15–33.

11. Myers, in "Representation of New World Phenomena," discusses the complex "visual epistemology" implicit in Oviedo's illustrations and descriptions of natural phenomena.

the species imported from Europe "no como madrastra, sino como más verdadera madre" ("not like a stepmother, but like a true mother") (*HGN*, 1:8, book 1, pro.). Thus, the marvelous nature of the reality and events he seeks to depict will inevitably seem like improbable exaggerations to those who have not left Europe.[12] Nonetheless, Oviedo promises a narrative that, although poor in style, will be rich in "truth," a rough draft ready for a trained stylist to turn into an elegant history: "Irán desnudos mis renglones de abundancia de palabras artificiales, para convidar a los lectores; pero serán muy copiosos de verdad, y conforme a ésta, diré lo que no tendrá contradicción, quanto a ella, para que vuestra soberana clemencia allá lo mande polir e limar" ("My lines will be naked of an abundance of artificial words to invite the readers, but they will be copious with truth, and in accordance with truth, I will relate what will not contradict it so that your sovereign clemency may send it to be polished over there") (*HGN*, 9). In clarifying that his history will not contain facts that contradict the truth, Fernández de Oviedo is careful to distinguish between apparent contradictions in the narrative itself and contradictions with regard to the historical reality that the text proposes to re-create. Unlike Vives, who does not distinguish the sort of coherence or probability that operates in imaginary as opposed to historical works, Oviedo, as we shall see, argues for historiographical reliability, grounded on a series of partial views, that embraces rather than eliminates contradictions.[13] In what he has not witnessed directly, he claims not to take the posture of an imaginary witness to adjudicate discrepancies.

The importance he attaches to his own role as scribe ("esta pluma, o escritor vuestro") turns out to be a favorite topic for Oviedo, as critics have often noted. In book 4 he suggests that the greatest historians of the past would not have needed to resort to embellishment or exaggeration to describe the history of New World; it is a topic more challenging than any dealt with by Orpheus, Homer, Hesiod, or Pindar. Not even a thousand Ciceros working together, he boasts, would have been up to the job of recording the "abundantísima e casi infinita materia destas maravillas e riquezas que acá hay y tengo entre manos que escrebir" ("very abundant and almost infinite material of these marvels and riches that are here and which it is my task to record") (*HGN*, 1:158). Even the venerable Pliny, his avowed model,

---

12. On the problem of narrating the marvelous, see Campbell, *The Witness and the Other World* (219).

13. See Merrim, "Mare magno," 119.

falls short because he lacked the kind of experience Fernández de Oviedo believed was crucial for understanding events unfolding in the Indies:

> No he sacado de dos mil millares de volúmines que haya leído, como . . . Plinio escribe, en lo qual paresce que él dijo lo que leyó . . . ; pero yo acumulé todo lo que aquí escribo de dos mill millones de trabajos y necesidades y peligros en veinte e dos años e más que veo y experimento por mi persona estas cosas, sirviendo a Dios y a mi rey.

> [I have not taken (my history) from the thousands of volumes that I might have read, as did Pliny in his writings, in which it appears that he related what he read . . . , but I accumulated all that I write here in thousands of hardships and dangers over the more than twenty-two years that I have seen and experienced these things in person, serving God and my King.] (*HGN,* 1:11, pro.)

Critics have long commented on Oviedo's privileging of experience, of what he has directly seen or witnessed as opposed to read or heard as a trademark of his work.[14] His case for empirical observation as the best source for history draws not just on the premise that a direct view of events allows for a more accurate subsequent representation of them, but on the notion, to be found, for example, in Job, that suffering and experience are related to revelation.[15] But the idea of revelation here is mitigated by an underlying sense, seen in the quote that opened this section, that the full meaning of the nature and history of the New World is veiled to mankind. Although in places, such as the *proemio* to book 1, Oviedo presents himself as a privileged witness in the eyes of God, he more frequently presents himself as just one witness among many: "No puede bastar la pluma ni estilo de uno, ni dos ni muchos historiales, sino de todos aquellos que oviere e lo supieren hacer y escribir en todos los tiempos y siglos venideros hasta el final juicio e fin de los humanos" ("Neither the pen nor the style of one or two or even many

---

14. As Gerbi notes in *Nature in the New World* (240), the implications of this method are "vast:" "personal experience takes precedence over tradition, both oral and written, [and] description of what the historian has seen with his own eyes has greater intrinsic value than reports of happenings, since no man can be present at more than a small proportion of events." The method, however, is not at all consistent, as we shall see. See also Iglesia, "Cronistas"; Salas, "Tres Cronistas"; and Pagden, *European Encounters,* 51–68.

15. Job, 42:4–5. For another apparent reference to Job in Oviedo, see Pagden, *European Encounters,* 61. Merrim, in "Mare magno," points to other uses of the idea of revelation in the *Historia.*

historians will be enough; but rather all those that have been or that will be written through the coming ages and centuries until mankind's Judgment day") (*HGN,* 4:417, book 50, chap. 30). As we shall see, the combining of multiple versions and styles within his history becomes a fundamental strategy in his attempt to provide a comprehensive account of the New World.

Oviedo was not the first to structure his history on the double move of emulating and criticizing classical authorities such as Pliny. He had ancient models in Thucydides and Josephus and, as Isaías Lerner has shown, a modern one in Pedro Mexía. But in his frequent jibes against rival contemporary historians, he can be said to inaugurate a tradition of "refutation" in the historiography of the Indies, as Frankl termed it, or "intertextual antagonism," to borrow Rigney's apt phrase from a different context.[16] In disparaging the accounts of the Spanish discovery and conquest of the Indies by courtly historians such as Peter Martyr d'Anghera and Lucio Marineo Sículo, Fernández de Oviedo primarily underlines the authors' lack of experience, which, he claims, disqualifies them as authorities on the New World. It is not enough, Oviedo suggests repeatedly in his history, to come up with a coherent narrative of events. True history must reflect extensive research and the ability on the part of the historian to judge the trustworthiness of sources; it should state what is correct about the existing record and refute where possible what is false. Central to Oviedo's project, then, is the author's portrayal of himself as historian at work, fulfilling the honorable yet elusive goals of his office. Unlike the courtly historians who write elegant and seamless accounts, Oviedo presents himself as an author who has no time for bothering with what he suggests is the merely rhetorical task of writing a coherent story, that is, a narrative that adheres to the norms of probability and presents no contradictions. But at the same time that he rebuts the erudite but inexperienced accounts of those who write from Europe, he also insists on the incompleteness of any single version (his own included) and on the need for bringing canonic "textual" witnesses (e.g., relevant quotations from Classical and Christian authorities) to bear on the places and events that he describes, as when he argues—based on an interpretation of the myth of

---

16. See Frankl, *El antijovio,* 96 and Rigney, *Rhetoric,* 47. While Michel de Certeau, in "L'histoire" (19–21), is right in noting that this sort of "fight against fiction" is a characteristic of Western historiography, it does not become a systematic strategy, to my knowledge, before the period under study here. The references that Herodotus, for example, makes to Homer, or those of Thucydides to Homer and to Herodotus, while important statements of method, are not, by contrast, sustained narrative strategies in the way that we find them in Oviedo's, and later Las Casas's, work.

the Hesperides—that the ancients had been aware of the Indies, but later "forgot" them (*HGN*, 1:17, book 1, chap. 3).[17]

Traditionally, Oviedo's reflections on the writing of history have been viewed in the context of the commonplace moralist condemnations of fiction. In attacking his rivals, Oviedo frequently characterizes the contemporary accounts as "fábulas" or "novelas," and associates both the texts and their authors with the range of moral and epistemological objections to chivalric romance that the Erasmists had raised.[18] Merrim aptly describes this approach as a "counternovelistic strategy," one in which the author "opposes his history, a feast of novelties, to the apocryphal marvels of romance."[19] Gerbi points to the methodological importance of this kind of reference, noting that his repeated and blunt condemnations are based not just on predictable moral grounds, but on scientific ones as well, having to do with objectivity in discourse.[20] And yet, Gerbi does not pursue this intriguing point. Clearly, Oviedo echoes the criticisms of fiction to protest his own credibility and to evoke (and dismiss) in a shorthand fashion the historical texts of his rivals.[21] While the *cronista*'s use of the commonplaces makes clear that he knows the rhetorical rules for historiography, it also signals the inadequacy of the humanist framework vis-à-vis his own text, and thus seeks

17. On Oviedo's imitation of Pliny, see Gerbi, *Nature in the New World* (271–73); Myers, "Imitación"; Bolaños, who in "Historian" notes Oviedo's problematic imitation of Pliny in the theory of the Hesperides; Ife ("Alexander"); and Bataillon, who in "Historiografía oficial," 32–38, discusses the role of this episode in the construction of a "verdad oficial [y] pragmática."

18. José Amador de los Ríos points to Oviedo's "aversion" to the genre in his introduction to the Academia de la Historia's edition of 1851–55, and O'Gorman suggests that the *cronista* capitalizes on the language of the humanists to make clear his own repudiation of the genre. The fact that, once engaged in the writing of history, Oviedo avoids any mention of the chivalric romance with which he began his literary career, the *Claribalte* (Valencia 1519), leads O'Gorman to hypothesize in "Prólogo" (ix–x) that Oviedo might have felt more than an abstract intellectual stake in the quarrel. Rodríguez Prampolini, who correctly identifies Oviedo's use of this register to indicate a generic boundary, proceeds in *Amadises* (148) to cite extensive passages that, according to her, present such clear thematic and stylistic parallels with sixteenth-century chivalric romances that they could be freely interchanged ("encajaría[n] perfectamente sin cambiarle[s] ni punto ni coma"). See also Pérez de Tudela Bueso, "Vida y escritos," cxlv, and Gerbi, *Nature in the New World*, 202–5.

19. Merrim, "Mare magno," 110, 117.

20. Gerbi, *Nature in the New World*, 203–4.

21. "Den, pues, los vanos sus orejas a los libros de Amadís y de Esplandián, e de los que dellos penden que es ya una generación tan multiplicada de fábulas, que por cierto yo he verguenza de oir que en España se escribieron tantas vanidades, que hacen ya olvidar las de los griegos. Mal se acuerda quien tal escribe y el que semejantes ficiones lee, de las palabras evangélicas que nos enseñan que el diablo es padre de la mentira. Pues luego quien la escribe hijo suyo será. Líbreme Dios de tamaño delicto y encamine mi pluma a que con verdad (ya quel buen estilo me falta), siempre diga y escriba lo que sea conforme a ella y al servicio y alabanza de la misma verdad ques Dios." *HGN* 2:182, book 18, pro.

to preempt potential criticism of his clearly nonconformist approach. The *cronista* manipulates the ambiguities of the preceptive discussion with care. Even as Vives and other humanists had sought a viable distinction between history and fiction, they commonly employed the same lexicon for referring to works of the imagination and to willful lies: terms such as *fábula, novela,* and *mentira* refer both to fictional works of invention and entertainment and to the act of deliberate falsifying in nonfictional discourse.[22] In places, the *cronista* follows suit:

> Pero será a lo menos lo que yo escribiere, historia verdadera e desviada de todas las fábulas que en este caso otros escriptores, sin verlo, desde España a pie enjuto, han presumido escribir con elegantes e no comunes letras latinas e vulgares, por informaciones de muchos de diferentes juicios, formando historias más allegadas a buen estilo que a la verdad de la cosa que cuentan; porque ni el ciego sabe determinar colores, ni el ausente así testificar estas materias, como quien las mira.

> [But at least I will write true history that deviates from all the fables that in this case other writers, without getting their feet wet, have presumed to write from Spain in elegant Latin and romance languages. They have used information from many sources, molding histories that are closer to good style than to the truth of what they tell: just as a blind man cannot see colors, one who has not witnessed cannot testify in these matters as well as someone who has seen them.] (*HGN,* 1:9, pro.)

Oviedo simultaneously invokes the texts of his adversaries and dismisses them as "lies" and fabrications akin to implausible fictional imaginings, but rarely rebuts them directly in terms of content. Instead he focuses on questions of character (the sedentary historians lack rigor and concoct elegant accounts from the most disparate testimonies), of language (his own unadorned style is a visible sign that he records the plain truth), and of epistemology (not to have witnessed is to be in the dark).

In contending against the versions of his rivals, Oviedo argues that the only narrative perspective appropriate for the historian is one that is true to his own voice and natural range of vision, and it is here that he

---

22. See the entries for these terms in the *Diccionario de autoridades.*

alludes to a problem that continues to interest students of narrative today: the considerable restrictions under which a historical narrator operates (or should operate) vis-à-vis a fictional one.[23] The figure of the narrator, whether fictional or factual, is always intimately connected to the structure of a work and the representation of character and worldview embodied within it. But the fact that the author of a historical work narrates in his or her own voice (or at least takes responsibility for his or her version of events) has important logical consequences for the story that he or she tells.[24] Beyond the basic conflation between the (real) author and the figure of the narrator in historical writing, Fernández de Oviedo clarifies that there are at least two narrative situations in his work:

> No escribo de auctoridad de algún historiador o poeta, sino como testigo de vista en la mayor parte de cuanto aquí tractaré; y lo que yo no hobiere visto, dirélo por relación de personas fidedignas, no dando en cosa alguna crédito a un solo testigo, sino a muchos, en aquellas cosas que por mi persona no hobiere experimentado. Y dirélas de la manera que las entendí y de quién, porque tengo cédulas y mandamientos de la Cesárea Majestad, para que todos sus gobernadores e justicias e oficiales de todas las Indias me den aviso e relación verdadera de todo lo que fuere digno de historia por testimonios auténticos, firmados de sus nombres e signados de escribanos públicos, de manera que hagan fe. Porque como celosos príncipes de la verdad é tan amigos della, quieren que esta *Historia natural e general de sus Indias* se escriba muy al propio.

> [In most of what I discuss here, I will not write by the authority of some historian or poet, but as an eyewitness. What I have not seen, I will relate through the accounts of reliable persons, and on those things that I myself have not experienced, I will never give credit to just one witness, but to many. And I will relate them in the way that I understood them and will say from whom I heard them, because I have licenses and orders from the Emperor his Majesty, so that all his governors and officials and judges in all the Indies should give me in authentic testimony, signed in their names

---

23. For a discussion of this problem in narratological terms, see Cohn, *Distinction,* 119.

24. Martínez Bonati, in *Fictive Discourse,* provides the philosophical argument for the disjunction between author and narrator in works of fiction. Cohn discusses this problem, as well as alternative models in *Distinction,* 123–31.

and duly notarized—so that they can be trusted—true account of all that is worthy of history. Because as friends and guardians of the truth, the princes want this *Natural and General History of the Indies* to be written accordingly.] (*HGN,* 1:13–14, book 2, chap. 1)

In claiming that he is neither a historian nor a poet, but a witness and examiner of other witnesses, Oviedo seems to recuse himself from the specifically "literary" task of constructing a cohesive narrative from his mass of data. He promises, for the most part, to narrate events that he directly observed or in which he participated. (To borrow Genette's equation: the author is both narrator and character present at the events that he narrates, a sign of autobiography.) But Oviedo makes clear that this eyewitness stance is not to be a consistent strategy. In what he has not seen himself, he will adopt the more traditional historian's role of comparing, judging, and reproducing the accounts of others. (Genette, again, provides us with a formula: the author acts as narrator but not as character.)[25] But this double perspective of the narrating person or voice (which, according to Genette's categories, would present a case of a narrator who alternates from the hetero- to the homodiegetical) is quite consistent in Oviedo's history, because when he recounts events beyond his experience, he maintains a restricted narrative point of view. In general, he portrays his authorial self not as an invisible observer, but as a historian at work, reading, corresponding, interviewing, juxtaposing conflicting accounts, weighing their reliability, directing the reader's sympathies, offering parallels from ancient texts and moralizing glosses, and more often than not, distancing his own voice from the versions of others. Formally, we have here a first-person narrator, but in places where the author's role in the story is marginal or null, it takes on the characteristics of third-person narration. The heterodiegetical stance (the narrator is absent from the events he recounts) becomes a variation of the homodiegetical one (the narrator is present at the events narrated),[26] an aspect that points to the multifaceted quality of the historical narrator, who is often faced (as in the case of the early historiography of the Indies) not just with his or her dual roles of participant and retrospective commentator, but with the problem of narrating material drawn from different sources.

---

25. Genette, *Fiction and Diction,* 73.

26. See Martínez Bonati's description of a similar phenomenon in fiction. Cohn, too, has noted in *Distinction* (122–23) the inapplicability of Genette's earlier categories in *Narrative Discourse* for historical discourse, and suggests that the closest analogy for the historiographical narrator would be the homodiegetical fictional type.

In this latter sense, one finds that the status of historiographical discourse is what Michel de Certeau has called a "laminated" text, one in which other discourses are quoted, stratified, and recomposed in order to produce a "sense of reliability."[27]

Indeed, Oviedo's figure as narrator takes on a very prominent presence in his work. His discourse is quite varied and includes not just narratives of human events and descriptions of natural phenomena, often interjected with autobiographical material, but also extensive direct quotation from the writings of others, summaries of other texts, addresses to the reader, commentary on the process of writing his work, reported interviews, direct dialogues, and various interpretive observations regarding the subject matter, his sources, and the diverse canonical authorities on whom he calls for comparative views. Both the abundance of autobiographical detail and his frequent judgmental commentary contribute to establishing a pronounced image of the authorial "I." In the books of chivalry, as Pagden has observed, the *topos* of the discovered manuscript plays at negating the imaginary quality of this kind of work, by denying the very existence of an author (i.e., such a book is not invented, but found). Pagden further notes that Oviedo, in contrast, grounds the credibility of his work by constantly commenting on the process of writing, making visible his own presence as author, one whose experience, hard work, and religious conviction distinguish his truthful account from those of lazy historians who cut and paste their works from secondary sources, as well as from the absent fictional historians of romance.[28] In speaking of his authorial role as one that is both difficult and risky, Oviedo draws on a telling analogy from the natural world. In writing his history, he tries to stay

> arrimado al bordón de la misma y esclarescida verdad, poco a poco, nunca me desacordando de la propiedad y costumbre que tiene la zorra para pasar el hielo: la cual . . . porque es animal de sotil oír, antes que pase pone la oreja sobre el hielo, y de aquella manera arbitra qué tan gordo está, y si es suficiente para sostenerla a cuestas y pasar sin peligro.

27. Michel de Certeau suggests in *Writing of History* (94) that this process of quotation is "constructed as the knowledge of the other." As we shall see, Oviedo seems to be critiquing precisely this sort of imaginative leap.

28. Pagden, *European Encounters*, 63–65.

[close to the staff of the same enlightened and illustrious truth, moving slowly but surely, never forgetting the behavior and custom of the fox when crossing the ice. Since this animal has subtle hearing, before crossing she puts her ear to the ice, so as to judge how thick it is, and whether it can support her weight so as to pass without danger.] (*HGN,* 2:183, book 18, pro.)

In contrast to the absent authors of chivalric romance, or the distant humanists who compose in the comfort of their studies, Oviedo here likens his narratorial self as akin to the painstaking fox, one whose keen ear distinguishes the thick from the thin ice of discourse, thus underscoring the notion that the author is circumscribed by natural limits of vision, experience, and instinct.

Method over Magic

Like the humanist preceptors, Oviedo associates the scope of the historian's knowledge and perception with the notion of reliability.[29] However, the concept of the ideal humanist historian as *sabio,* whether magus or seer or prophet, able to conjure up an image of the past beyond his experience and to forecast the future, which has such positive connotations in the preceptive tradition, takes on a strikingly negative tone in the *cronista*'s work. In book 33, chapter 44, Oviedo notes the difficulty of relying on secondary sources to gain precise geographical information:

> Quiero decir, que no soy adivino, ni nuestros soldados cosmógrafos; pero esforzarme he, donde hallare lugar, para poner cada cosa en su debida cuenta; y esto no puede ser de un golpe tampoco, sino dilatándose el tiempo, como en la pintura, para que con el, con los mesmos nombres que aquí se dirán, otros perficionen e pongan al propio los grados e alturas en cada provincia destas.

> [I want to say that I am not a soothsayer, nor are our soldiers cosmographers, but I will try whenever possible to give a proper account of each thing. And this cannot be done all of a sudden, but rather as time passes, as in a painting, so that with the names that are recorded here, others will perfect and add the precise

---

29. For a discussion of this question in fictional works, see Yacobi, "Fictional Reliability."

degrees and altitudes in each of these provinces.] (*HGN,* 4:208, book 33, chap. 44)

To come up with an accurate description based on secondhand information alone would require the fantastic vision of a soothsayer, he suggests, noting that his own necessarily faulty account will have to be perfected by successive versions. In his *Quincuagenas*[30] Oviedo echoes this point, with a more direct attack on the historians writing from Europe:

> Me maravillo de algunos tractados que en España han escripto otros auctores en latín e rromance sin aver visto las Indias. En los cuales ay cosas muchas muy al rrevés de cómo se verán en mi *Historia general,* porque yo hablo de vista o muy informado de lo que digo, e los que desde Castilla escriven, aunque hablen por mejor estilo, se podrían engañar. Yo no hago este oficio como adevino, ni a tanto peligro de mi consciencia como los ausentes.

> [I marvel at some treatises that in Spain other writers have written in Latin and romance languages without having seen the Indies. In them there are many things that are in stark contrast with how they will be seen in my *General History,* because I speak as an eyewitness or very informed of what I say, and those who write from Castile, although they do so with better style, might well be deceived. I do not fulfill this office as a soothsayer, nor with as much danger to my conscience as do those who are absent.][31]

Oviedo deftly manipulates the commonplace of the humanist historian as wise man, suggesting that the accounts of his rivals reveal them to be not so much Christian sages as heretic soothsayers, who, rather than revealing divine (redemptive) truths, conjecture about and perpetuate false views. He associates the narrative feats of those writing from Europe with the sorts

---

30. *Las Quincuagenas de los generosos e illustres e no menos famosos reyes, príncipes, duques, marqueses, y condes e caballeros e personas notables de España* was completed in 1555, but not published (and then only partially) until the nineteenth century. See Turner, *Gonzalo Fernández de Oviedo,* 15. The work is composed of verse, which Oviedo called *segunda rima,* alternating with textual commentary. Avalle-Arce has selected and published extensive excerpts from this work under the title *Memorias de Gonzalo Fernández de Oviedo* (1974).

31. Fernández de Oviedo, *Memorias,* 301.

of unsophisticated tricks characteristic of low magic,[32] suggesting that to re-create a sense of immediacy about events not witnessed is a clear-cut sign of unreliability in historical writing.

Oviedo's criticisms of the writers from Europe draw on the language of condemnation of superstitions, witchcraft, and heresy common to the period. In Pedro Ciruelo's *Reprobación de las supersticiones y hechicerías* (1530),[33] which Oviedo cites on a number of occasions, the author catalogs and describes a number of superstitious beliefs and behaviors, highlighting the supernatural or uncanny quality of the knowledge that they presume, and thus, what he views as their diabolical character. In the section of his work that deals with the art of divination, Ciruelo suggests that, while it is natural for mankind to desire knowledge, the search for understanding must always be grounded in Christian belief and an awareness of natural human limitations. Human intellectual endeavors, he writes, must be governed by "the rule of reason and the law of God"; otherwise even the greatest minds risk "running wild like horses without reins" ("como cavallos desbocados que corren sin riendas"). Ciruelo elaborates:

> La regla es esta: que el hombre cuerdo no quiera saber lo que no se pueda saber por razón natural si dios no lo revelasse. . . . Mas los hombres curiosos y livianos con desordenada cobdicia de querer saber: no paran mientes en ver cuáles cosas se pueden saber y cuáles no: y sin hazer differencia estienden su cobdicia a todas las cosas. Y en las que se pueden saber por vía de razón natural: no quieren guardar la orden y manera que se ha de tener para las saber: porque no quieren trabajar en el estudio de las ciencias: ni se sufren a esperar tanto tiempo como se requiere para alcanzar el saber de las cosas: por eso han buscado artes diabólicas y maneras supersticiosas por las cuales piensan que sin trabajo y en breve tiempo podrían saber todas las cosas que ellos quieren. Estas artes halló el diablo para engañar y cegar a los hombres vanos: que se desvanescen en estas fantasías. A estas artes llaman los sanctos doctores artes divinatorias: y a los que las usan llaman divinos en latín: quiere decir hombres que son como

---

32. On the distinctions between "high" and "low" magic during this period, see Russell, "The Meaning of Witchcraft," in *Witchcraft in the Middle Ages,* 1–26.

33. Ciruelo (b. ca. 1475) was a professor of Thomist philosophy at the University of Alcalá and author of a number of scientific, theological and philosophical works, of which the *Reprobación* was one of the most popular. First published in 1530, this work had been reprinted in seven editions by 1556. See Ebersole, "Introducción," 9–10.

dioses: porque fingen que saben lo que a solo dios pertenesce saber. . . . En lengua de España estos se llaman adivinos.

[The rule is this: that the prudent man should not want to know what cannot be known by natural reason if god does not reveal it to him. . . . But curious and fickle men in their unruly greed seek to learn without stopping to consider which things can be known, and which cannot. They indiscriminately extend their greed to all things. . . . And in those that can be known through the path of reason, they do not want to keep the order and manner that must be kept in order to know them, because they do not want to work in the study of sciences, nor do they suffer to wait as long as is necessary to acquire the knowledge of things. That is why they have sought diabolical arts and superstitious ways by which they think that without effort and in a short time they will be able to know all that they want. The devil found these arts to deceive and blind vain men, who are dissipated in these fantasies. The saintly doctors call these arts divinatory arts, and those who use them are called diviners in Latin; this means men who are like gods, because they feign to know what only god can know. . . . In the language of Spain they are called *adivinos*.][34]

Ciruelo further explains that those who seek to inquire into what cannot naturally be known must have been either privy to divine revelation or, alternatively, have succumbed to a pact with the devil.

Oviedo may well have consulted Ciruelo's treaty in his efforts to account for the customs of native peoples (we find him in a telling scene in the *Sumario* as a protomissionary who tries to disabuse a captive native of his superstitious beliefs). In his later works he uses logic similar to that of Ciruelo in criticizing the narrative stance and breadth of vision of those writing from Europe as implausible, directing his criticism both at the rival texts themselves and at the humanist rhetorical model they embrace. To represent without reservations or disclaimers as one's own the information gained from others, he suggests, amounts to historiographical hocus pocus; it signals a reliance not on careful research but on dissimulation and spectacular rhetorical display. Like an *adivino,* the historian writing from Europe adopts

---

34. Ciruelo, *Reprobación,* 53–54, spelling modernized (my translation).

a necessarily unnatural narrative point of view, reaching beyond what can be reliably known, and thus, misrepresenting the facts.

In his own history, the image of the author's highly personal and judgmental narrative voice is accentuated by what appears to be a conscientious (if not always consistent) distancing of his own narrative perspective from those of his sources in matters that he has not witnessed directly. In doing so, Oviedo appears to privilege something like what Martínez Bonati has defined as "natural discourse," a type of speech in which a person recounts his own lived experience in his own voice at a specific time and place, using his own descriptive categories and opinions and taking responsibility for his act of speech.[35] For Oviedo, natural discourse in which narrative voice corresponds to narrative perspective is more credible material for history than is the indirect recounting of the experiences of others. As Oviedo reminds us: "Lo que no ve el historiador, forzado es que escriba por diversas informaciones" ("What the historian does not see, he is forced to compile from diverse accounts") (HGN, 3:265, book 33, chap. 55). He even describes "the rule" (la regla) of the historian as follows: "Lo que viere, testificarlo de vista llanamente, y lo que leyere, dar el autor" ("What he witnesses, to recount it simply; what he has read, to give the author") (HGN, 5:165, book 47, chap. 11). Iglesia and Gerbi have noted the care with which he addresses his source materials, contrasting accounts from contemporary witnesses and ancient texts alike. But Salas rightly points out that Oviedo tends to accumulate rather than confront his witnesses, meaning that the accounts often overlap, reiterating the substance of events already narrated albeit with small changes in emphasis.[36] One might add that he more often "confronts" his New World witnesses against ancient authorities than against each other.

Perhaps the most extreme example of this approach can be found in the sections on the conquest of Mexico. For example, in mentioning conflicts in the accounts of Diego Velásquez and Cortés, Oviedo explains that he will quote directly from Cortés's letter to avoid any confusion between his own perspective and that of the Marqués: "Porque es de manera que no se deben mezclar mis palabras ni otras en ello, ni quiero que en ningún tiempo él ni otro pueda decir que quité ni añadí palabra ni letra, ni quiero voto ni parescer en lo que en este caso dixo, pues no soy juez para ello" ("Neither my words nor others should be mixed with this account, nor do I want at any time that he or anyone else be able to say that I added or took away a

---

35. Martínez Bonati, "El sistema del discurso," in Ficción, 73.
36. Salas, Tres cronistas, 121.

word or letter; nor do I want to opine on what he said in this case, as I am not a judge of it") (*HGN*, 4:192, book 33, chap. 41). Although much of the Cortesian material Oviedo includes is in fact a summary (and not a direct citation) of Cortés's *Cartas de relación,* he tends to resort to direct quotation or even dialogue on highly controversial points to problematize sections of the account, as Myers has shown.[37] In general, Oviedo justifies the frequent distancing between his own vision and that of the historical actors present at the events on epistemological grounds, seeking in this fashion to make up for the apparent lack of narrative coherence and structure that result from this strategy.[38]

Salas's outline of book 33, which encompasses the narrative of the conquest of Mexico and incorporates a particularly wide range of versions, illustrates the consequences of this approach. It includes a close summary of Cortés's letters (forty-one chapters); *relaciones* from Pedro de Alvarado and Diego de Godoy to Cortés (three chapters); an alternate perspective on the campaign against the Aztecs derived from unnamed sources who participated in it (four chapters); the testimony of a priest, Diego de Loaysa (one chapter); a letter concerning indigenous practices (one chapter); a subsequent treatment of the same topic, from different sources (one chapter); a letter from Antonio de Mendoza to Oviedo (one chapter); the author's reply (one chapter); and a transcribed dialogue between the author and Juan Cano, who contests some of the elements in the prior versions of the conquest narrative (one chapter). Salas notes that "if Oviedo had made thorough corrections, or at least connected the diverse versions that he includes of a single event, he would not have incurred the disorder and zigzagging that we have highlighted."[39] Salas concludes, echoing Oviedo's own formulation, that he cannot be considered a "historian," but rather a "compiler" who had no intention of writing a critical and coherent historical narrative.[40]

What Salas does not seem to appreciate is that in coming up with his cumbersome method, Oviedo makes a valid point, as Iglesia judiciously recognized.[41] I would add that this methodological insight is inextricably linked

---

37. Myers, "History," 618.

38. In *Cronistas* (85–93) Iglesia notes that, in general, Oviedo endeavors to maintain a more distanced attitude toward Cortés than other *cronistas.* On other aspects that contribute to problems of "coherence" in the work, see Merrim, "Mare magno."

39. Salas, *Tres cronistas,* 116–17 (my translation).

40. For Oviedo's own formulation, see *HGN,* 5:166.

41. Iglesia, *Cronistas,* 84.

to the problem of narrative perspective: to confront differing accounts in order to achieve a seamless version requires speculation and thus a narrative stance akin to that of the *adivino* that Oviedo criticizes in other historians. To try, on the other hand, to simply juxtapose different versions of discrete events is no less risky: accounts are frequently incompatible, and "story" tends to be bound up in discourse in subtle and inextricable ways. Indeed, one senses a conscious narrative experiment on Oviedo's part, namely, to question the "truth" of a historical text that adopts an unnatural perspective. The only reliable way to treat witnesses, the *cronista* seems to suggest, is simply to let them speak for themselves and not to disassociate the perspective of a particular vision or experience from the voice that narrates it. The only true coherence to be found in historical testimony comes from preserving a connection between voice and perspective.

There is more here than mere rhetoric or a repetition of the humanist commonplaces. In a sense, one could say that Fernández de Oviedo's own reluctance to decide on the "facts" in the rival accounts of events he has not witnessed would appear to constitute an insight in terms of narrative logic and technique. When recording such a vast and novel arena as the natural and human history of the Indies, to rely on secondhand accounts is to stretch the limits of the plausible, he suggests, if the author is not careful to distinguish his own narrative perspective from those of his sources. In an acid imperative to those writing from Spain, Oviedo states that, at the very least, one should explain how and where one gets one's information: "pongan el nombre del autor que les informó" (*HGN,* 2:319, book 21, chap. 5). Oviedo distinguishes his own treatment of secondhand information from that of his rivals by distancing his own voice (or so he tells us) from the words of his sources. In doing so, the *cronista* repeatedly hints in a rough fashion at a concept that has come to be described by Genette in more precise narratological terms as "mood," and which refers to narrative distance and perspective.[42] Narrative distance in Genette's terminology refers to techniques of representation, whether "showing" (scene, mimesis) or "telling" (summary, diegesis), and perspective refers to the question of who perceives these events or scenes. Genette distinguishes narrative perspective from voice: a story may be told in the voice of a narrator but "focalized" through the consciousness or perception of another character (or not focalized, as the case may be). In a later work, in which Genette seeks to specify the differences between fictional and factual discourse, he notes that mood is

---

42. Genette, *Narrative Discourse,* 161–211.

"a locus of narrative divergence between the two types." The requirement of truth in historical narrative, wherein the author takes responsibility for the accuracy of the account, and which involves "the obligation to report only what one knows, to provide all the relevant information—and to state how one has come by that knowledge" means that, at least in theory, it is problematic for the conscientious writer of history to adopt the narrative perspective (or "focalization") of one of the agents in the events without clearly crediting and justifying such a strategy.[43] In practice, one suspects, the problem is more complex than Genette suggests. As we shall see, it is one that preoccupied Oviedo, who refers repeatedly if crudely to the difficulty (or impossibility) of separating an image of historical truth from the source or voice that relates it and thus proposes the legitimacy of a historiographical vision based not on a linear, unified, and coherent account of events, but on a series of independent approximations.

Oviedo was not alone in likening the unreliable historian to a conjurer; one finds a similar formulation in the critique by humanist Pedro de Rhúa of Antonio de Guevara's pseudohistorical works, which were considered by Erasmists in Spain to be "prototypes" of lying literature.[44] (Guevara, appointed *cronista* before Oviedo, never wrote a history of the Indies.) Composed in 1540, Rhúa's letters to Guevara, which Oviedo mentions approvingly in his *Quincuagenas,* reveal a careful adherence to Vives's ideas on history. In this largely one-sided correspondence, the *bachiller* from Soria engages in a hard-hitting, point-by-point correction of the facts, accusing the Bishop of Mondoñedo of being a Pyrrhonist,[45] and chastising him for distorting the past, if not as an enchanter (*encantador*) (this would require serious, learned magic), then at least as a poet who conjures up *fábulas* at the mere stroke of a pen. Here, Rhúa's linkage of the idea of the magus, or enchanter, to a historiographical impostor is notable:

> El que en cada hoja de sus libros promete verdad y en cada hoja da falsedad, y el que pregona historias y vende fábulas, y el que nombra testigos ultramarinos y nunca los presenta, el que invierte las edades, trastrueca los tiempos, trasmuda los lugares, y no como los encantadores, de quien dicen las doce tablas . . . que pasaban unas

43. Genette, *Fiction and Diction,* 67.

44. See Bataillon, *L'Erasme et L'Espagne,* 661. Written in 1540 and published in 1549, Rhúa's letters are available in *Epistolario español.* On Rhúa's place in Spanish humanism, see Frankl, *El antijovio,* 85, and Lewis, "Humanistic Historiography," 24–26.

45. Rhúa, "Cartas," 237.

piezas de panes de la ribera de un rio á la otra, ó de una ladera de un monte á la otra, mas una ciudad con sus cimientos la pasan de Asia en Europa y de Europa en África, y no por arte mágica ni con ayuda de demonios . . . sino con solo mover una pluma de ansarón, tan fácilmente y con aquella misma arte que Homero en su Ilíada . . . ¿qué merece de los presentes sino la censura?

[He who in each page of his books promises truth but gives false-hood, and he who proclaims histories but sells fables, and he who names overseas witnesses but never presents them, he who inverts the ages, switches times, mixes up places, not like the enchanters, of whom the twelve tablets say that . . . they used to pass loaves of bread from one bank of the river to the other, or from one side of the mountain to the other, but by moving a whole city with its foundations from Asia to Europe and from Europe to Africa, and not by magical arts or with the aid of demons, . . . but with a mere stroke of a pen, as easily and with the same art as Homer in his Iliad. . . . What does such an author deserve from those present but censure?][46]

Guevara's work is so full of blatant inaccuracies, Rhúa suggests, that even the enchanters of ancient Rome, who limited themselves to more modest feats, would recognize them as highly improbable. Much like Oviedo, Rhúa associates historiographic failures with the sorts of showy displays character-istic of low magic, implying that Guevara's narrative tricks would require inconceivable magical powers, and thus must be read as mere invention.[47]

Oviedo lavishes praise on Rhúa for his historical detective work, and even suggests that he be sent in person to the Indies as a sort of expert censor able to refute the erroneous accounts through both erudition and experi-ence. Given the lack of available proof—written sources and traditions on the Indies—the task of guarding against fabrication in the accounts of the New World, Oviedo suggests, would be less tiresome than having to track down the archival material to expose Guevara's work as an invention.[48]

---

46. Ibid., 241.
47. There would seem to be here a fusion of popular and erudite notions of the magician similar to that described by Traister in *Heavenly Necromancers* (1–31).
48. "Que harto más tuviera que hazer [Pedro de Rhúa], y más sin fatiga, que en los hurtos y faltas del Obispo, porque no tuviera que buscar como buscó, como dotto, los auctores para con-fundir esas mentiras que juntamente, no por capítulos e parte, pudiera condenar estos escriptores

The new kind of historian required for the Indies, in his view, would possess both humanistic training and eyewitness experience, as well as a firm moral commitment to the truth.[49]

Oviedo frequently associates in a more general fashion the problem of falsehood in discourse with questionable or magical practices when discussing those who, though present in the Indies, will notarize any version of events so long as the price is right. In denouncing Castilian captains in the Indies who endeavor to transform criminal records into résumés worthy of royal recognition, the *cronista* chastises the unscrupulous sort of notary public ("escribano de mango y loco") willing to assist them in establishing such false claims. Oviedo likens this sort of chronicler to an alchemist who claims to be able to transform cheap materials into great riches: "Cosa facilísima es juntar los materiales, e de muy poca costa efectuar esta alquimia, sin congelar el mercurio, sin soplar el fuego." ("It is very easy to put together the materials, and to effect this alchemy out of almost nothing, without freezing mercury, without fanning the fire.") The *cronista* clarifies that he refers not to black magic in fact, but rather to a profession that is "permitido y muy usado, y no hay en el más que tinta y papel. . . . Son estos alquimistas de papel muy presto, ricos; y antes acá, porque es tierra de menos verdad" ("permitted and often used, and there is nothing to it but ink and paper. . . . These paper alchemists are soon rich, and even more so here, because this is a land less concerned with truth"). One can easily accumulate a fortune with minimal investment and risk, suggests Oviedo, using only paper and ink to record "what does and does not happen." Oviedo addresses himself directly to these "alquimistas de tinta y de engaños" ("alchemists of ink and deceits") warning that their temporal earnings will not save them from divine punishment (*HGN*, 3:198–99, book 28, chap. 6). In associating falsehood in discourse with unscrupulous "magical" practices, Oviedo once again highlights his own methodological standards: under royal obligation to tell the truth, he claims no interference in the production of a transparent account: "Vosotros habéis de poner la materia y yo poner la tinta y el papel . . . vosotros sois el pregonero e pintor de [vuestras obras]" ("You must provide the material and I, the ink and paper. . . . You

---

que biven de sudores ajenos, pero todos sus volúmines de tabla a tabla, o de la primera hasta su última letra se pueden desechar por falsedades, y lo que en sus trattados es verdad es tomado de otros autores, pero contado con cautela e mudando la limpieza e bordándola, e rremendando, e poniendo de más e de menos como se les antoja en lo que escriven." Oviedo, *Quincuagenas*, in *Memorias*, 1:301–2.

49. Thus, one cannot agree with Frankl that Oviedo's emphasis on the value of experience, of "lo visto y lo vivido," is part of a critical attitude against bookish knowledge in general and against the intellectual orientation of the Renaissance and humanist authors. See Frankl, *El antijovio*, 85.

are both the proclaimer and painter of your own deeds") (*HGN*, 3:186–87, book 28, chap. 4).

In addition to the implicit associations between magical practices and historiographical falsification, and the indirect metadiscursive references to the narrative stance of the *adivino* as a sign of both an unreliable or impossible perspective on historical events and a moral failing, Oviedo brings up numerous examples of seers from both modern and ancient times in his history. His concern for reporting omens, prophecies, miracles, and visions may have had a source in classical historians or in Giovanni Pontano (who wrote in his dialogue *Actius* that the historian was obliged to report supernatural signs of a providential plan) or may have even been inspired by the prevalence of popular literature on prophecy common in Italy in the sixteenth century.[50] But Oviedo seems to have a genuine interest in the mysterious as well, and it is possible that his methodological insights are linked not just to his own efforts to establish his own credibility vis-à-vis the more learned writers, but to his project of describing the customs and practices of New World peoples.[51] At any rate, given that the author often frames his "rule" for writing history in terms that recall the language of censure of superstitions of the period, it seems pertinent to examine his own treatment of the supernatural in history. As Lorraine Daston has shown, attitudes toward the supernatural, marvels, and prodigies tell much about the epistemology of writing history.[52] Although Oviedo's representations of soothsayers and supernatural events obviously perform a function quite different from the author's direct comments on the problems of writing history, they nonetheless elucidate what he means when he compares the rival historians to *adivinos*. While he discusses soothsayers from the most disparate sources—among the indigenous peoples, among Spaniards, and in both pagan and sacred histories—for the most part he associates their predictions with an overreaching of the bounds of what can be known and with the devil, that "father of lies" (*HGN*, 2:183). Oviedo's treatment of soothsaying fits in with his overall critique of the humanist concept of the historian and a postulation of a new type of model inquirer needed for the task of recording the history of the Indies. In the *Libro de la cámara del real príncipe*, completed

50. See Gilmore, *Humanists*, 48, and Niccoli, who in *Prophecy* (xii) studies the role of prophecy in popular culture in Italy between 1500 and 1530, pointing to the "exceptionally open circulation" and acceptance of notions of prophecy among different social and cultural groups.

51. On the censorship of writings about Amerindian cultures, see Adorno, "Literary Production."

52. See Daston, "Marvelous Facts," and "Historical Epistemology," in *Questions of Evidence*, 243–74, 282–89.

at about the same time as the publication of part I of the *Historia general y natural,* Oviedo deals directly with the question—so dear to preceptors—of who was qualified to write history. He notes that writing history is "preeminent" among the services required by the king: "oficio es evangelista."[53] In equating the historian with the Gospel writers, Oviedo intimates an alternative to the humanist notion of the superior and distant *sabio.* Rather than a sage or magus who conjures up scenes from afar, the ideal historian should be a wandering witness who sees and records the revelation of the grace of God. On another occasion, he provides a narrative anecdote that contrasts the kind of knowledge that can be gained from augury with that of revelation. In book 6, chapter 48, of the *Historia,* he relates the example of an unsung hero of the conquest, García de Montalvo, who experiences a "dream or revelation" in which he learns of an antidote to poison arrows. The antidote is found to be effective, and later, as word of it spreads, it saves untold lives and grants the Spaniards another advantage in the wars of conquest. In the long run, Oviedo suggests, Montalvo's heaven-sent pharmaceutical insight made a contribution to the success of the imperial expansion second only to that of Columbus. To bolster this claim, so characteristic of Oviedo's work in its mix of scientific and providential explanations, the *cronista* cites Pedro Ciruelo on distinguishing divine from diabolic dreams. According to Ciruelo's definition, messages from God are rare and deal only with information of the highest significance for his chosen people, and are characterized by the absolute certainty of the witness of the revelation as to its truth. In contrast, the dreams of soothsayers tend to occur more frequently and to deal with "vain" subjects.[54]

---

53. Rómulo Carbia appears to have been the first to signal this passage, although he does not note its relevance to the humanist context under discussion here. Oviedo writes: "Historiadores e cronistas son en la casa rreal ofiçio muy preheminente. . . . [H]a de escrevir la vida e discursos de las personas rreales e suçesos de los tiempos, con la verdad e limpieza que se rrequiere. Offiçio es evanjelista, e conviene que esté en persona que tema a Dios, por que ha de tractar en cosas muy importantes, e develas dezir, no tanto arrimandose a la eloquencia e ornamento rretorico, quanto a la puridad e valor de la verdad, llanamente e sin rodeos ni abundançia de palabras." Oviedo, *Libro de la cámara real del príncipe,* as cited in Carbia, *Crónica oficial,* 27. Pérez de Tudela Bueso, in "Vida y escritos" (cxvii, n389), dates the completion of this manuscript in 1535. See also Gerbi, who notes Oviedo's view of himself as a "high priest of truth" in *Nature in the New World* (216).

54. The *cronista* quotes Pedro Ciruelo's *Reprobación de las supersticiones y hechicerías,* part 2, chap. 6: "en la revelación de Dios o del buen ángel no se hace mención de cosas vanas, ni acaesce muchas veces, sino por alguna cosa de mucha importancia y que pertenesce al bien común del pueblo de Dios, y con la tal visión queda el hombre muy certificado que es de buena parte, porque Dios alumbra el entendimiento del hombre y le certifica de la verdad. Mas en los sueños de los nigrománticos e adevinos no hay tal certidumbre, y vienen muchas veces y sobre cosas livianas y queda el hombre cegado y engañado del diablo." *HGN,* 1:211, book 6, chap. 48.

The Montalvo anecdote is important because it encapsulates a number of elements that allude to the particular problems of writing history and to the solutions that Oviedo finds to these problems. Clearly, the concern here is epistemological and relates to the possibility of supernatural knowledge—something practically required by Vives's precept of presenting the past as *perceived*. Ann Rigney has written that in order to understand its specifically historiographic function, "historical discourse must be seen as 'anachronistically' situated with respect to its object: it represents past events at the same time as it considers them retrospectively from a particular distance and reveals their significance for a later public."[55] Montalvo's dream can be appreciated only in hindsight. Although a *hidalgo* with a distinguished record, he holds no position of rank in any of the major expeditions. Oviedo mentions him only once, in this short anecdote, and he does not appear in earlier histories. If not for the dream, Montalvo might not have made it into the book at all. His significance would not likely have been apparent at the time of his vision. It becomes clear to Oviedo only in retrospect, as he contemplates the enormity of his project, that this was not just a "vain" or "light" story, but one that hints at hidden meanings. The textual parallel to Ciruelo is thus connected to the time of the narrative, not of the event. It is unlikely that Montalvo, under duress and unsure about his very survival, would have worried about the origin of this dream; rather, it is Oviedo who has to account for his narrative choices. In arguing that the dream was in fact revelatory and not a result of soothsaying, the *cronista* justifies the inclusion (and elevation to second place in the hierarchy of heroes) of this otherwise obscure figure in the account of the conquest, and, by extension, claims for his own history a part of the certainty of revelation. This is no trifle fabricated for special effect, Oviedo suggests, but a visible sign of God's will, duly deciphered and recorded after the fact by an inquirer who is, in this case, confident of his ability to perceive at least part of the providential design. Indeed, the outlook of the *adivino* is hard to resist, even for Oviedo.

Treatment of Historical Actors

The question of what the reliable historiographical narrator can know and the problem of coherence relates to the often ambiguous representation of "characters" or actors in Oviedo's history. Rigney has suggested that, unlike

55. Rigney, *Rhetoric*, 14.

works of the imagination, historical works tend to be more concerned with portraying groups than individuals: "The historical representation of collective events and collective characters raises specific problems which a model based solely on fictional narratives and individual subjects cannot fully account for." She notes that the same figures do not necessarily appear throughout a historical work, or even from one episode to the next, and that the sense of unity in a work of history comes not from the fate of one person, but from "the collective evolution of a social entity . . . which is by definition impersonal or, rather, transpersonal."[56] Dorrit Cohn has further suggested that the ability to portray the minds of individuals is a possibility specific to fiction (and particularly to the modern novel), and that in historiographical works the representation of inner thoughts and awareness tends to be carefully qualified with the language of conjecture.[57]

The portrayal of historical actors in the *Historia general y natural* would seem to bear out these observations. The sheer volume of individuals that Oviedo mentions (some of them major figures portrayed in great detail, others secondary or even minor actors, often appearing in lists as "witnesses" or participants in a particular expedition) means that few stand out as crucial to the encyclopedic sweep of the whole. Indeed, as if cognizant of the dizzying scope of his work, the *cronista* ends his history with a brief recapitulation in which he highlights seven individuals who contributed the greatest "services" to the imperial enterprise in the West Indies. Oviedo's particular treatment of sources brings up other problems as well. The "portrayal" of Cortés, for example, emerges from a number of various discrepant testimonies, and there is, as Iglesia noted long ago, an "open contradiction" between the enthusiastic narrative of the captain's qualities and achievements in the first version he presents and the deflating record of Cortés's death with which he ends this section.[58] One might speculate that the extended period over which the *cronista* composed his work might explain the divergent interpretations, or that this kind of phenomenon is a logical consequence of Oviedo's stated refusal to take sides on matters beyond his experience. But, one suspects that this kind of attitude points, as Cohn has suggested, to another discursive divide: historical figures simply cannot be known as thoroughly as fictional beings.[59]

56. Ibid., 103–4.
57. Cohn, *Distinction*, 121.
58. Iglesia, *Cronistas*, 92–93.
59. Cohn, *Distinction*, 121.

And yet Oviedo is not entirely consistent in this regard. His vision of the conquistadors as a collective group becomes increasingly pessimistic as the history progresses. Toward the beginning of the *Historia general y natural,* specifically the part 1 that was published in his lifetime, a panegyric celebration of the nature of the Indies and of the heroism of the conquerors, predominates, albeit with some notes of contrast.[60] We find, for example, nationalistic praise for the superiority of the Castilian conquerors: "En nuestra nación española no parece sino que comúnmente todos los hombres della nascieron principal y especialmente dedicados a las armas y a su ejercicio, y les son ellas e la guerra tan apropriada cosa, que todo lo demás es accesorio, e de todo se desocupan de grado, para la milicia" ("In our Spanish nation it appears that commonly all men are born principally and especially dedicated to the exercise of arms and war, and they are so taken with and talented for military affairs that for them everything else is accessory. They gladly leave all other occupations to enroll in the army") (*HGN,* 2:96, book 16, chap. 7). Those who participated in the conquest of San Juan (Puerto Rico), though few in number, were "of great spirit and effort" ("de grandísimo ánimo y esfuerzo") and, he suggests, never received adequate recompense for their services. Much like Bernal Díaz del Castillo, Oviedo here endeavors to capture the deeds of men who might otherwise be forgotten:

> A lo menos, si quedaron sin galardón o pago de sus trabajos y méritos, no les falte por culpa de mi pluma e pigricia la memoria de que fueron y son muy dignos sus hechos, porque en la verdad, es mejor satisfacción que otras; y en más se debe tener lo que se escribe en loor de los que bien vivieron e acabaron como buenos y valerosos, que cuantos bienes les pudo dar o quitar la fortuna.

> [At least, if they were left without reward or payment for their labor and merits, they should not lack through the fault of my pen and laziness the memory that their deeds were and are noble, for in truth, this is a greater satisfaction than the others. What is written in praise of those who lived well and died as good and valiant men should be held in greater regard than whatever material goods fortune enabled them to acquire or to lose.] (*HGN,* 2:96, book 16, chap. 7)

---

60. Two such contrasting notes are, for example, Oviedo's satire on Las Casas's colonization project in Cumaná and the "Naufragios" included as book 20.

But this panegyric homage to the manly prowess of the imperial enterprise begins to erode in subsequent additions to the first part, not published until the nineteenth century. He adds, for example, seven chapters to book 17 to include a scathing critique of Hernando de Soto's expedition: "¡Oh gente perdida, oh diabólica cobdicia, oh mala conciencia, oh desventurados mílites! ¿cómo no entendíades en cuánto peligro andábades, . . . Oid, pues, letor, católico, y no lloréis menos los indios conquistados que a los cristianos conquistadores dellos" ("Oh lost people, oh diabolical greed, oh bad conscience, oh unhappy soldiers! How did you not understand what grave danger you were in? . . . Listen, therefore, Catholic reader, and do not cry less for the conquered Indians than for the Christians who conquered them") (*HGN,* 2:172–73, book 17, chap. 26). Oviedo likens the crimes of de Soto's men to those of Pedrarias Dávila in Central America and to those of the Pizarros in Peru, thus giving greater emphasis to what had been a less prominent theme in the 1526 *Sumario*. He decries all who followed Columbus to be "alteradores y destruidores de la tierra" ("alterers and destroyers of the land") (*HGN,* 3:130, book 27, chap. 1); starving soldiers who resort to cannibalism are described as "wolves" and addressed directly: "¡Oh malditos hombres! ¡Oh improprios cristianos! ¡Oh verdaderos lobos y no hombres humanos!" ("Oh cursed men, oh improper Christians, oh true wolves and not human men!") (*HGN,* 3:195, book 28, chap. 6). The sort of perspectivist benefit-of-the-doubt approach accorded to Cortés, for example, is not granted to the Peruvian exploits of what he lambastes as Pizarro's "sect" (*HGN,* 5:254, book 49, chap. 9). Instead, we find, as Raúl Porras Barrenechea notes, a consistent animosity toward this line of "tyrants,"[61] and the account of the conquest of Peru takes on a markedly tragic cast, reflecting in part the *cronista*'s loss of his own son on Almagro's Chilean expedition, as well as, perhaps, an acknowledgment of the abuses so forcefully documented by Las Casas. Indeed, by the end of the work, Oviedo appears to lose his reticence to interpret the meaning of events, naming the evildoers by name and emphasizing the judicial and administrative processes by which they either receive or escape punishment.

As Bolaños has noted, Oviedo represents his own good leadership as contrasting with the seemingly endless crimes of the others entrusted by the crown with administrative responsibilities.[62] Oviedo notes that the stories of the governors sent by the Crown "mucho parescen tragedias" ("in much

---

61. Porras Barrenechea, "Cronistas," 242–44.
62. Bolaños, "La crónica."

appear to be tragedies"), with terrible fate brought on by insatiable greed. The very title of *adelantado* is a "mal augurio" ("bad omen") (*HGN*, 2:176, book 17, chap. 27); and *aciago* ("bitter"), because so many of those who have held the title have come to awful ends (*HGN*, 4:355, book 41, chap. 3). By the end of part 3, which deals with the brutal civil wars in Peru, he calls his own work an "imitación trágica" ("tragic representation") of history (4:335). One is struck, in a work that begins on a note of wonder and astonishment at the abundance of hidden riches to be found in the New World, to find authorial cautions to the reader—addressed now as "friend and companion" ("compañero amigo")—that he resist the temptation to embark to the Indies. He warns prospective sailors and soldiers to choose their company wisely:

> Muchos destos capitanes prometen lo que no tienen, ni saben ni entienden, y en pago de vuestra persona, os compran con palabras que son menos que plumas; porque las plumas, aunque las lleve el viento, veis adonde van guiadas . . . pero las palabras del que miente, son incorpóreas, e dichas, son invisibles y pásanse como aire.

> [Many of these captains promise what they neither have, know, nor understand, and as payment for your person, they buy you with words that are lighter than feathers; because even if feathers are blown by the wind, you can see where they are going; but the words of the liar are bodiless, and, once uttered, are invisible and pass by like air.] (*HGN*, 2:402, book 24, chap. 4)[63]

He provides a list of conditions for ascertaining the viability of expeditions and competence of captains. Indeed, one senses a broader pedagogical goal at work in Oviedo's historiographic method: the education not just of the prince, but of the reader-companion in order that he might learn to judge the reliability of testimony. Like the historian, the explorer and colonist depends on an appreciation for the slippery slope of discourse. Thus the different threads in Oviedo's interpretations often encroach upon and erode one another. Like the inclusion of multiple individual perspectives on events, the inclusion of multiple and seemingly contradictory interpretations

---

63. For a similar caution to governors: "el que se ceba de palabras de personas lagoteras de poco entender, fúndase en el aire; e así lo que se edifica de esta manera, ha de caer presto y no llegar a colmo." *HGN*, 3:185–86, book 28, chap. 4.

of the meaning of historical developments (panegyric, tragic, and providential) adds to the complexity and scope of his project.[64]

Perspectivism and the Styles of History:
"No puede bastar la pluma ni estilo de uno"

Kathleen Myers has pointed to the visual epistemology implicit in Oviedo's theory and practice of communicating natural history.[65] The visual perspectivism that this critic has highlighted in Oviedo's use of illustrations and sketches in his autograph manuscript would appear to be part of a range of perspectivist techniques that permeate his history. The sort of perspectivism implicit in providing multiple accounts of the same event, already discussed, coexists with what one might call the use of microperspectivism to relate doubtful events, as well as with a broad-scale perspectivism that seeks to bring a range of competing styles or interpretations to the material at hand.

Significantly, Oviedo includes not just accounts that he deems probable and trustworthy, but others that he suspects are false as well. This sort of representation of an "absence" is one aspect that Rigney has highlighted as common to historiographical discourse in general.[66] As already suggested, the *cronista* claims his authority as historian on his experience in examining the credibility of his witnesses, and thus in places devotes considerable energy to refuting rumor and innuendo (although frequently he refuses to judge between accounts). One notable such "absence" is the case of the narrative of the anonymous Portuguese pilot who was rumored to have preceded Columbus in discovering the western isles and to have confided the details of the route to the future admiral before dying.[67] The passage is exemplary as an exercise in microperspectivism (and in fact follows Vives's advice for relating events that are doubtful):

> Unos dicen que este maestre o piloto era andaluz; otros le hacen
> portugués; otros vizcaíno; otros dicen quel Colom estaba entonces
> en la isla de la Madera, e otros quieren decir que en las de Cabo
> Verde, y que allí aportó la caravela que he dicho, y él hobo por

---

64. Bolaños discusses the providentialist aspects of Oviedo's *Historia general y natural* in "Milagro."

65. Myers, "Representation."

66. Rigney, *Rhetoric*, 55.

67. See Bataillon, "La idea del descubrimiento de América," in Bataillon and O'Gorman, *Dos concepciones*, esp. 41.

esta forma noticia desta tierra. Que esto pasase así o no, ninguno con verdad lo puede afirmar; pero aquesta novela así anda por el mundo entre la vulgar gente de la manera que es dicho. Para mí lo tengo por falso.

[Some say that this master or pilot was Andalusian; others say Portuguese; others, Basque; others say that Columbus was on the Island of Madeira at the time, and others say that he was at Cape Verde, where the boat came to port, and that is how he heard tell of this land. Whether things happened in this way or not, none can truthfully affirm, but this rumor as told here has spread among common people. I myself believe it to be false.] (*HGN,* 1:16, book 1, chap. 2)

Oviedo juxtaposes this chorus of contradictory rumors, with no witnesses cited by name, with his own categorical opinion that it is false. Throughout the history he distinguishes between hearsay (marked by tags such as "quieren decir," "dicen," "dícese") and the legally sworn testimony of individuals.[68]

Oviedo's method of privileging voice and perspective over chronology necessarily comes at the expense of the readability of his work, as critics have often noted. Gerbi, otherwise one of the *cronista*'s greatest enthusiasts, suggests that the lack of "art and discipline" in this regard leads the author to lapse "into the sort of turgid farrago typical of the medieval 'summae,'" and that the total disorganization of his work has "done more harm to his reputation than his prejudices and essential shortcomings."[69] Oviedo himself claims to structure his text on geographical, not chronological, principles and explicitly warns his reader to pay no attention to the sequence in which he relates events: "No mire en esta discusión cuál va puesto primero; porque yo, continuando con mis libros la costa, irán en algunas partes los modernos antes que los que en tiempo los preceden" ("Do not look in this discussion for what is placed first; because I, following the coast with my books, have put more recent events ahead of others that preceded them in time") (*HGN,* 2:342, book 22, chap. 1). But the method of following coastlines rather than chronology only adds to the innumerable repetitions and redundancies occasioned by his labyrinthine endeavor.

---

68. A similar perspectivist strategy can be seen in his efforts to discredit rumors of metallurgic riches in the Masaya volcano in Nicaragua. *HGN,* 4:399, book 42, chap. 6.

69. Gerbi, *Nature in the New World,* 386.

Oviedo, it is true, does not apply his "rule" consistently throughout his work. And yet, what might seem to be inconsistencies are often telling strategies, because they illustrate the ways in which he grapples with conflicting models of historical writing and the expectations they entail. It is instructive to examine in a more extended narrative context an episode dealing with Oviedo's depiction of historical agents and his representation of the supernatural. The events surrounding the Spaniards' march into and subsequent flight from Tenochtitlán clearly caught the *cronista*'s attention, as they should. A major (if temporary) reversal in the fortunes of Cortés and his company, this episode had already received prominent treatment in earlier accounts of the conquest of Mexico, and thus could not, in any case, have been avoided in a historical work that claimed reliability. Oviedo deals with these events, as already mentioned, in chapter 13 of book 33 (where he follows Cortés's second "Carta de relación" closely), but exploits some of their dramatic possibilities in a second account, in which he records an alternate view ("relación asaz diferente") based on information from "caballeros e mílites que se hallaron en la conquista de la Nueva España" ("gentlemen and soldiers who participated in the conquest of New Spain") (*HGN*, 4:213, book 33, chap. 45). The author protests:

> E no le parezca al que lee que es contradecirse lo uno a lo otro, porque los hombres así como son de diversos juicios e condiciones, así miran y entienden las cosas diferenciadamente e las cuentan; puesto que vengan los unos e los otros a una general e mesma conclusión, e aun a las veces se contradicen en muchas cosas puntualmente.

> [And it should not seem to the reader that one contradicts the other, because just as men are of different minds and conditions, so they look at and understand things in different ways and tell them as such. Even when they come to a similar general conclusion, different accounts often contradict each other on many particular points.] (*HGN*, 4:223–24, book 33, chap. 47)

As in legal cases, suggests Oviedo, differences in particular versions or testimonies do not necessarily indicate unreliability or falsehood. In history, he suggests, the inclusion of multiple and contradictory accounts is a sign of careful research, even if it makes the narrative appear to be all mixed up ("salteada"). Though the *cronista* protests the trustworthiness of the sources for this second account, they remain, nonetheless, unnamed.

The presence of multiple anonymous sources may well be an indication from the author that he has taken greater freedom in the composition of this episode than in the other chapters of book 33, which are clearly tied to names and documents as sources. Although this alternative version repeats information included in the Cortesian one, it is written in a markedly different style. Whereas in the first account Oviedo limits himself to indirect summary focusing largely on the figure of Cortés, in the second one he includes short scenes of direct dialogues. A sequence of dialogues between Cortés and Montezuma is followed, after the Castilian captain's departure to face the army of his rival Pánfilo de Narváez, with a scene of a conversation between natives and Castilians as the former plot treachery and ready the pots full of *ají* for cooking up the now highly vulnerable invaders left behind by Cortés to hold Tenochtitlán. The device of the direct dialogue between unnamed sources is notable here precisely because it is not a common one in the *Historia general y natural*.[70] Indeed in several places of his text, we find the presence of a dialogue between unnamed sources as a sort of signature by which Oviedo appears to indicate his own perspective on events he has not witnessed. Furthermore, in this passage Oviedo describes with some precision miracles, as well as the false counsel of the *adivino* Botello and the effects that these signs had on Castilians and Nahuas alike. The scene is rife with conflict between celestial and demonic powers, and the marvelous nature of events brings up unavoidable issues of credibility.

Prominent in this account are the series of providential signs that appear to herald a victory for the embattled retinue: saltwater turns to fresh just in time to assuage the embattled Christians' thirst; the Nahuas who try to take down the image of the Virgin Mary find that their hands stick to it mysteriously; and a faulty cannon shot, long deemed useless, suddenly explodes, killing many of the indigenous fighters, who, "con ímpetu leonino" ("with leonine impetus") had been on the verge of decimating the Spaniards. An image of Santiago on a white horse appears to assist the Christians. And yet the atmosphere among the soldiers—one of tense confusion and internal divisions—would not seem to reflect any clear premonition of certain deliverance. The retrospective understanding of a divine plan favoring the

70. On Oviedo's use of the dialogue form with named witnesses, see Myers, "History, Truth and Dialogue." An interesting point of contrast is the series of dialogues with indigenous leaders conducted in Nicaragua by a Mercedarian friar. *HGN,* 4, book 42, chaps. 2–3.

military and political ambitions of the conquerors emerges as the *cronista* pictures God intervening directly through his miracles on the battlefield. Oviedo, ever self-conscious on questions of credibility, is quick to preempt criticism concerning the plausibility of these events:

> Ya sé que los incrédulos o poco devotos dirán que mi ocupación en esto de milagros, pues no los ví, es superflua o perder tiempo, novelando; e yo hablo que esto e más se puede y debe creer, pues que los gentiles e sin fe e idólatras escriben que hubo grandes misterios e milagros en sus tiempos, e aquellos sabemos que eran causados e fechos por el diablo. Pues más fácil cosa es a Dios e a la inmaculada Virgen Nuestra Señora, e al glorioso apóstol Santiago, e a los santos e amigos de Jesucristo hacer esos milagros que de suso están dichos, e otros mayores.

> [I know that those who are incredulous or not very devout will say that to occupy myself with these miracles, which I have not seen, is superfluous or a waste of time, a fabrication; and I say that this and more can and should be believed, because the gentiles and faithless and idolatrous write that there were great mysteries and miracles in their times, and we know that those were caused and made by the devil. Well it is easier for God and Our Lady the immaculate Virgin, and for the glorious apostle Santiago, and for the saints and friends of Jesus Christ to perform miracles such as these, and even greater ones.] (*HGN,* 4:228)

While Fernández de Oviedo's protestations may well be a confession of his own narrative liberties in this passage, it also points to his tendency to rely, particularly on controversial points, on textual authorities to make up for gaps in his own vision. Although he did not witness these events, which might appear fabricated ("novelando") to the less devout, there are, he suggests, solid precedents for such things in gentile history.[71] Compared to the miracles in the Bible and in later Christian traditions, this sort of marvel is really nothing new. He follows this narrative of providential signs with an ancient example of diabolic feats:

---

71. In reference to Gentile histories, he writes: "qué subjetos a sus aurispices e adevinos fueron! e qué agoreros e obidientes a vanidades, fundadas sobre religiosidad e falsa sanctimonia! Quiero decir, que si miramos en las cosas de los gentiles en este caso, por tan profanas y diabólicas las tenemos como las de nuestras Indias." Oviedo, *HGN,* 4:221, book 33, chap. 46.

Escribe Tito Livio que debatiendo Lucio Tarquino Prisco, quinto rey de los romanos, con Action Navio, famoso en los augurios, dijo al adivino como por cosa de burla: "¿Adivinarás lo que yo agora pienso o deviso en mi corazón?" Y el adivino, que estaba guardando en sus puntos e ciencia, dijo que sí. Entonces, dijo el rey: "Yo devisaba que tú cortabas aquella piedra con una navaja; toma la navaja e haz aquello que tus aves adivinan." El adivino deliberadamente tomó la navaja e cortó la piedra; así que ved lo que el diablo puede, que hizo que la navaja cortase la piedra.

[Livy writes that, when Lucius Tarquinus Priscus, fifth king of the Romans, was debating Actius Navius, famous for his auspices, he said to the soothsayer in jest: Can you divine what I am now thinking or entertaining in my heart? And the soothsayer, who was keeping his thoughts to himself, said yes. Then, the king said: "I was imagining that you were cutting that stone with a knife. Take the knife and do what your birds divine." The soothsayer deliberately took the knife and cut the stone; look what the devil, who made the knife cut the stone, is able to do.] (*HGN*, 4:228)

In noting this model from Roman history, in which the king unsuccessfully challenges the authority of the augur, Fernández de Oviedo associates the soothsayer's miracle (an ability to perceive accurately and act on the thoughts of another individual) with supernatural powers granted directly by the devil.[72] In an odd—but typical for Oviedo—kind of logic, this "miracle" excerpted from Livy serves several disparate functions. First, it brings a classical authority to vouch for the credibility of the accounts of providential signs in the Indies: if the stories of diabolic miracles found in Latin history are true, suggests Oviedo, then why question accounts in recent history that confirm Christian belief? It also reminds us of Oviedo's claims to his own restricted point of view, while forming a narrative link to (and textual

72. Taken from Livy's *Early History of Rome,* the episode refers to a critical moment when Tarquin, an outsider who has recently gained the throne through scheming, finds himself under attack by the Sabines. He wants to increase the army, but tradition has it that the augurs must be consulted first. Tarquin defies the augurs, and loses. Livy comments: "But whatever we may think of this story, the fact remains that the importance attached to augury and the augural priesthood increased to such an extent that to take auspices was henceforth an essential preliminary to any serious undertaking in peace or in war; not only army parades or popular assemblies, but matters of vital concern to the commonwealth were postponed, if the birds refused their assent." Livy, *Early History of Rome,* 59.

precedent for) the next section of the episode, where Oviedo dramatizes the effects of the miracles on the indigenous peoples, as well as the intervention of the Spanish soothsayer, Botello, and his possible influence over Cortés at this decisive moment.

As the enemy forces surround the Spaniards in ever-greater numbers, Oviedo brings in a chorus of unnamed Nahua opinion that reflects, in a mixture of direct and indirect discourse, on miraculous signs, such as the appearances of Saint James and the Virgin Mary:

> E decían: "Si no hobiésemos miedo de esse del caballo blanco, ya vosotros estaríedes cocidos, aunque no valéis nada para comeros, porque los cristianos que tomamos esotro día, los cocimos, e amargaban mucho.". . . E que pues decían los indios que veían una mujer que les echaba mucho polvo en los ojos, cuando peleaban con los christianos porque no los viesen.

> [And they said: "If we were not frightened of that one on the white horse, you would already be cooked, although you are not worth eating, because the Christians that we took the other day, we cooked them, and they were very bitter." . . . And the Indians said that they saw a woman who was throwing dust in their eyes when they were fighting with the Christians so that they could not see them.] (*HGN,* 4:229)

The Nahua witnessing and interpreting of the signs of divine Providence would seem to function as a sort of independent confirmation of the miraculous events. Even unbelievers see, but fail to comprehend, the apparition of a feisty horse and horseman, and testify to the supernatural interference of a woman. Faced with the imminent threat of cannibalism, not to mention military annihilation, the Christians nonetheless take a moment to refute the enemy's "gentilicas y heréticas vanidades" ("gentile and heretical vanities"), explaining the roles the Virgin and the saint play in Christian tradition. This minute scene in which Christians endeavor to spread the Gospel to the natives on the battlefield serves multiple purposes, at once highlighting the "inhuman" practices of the enemy and suggesting that only miracles could ever save Cortés's enterprise. Here, too, the use of unnamed sources may well indicate the liberties Oviedo has taken in his interpretation.

The indigenous reactions also have a parallel in that of Cortés, just returned from his successful campaign against Narváez, to the soothsayer

Botello, who predicts that if the Christians do not leave the Aztec capital on a particular night, none of their band will survive. Cortés agrees to withdraw his troops, and Oviedo ponders whether the Spanish captain did so on Botello's misguided advice ("aquel adevino o desvariado parescer") or on his own intuition, "como varón experto é de grand conoscimiento, e aun porque la nescesidad es la que enseña a los hombres en tales trances lo que conviene a su salvación" ("like an expert and very knowledgeable man, even more so because necessity is what teaches men in these circumstances what is necessary for their salvation") (*HGN,* 4:229, book 33, chap. 47). Oviedo conjectures that Cortés would have acted on instinct, not the advice of a conjurer, and suggests that, though the casualties suffered by the Castilians were in fact devastating (a detail that might lend credence to Botello), the damage was augmented by their greedy insistence on carrying treasure as they fled. Indeed, the loss of the expedition might have been total, he suggests, had not the Aztec warriors been distracted from fighting as they sought to recover their riches. Oviedo records both the ostensible miracle, as well as the suspect soothsayer's prophecy, but ultimately emphasizes the contingent, unexpected actions of groups and individuals as decisive in the outcome.

The parallels between the passage by Livy and the situation of the Castilians under siege are as interesting as they are undeveloped by Oviedo. In Livy's account of the face-off between the Roman king and Actius Navius, the augur gains the upper hand, thus improving the fortunes of the soothsaying enterprise in this early period of Roman history. Though Oviedo includes the narrative about the tense moments under Aztec attack, ostensibly derived from unnamed witnesses, he appears to disagree with the image they suggest of Cortés as willing to listen to augurs. The *cronista* follows the Botello anecdote with another historical example of advice from a soothsayer, this time from Josephus's *Against Apion* (I. 201). In this case, the attitude of the Jewish hero Mesolano, who defies a soothsayer's authority and ultimately wins, appears to resemble that of Cortés, reinforcing the notion that the latter's decision to retreat was in fact based on wit, not on the advice of an *adivino.* The two textual parallels that Oviedo brings to bear on Cortés's situation are very different, and the author leaves it to the reader to infer which case is more applicable. One senses here a hope that an accumulation of authoritative witnesses might make up for a lack of duly sworn (i.e., reliable) versions.

The author's restricted knowledge of Cortés's true motivations is paralleled by a similarly guarded approach to the mind of the Aztec leader at the beginning of book 33, chapter 47, where Oviedo explains how the devil, in torment over the Catholic sacraments and ceremonies so devoutly practiced by the conquerors in Tenochtitlán, suggested to the Aztec lord ("puso en corazón a Montezuma") that the Christians be thrown out of the territory or else killed. The *cronista* cites a combination of unnamed sources and suppositions for this version ("Quieren decir, e aun es de sospechar"; "E débese pensar, si verdad es que esas gentes tienen tanta conversación e comunicación con nuestro adversario"; "e a esto decían que le respondía Montezuma") (*HGN,* 4:224). Thus, the portrait of the Aztec emperor in this crucial episode emerges, like that of the marvelous miracles, as grounded on a mixture of unverifiable rumor and "reliable" dogma. As in the case of Cortés, Oviedo suggests that one can only guess as to the real thoughts and motivations of the Aztec leader.

Oviedo's quite different treatment of "providential" signs in the Peru material contrasts with the more positive vision put forth of the conquest of Mexico. The *cronista*'s rendition of a report by Alonso de Montemayor of portents that preceded Gonzalo Pizarro's defeat tells of a lunar eclipse in Quito, when two clouds shaped like lions appeared in the sky. As the cloud-lions prepare to battle, onlookers hear a voice proclaim "long live the king" and witness a shower of blood drops from the sky. Oviedo comments:

> Dice el cronista que al prescio que hobo esta relación, la da, e libra al lector en don Alonso; e a quien quisiere saber muchas cosas de portentos, remite a las *Décadas* de Tito Livio e a Dionisio Halicarnaseo, en el libro IV de sus historias. Pero no dejando de verse en las nubes muchas figuras que bastan a los ligeros e varios hombres para más desvanecerlos si dejan de entender que son naturalmente causados del viento, e con él, en breve pasan. Pero como esta tiranía de Gonzalo Pizarro e sus crueldades le hacen tan odioso méritamente, no me maravillo que se juntasen esos portentos: e los aurispicios e adevinos, . . . no han de ser las nubes, sino la justicia divina e humana.

[The chronicler says that he will sell this account for the same price he bought it, and refers the reader directly to don Alonso. Who-ever wants to know many things about portents should refer to the *Decades* of Livy and to Dionisius Halicarnassus, in book 4 of his histories. But since clouds never fail to make shapes, this is enough for light and fickle men to become distracted and lose their wits, if they forget that clouds are naturally caused by wind patterns and, so, soon pass. But since Gonzalo Pizarro is so justly odious because of his tyranny and cruelties, it does not surprise me that these portents came together. And the auspices and soothsayers . . . will not be the clouds, but divine and human justice.] (*HGN*, 5:284, book 49, chap. 10)

Oviedo's ironic jab that he has paid nothing for this ostensibly supernatural account, which only Montemayor can vouch for, at once posits a possible natural cause (wind patterns) while at the same time leaving open the possibility of a providential explanation. As someone who has repeatedly defied both divine and terrestrial justice, Pizarro appears to have finally met his match. In general, in his account of the Peruvian expeditions, Oviedo laments the lack of information and alternative sources, noting wryly that history is written by the winners. Those who might provide an alternate point of view have either died or fled, and the victors tend to be in a good position to offer bribes or gifts for those who help them. Finally, no one wants to get in trouble by talking too much (*HGN*, 5:209, book 47, chap. 21). We find here not the foxlike chronicler, nor the imperial evangelist of history, but rather a deeply melancholic narrator who signals the fragility of any historiographic endeavor in the conflictive colonial context.

This degraded view of history as merely a tool of the victors coexists with the author's increasingly critical view, toward the end of his work, of the possibility of arriving at truth. The idea of falsehoods as being manifest or self-evident in narrative is often linked to his criticisms of his rivals and his metacommentaries about the writing process. In book 29, chapter 25, for instance, he returns to the topic of the "vicious novels," quoting the authority of Saint Gregory with a metaphor that once again associates textual deceit with heresy. He suggests that lying literature serves a social purpose, much like heretics, who, once exposed, must repent (or face public punishment).[73] Although he refrains from naming the works he criticizes here, he suggests that "lying histories," like those who have been tried and revealed to be dissimulators in public, can serve an exemplary function.[74] But elsewhere he describes a case of simple misunderstandings interpreted as lies. In book 33, chapter 22, for example, in treating questions of evangelizing the indigenous

---

73. "Conviene, dice este dotor sagrado, que haya herejes, para que seyendo probados, sean manifiestos. No quiero nombrar los libros, ni los auctores que reprehendo." *HGN*, 3:312, book 29, chap. 25.

74. For an example that stresses the idea of lies as exposing the vanity of men, see book 50, chap. 30.

peoples, Oviedo includes an account of two unnamed Christians who were "lost" and living among dangerous Caribs. The latter, however, did not harm these two anonymous Castilians, but instead treated them well in exchange for instruction in the Catholic faith. In an effort to test the foreigners, the Caribs, like expert detectives, separate them to inquire about the nature and appearance of the Christian god. The first captive tells his native interlocutors that God created the world, that he had no beard, and that no one was worthy of seeing him. The second explains that the Christian God was born of the Virgin Mary, lived on earth and had a beard, but went to heaven after death. Perplexed by these ostensibly contradictory versions, the Caribs accuse the Castilians of lying. The latter endeavor to explain the concept of the Trinity, but become so tangled in their expositions that the Caribs stop listening. When the Christians subsequently get into a dispute among themselves over whom was to blame for the confusion, they turn to blows and end up killing each other. Once again, Oviedo would seem to signal the "invented" quality of this passage by the anonymity of his source: the would-be evangelists here start out "lost" and end up dead, and their fate points not so much to the difficulties of the task of conversion as to the confusion and shortsighted belligerence of the believers. What may seem like blatant contradictions to the uninitiated are but partial perceptions of a Christian truth. This anecdote, together with the commentary concerning the benefits of making public even "lying" histories, may well allude in an eloquent and symbolic fashion to the difficulties of distinguishing truth in discourse when dealing with unfamiliar material and, thus, to the controversies that would emerge over the meaning of events in the newly conquered territories. At the same time, the frequent association of falsehood and dissimulation with superstitious practices and heresy in Oviedo reinforces his own implicit aspiration to be an "evangelist" of history (albeit a foxlike one) who seeks to rectify the dangerous misrepresentations of his rivals, and recalls the humanist ideal, expressed by Vives, that historical narrative recapture timeless religious truths.

Oviedo's restricted narrative stance, which sets the standards for the structure and portrayal of "characters" or agents in the *Historia general y natural,* necessarily affects the concept of exemplarity within his work. In order to know whether a figure such as Cortés is exemplary or not, one must have a relatively firm grasp of his achievements and errors. Oviedo, however, while expressing certainty in a providential plan at work, tends more often than not to reserve judgment about the deeds and intentions of men, to accumulate partial perspectives rather than to attempt a synthetic whole. He writes, in one of his frequent digressions on lying literature, that he hopes that his own work will be well received in the eyes of God as a history that has not deviated from the path of truth. The opinion of his readers, he suspects, will likely be far more severe:

> Ya yo sé que las hierbas que substentan a unos animales, matan a otros . . . y he visto que la sentencia que unos llaman injusta, otros la alaban: y sé que todo esto habrá en mis renglones, porque los gustos no son uno mesmo, ni los juicios de los hombres siguen un parescer, ni son de igual ingenio ni inclinación. Sólo Dios es el justo y el que puede e sabe justamente juzgar a todos, porque ninguna cosa le es oculta, y es impassible.

> [I know that the herbs that sustain some animals will kill others . . . and I have seen that the judgment that some call unjust is praised by others, and I know that all this will be found in my lines, because neither tastes are all the same, nor do the minds of men follow a single opinion, nor are they of equal wit or inclination. Only God is just and able to justly judge others, because nothing is hidden from him and he is impassive.] (*HGN*, 3:312, book 29, chap. 25)

Oviedo's conviction that the Almighty is, ultimately, the only competent judge of credibility and exemplarity in human affairs points once again to the *cronista*'s conscious critique of the humanist method and techniques for writing history. Indeed, one finds an increasing tendency to base exemplarity not in judging actions, but in judging words. What began as a contemplation of the marvels of the emperor's holdings becomes a lament for the fallen, a dispatch to inform the living of those they have lost, as well as a caution to the curious reader. As we have seen, Oviedo is not entirely consistent throughout the *Historia* in implementing his narrative experiments, but the range of strategies that he adopts is testimony to the seriousness with which he undertook his task. On the one hand, Oviedo was endeavoring to write a history that, for all of its novelty, would address, if not always comply with, the humanist expectations for history and the narrative perspective appropriate thereto, even as he questioned and, to some degree, reformulated the humanist norms. On the other, in making his own claim that his history was a truthful one, he was anxious to distinguish it in all respects from the infamous "lying" kind, filled with inventions and told as if by a soothsayer. In the next chapter I examine the ways in which Las Casas exploits and transforms Oviedo's strategies, turning them against their author.

3

VISION AND VOICE: THE *HISTORIA DE LAS INDIAS* BY BARTOLOMÉ DE LAS CASAS

LIKE FERNÁNDEZ DE OVIEDO, Bartolomé de Las Casas (1484–1566) in his *Historia de las Indias*[1] endeavors to come to practical terms with both the humanist norms for "true" history and with the prior historical accounts concerning the New World.[2] But where Oviedo had built a strategy of dismissing the works of authors writing from Europe on broad epistemological grounds, Las Casas claims his authority as historian based on an acute notion of orthodoxy in both content and form. One finds in his work an extraordinary effort to put into practice both the humanist ideals concerning the writing of history and the sort of insight arrived at by Oviedo concerning the necessarily limited scope of the historian's vision. He portrays himself as an erudite spiritual authority, sometimes as a prophet and sometimes as an inquisitorial figure, while at the same time emphasizing the value of his own testimony as a direct witness. The effort to reconcile the narrative perspective of the retrospective and visionary historian with his more limited viewpoint in scenes wherein he is a witness or actor leads him to odd narrative solutions. In the autobiographical sections of his history, for example, we often find him representing himself—in both the first and the third person—as a historical actor who is the object of the author's commentary. His work thus dramatizes a widely varying range of vision on the part of the historiographical narrator: in places, as we shall see, the critical attitude that he adopts toward others coexists with a remarkable hesitancy in his portrayal of himself as a participant in events.

1. All citations from the *Historia de las Indias* (*HI*) are taken from Saint-Lu's edition (Caracas, 1986) and are hereafter noted parenthetically in text by volume, page number, and chapter. While a number of editions are based on Fray Bartolomé's autograph manuscript, which is located in the Biblioteca Nacional in Madrid and recognized as the most complete of existing copies, Saint-Lu's edition corrects errors and omissions in the earlier editions of Millares Carlo (Mexico, 1951) and Pérez de Tudela Bueso (Madrid, 1957). Unless otherwise noted, English translations are from Collard's version, although I have modified her renderings in places as noted.

2. The major histories of the Indies published in Spain before 1552 included Martyr de Anghera's *De orbe novo* (1516); Oviedo's *Historia general y natural* (1535, 1547); and López de Gómara's *Historia general de las Indias* and *Historia de la conquista de México* (1552).

Las Casas's search for orthodoxy both in form and in subject matter has been explained in an alternative fashion by Ramón Menéndez Pidal in terms of the dual rhetorical strategies of accusation and apology that inform the *Historia de las Indias*. Menéndez Pidal notes these two tendencies in his controversial biography, provocatively titled *El padre Las Casas: Su doble personalidad*,[3] and one suspects that a number of otherwise apt observations about the text have been overshadowed by the author's evident animosity toward Las Casas, by his efforts to discredit the latter's achievements, and by his interpretation of the cleric as a paranoiac personality, one that most historians have correctly rejected.[4] Indeed, Menéndez Pidal would seem in his analysis to have confused the figure of the (real) author with that of his narrative persona. In a work of history, of course, the textual figure of the narrator provides hints as to the being of the author, and in the *Historia de las Indias,* which includes an extended account of the cleric's public life, one is tempted to look for the sort of telltale "deformations" and "breaches of contract" that Philippe Lejeune describes as inherent to the autobiographical pact.[5] While to hazard a guess at the author's mental health would seem to violate one of the historiographical taboos under examination in this book (reading minds), a study of the textual construct of the narrator and the problems of voice and perspective embodied within it enables one to look at the larger theoretical issue of narrative reliability in historical versus fictional texts. In particular, I would like to suggest that a study of the strange shape of Las Casas's textual self-fashioning illustrates manners in which unreliability in historical narrative appears to obey a logic different from that of fiction, and thus hints at another of the borderlines that I have been attempting to identify and describe in this book.

In his "accusatory" mode, Las Casas as narrator invokes the humanist historiographic norms both to attack the histories of his rivals, such as Oviedo and Gómara, and to establish an authoritative, even prophetic voice (as true evangelist of the New World); in his "apologetic" mode, he presents a "biography" of himself, as María Teresa Silva Tena first described it, a third-person narrative that seeks both to defend and to atone for his own actions in the Indies.[6] This multiple narrative persona brings up a number of critical issues that I address in this chapter. By examining the basic

3. Menéndez Pidal, *El padre Las Casas,* 47.
4. Raymond Marcus, in "Las Casas: A Selective Bibliography" (612–13), lists and briefly annotates the extensive and heated reactions generated by Menéndez Pidal's book.
5. Lejeune, *On Autobiography,* 14.
6. Silva Tena, "Las Casas, biógrafo."

outlines of Las Casas's multifaceted authorial voice in both its accusatory and apologetic modes, I hope to highlight the narrative complexities of the solution he finds to the rhetorical and historical parameters in which he found himself.[7]

Life and Works

Las Casas was born around 1484 to a family of merchants, possibly of *converso* origin, in Seville. In 1502 he sailed to Hispaniola, where he may have been involved in mining and military expeditions. He returned to Spain in 1506, was ordained a *clérigo* (lay priest) in Rome in 1507, and later studied canon law at the University of Salamanca, from which he received a licenciatura. By 1512 he participated as chaplain in the conquest of Cuba and received an *encomienda* in return for his services.[8] By his own account, Las Casas was inspired in 1511 by a sermon given by the Dominican Antonio Montesinos censuring the enslavement by Spaniards of the indigenous peoples, and professes to have undergone a "conversion" in 1514 that would motivate him to relinquish his *encomienda* and become an outspoken critic of conquest and colonial practices.[9] In 1520 he obtained, despite some controversy, a concession from Charles V to peacefully colonize Cumaná (on the coast of Venezuela). After the failure of this experiment (the settlement was attacked by natives; many of the colonizers and priests who accompanied them died in the conflict), Las Casas joined the Dominican Order in 1522 as a novice, taking his vows a year later (some refer to this as his "second conversion").[10] He then retreated to a Dominican monastery in Hispaniola, where

---

7. Oviedo's *Historia general y natural* featured a highly unfavorable, even satirical, picture of Las Casas and his evangelization experiment at Cumaná, and was cited by Juan Ginés de Sepúlveda (1490–1573) as the documentary support for justifying the wars against the indigenous peoples. By 1552, when Las Casas penned the prologue to his history, Oviedo's history had become the foundation for an emerging tradition of historical accounts on the Indies, one that achieved a more clearly defined narrative configuration in works such as López de Gómara's history. On Oviedo's harsh representation of Las Casas and subsequent reception of Las Casas's work in the sixteenth century, see Keen, "Approaches," in Friede and Keen, eds., *Bartolomé de las Casas in History*, 3–11, and his later and more complete "Approaches to Bartolomé de las Casas," in *Essays*, 1–56.

8. On Las Casas's biography, see, among others, Huerga, whose essay in volume 1 of *Obras completas* clarifies sources of contradictions in earlier studies; Hanke, "Bartolomé de Las Casas: Historiador"; Giménez Fernández's "Biographical Sketch," in Friede and Keen, eds., *Bartolomé de las Casas in History*; Parish and Weidman, "The Correct Birthdate"; Salas, *Tres cronistas*, 177–227; Saint Lu, "Vida y obra," *HI*, 3:621–26; and Adorno, who in "The Intellectual Life," 2–6, summarizes and clarifies the scholarship related to Las Casas's ordination and subsequent studies in law.

9. Las Casas, *HI*, 3:282–85, chap. 79.

10. On this subject, see Hanke, "Bartolomé," and Bataillon, *Estudios*, 157–77.

he would spend the next seven years. Subsequently he renewed his vocal advocacy of indigenous causes as activist at the court of Charles V, obtaining legal reforms to protect the indigenous population, such as the New Laws of 1542, and championing a model of peaceful evangelization. He became bishop of Chiapas (1543–50); attorney-at-large for the indigenous peoples (1547–66); and tenacious writer of letters, juridical and theological treatises, and historical works until his death in Madrid in 1566.

Las Casas began to write the *Historia de las Indias* in 1527, by his own account, shortly after the publication of Oviedo's *Sumario de la natural historia de las Indias* (1526), and while he was at the monastery at Puerto de Plata, Hispaniola. While he continued to work on and collect materials for his history over the next thirty-five years, it seems that, as Hanke suggests, he began to write in earnest only after 1547, spurred by the publication that year of the second edition of part 1 of Oviedo's *Historia general y natural*. Las Casas had aimed, he himself tells us in the prologue, to cover the first six decades of the discovery, conquest, and colonization of the Indies in *Historia de las Indias,* but when he stopped working on the manuscript in 1561, he appears to have completed only the first three books, dealing with events of approximately the first three decades. Scholars who have struggled with editing the autograph manuscript attest to the labyrinthine corrections and interpolations, where the confusing chronology and frequent quotations often smother the narrative of events.[11] Saint-Lu, following Hanke, suggests that the manuscript reveals few indications of the initial stages of the work and proposes that the author likely gave the history its definitive form in the later years.[12] Bataillon, in his review of the 1951 edition of the *Historia de las Indias,* hypothesizes, based on the wealth of detail in book 3 concerning events in which the author participates, that Las Casas in fact composed a basic version of the work much earlier and simply recopied while revising it at a later time. There are certainly passages to support this hypothesis: "No me pude acordar cuando esto escribía" ("I could not remember when I was writing this") (3:120, chap. 31). In his testament, Las Casas bequeathed the manuscript of the *Historia de las Indias* to the monastery of San Gregorio in Valladolid, with instructions that it should not be published until forty years after his death. While the first edition would not appear until 1875, and the text based on the autograph manuscript would not be published until the

---

11. Hanke, "Bartolomé," xxxi.

12. Saint-Lu, "Prólogo," xx–xxi; Pérez Fernández's exhaustive analysis of this question in "Estudio preliminar y análisis crítico" (180–84) largely seems to bear Saint-Lu's impressions out.

mid-twentieth century, Hanke notes that few histories have been used as extensively before publication as the *Historia de las Indias*.[13]

To try to address the vast library of scholarship on Las Casas—whose *Brevísima relación de la destrucción de las Indias* is today one of the most canonical works in the Spanish American tradition—is a daunting task. Keen has reviewed the scholarship as well as the "black" and "white" legends associated with the figure of Las Casas, noting that the cleric is justly credited as a founder of the struggle for social justice in Latin America, and that his stance on issues of human rights and anticolonialism still resonates today.[14] The essential outline of the author's demonstration of the rationality of Amerindian peoples according to Aristotelian categories is well known, and his very important political and historiographical achievements have been documented extensively by scholars such as Hanke, Bataillon, Giménez Fernández, O'Gorman, and Pérez de Tudela Bueso, among others. The utopian aspects of his construction of the "other" have received critical attention, as has the autobiographical vein in his text.[15] In focusing on Las Casas's keen sensibilities on problems of writing history as well as his own narrative experiments, it is not my intention to minimize the author's achievements. Rather, my aim in this chapter is to examine the diverse manners in which the cleric participates in debates over epistemological questions concerning the writing of history, and in particular the manner in which he harnesses both the humanist rhetoric concerning the corruption of the "Greek tradition" and the language of inquisitorial examination to his critique of the chroniclers of empire. I will argue that the language of the humanist debates and that of inquisitorial examination provide him with a framework for gaining precision in evaluating problems of truth and falsehood in historical discourse. In the process, Las Casas engages in and contributes to the debate over the question of narrative perspective and the forms proper to "true" history. Finally, I would like to suggest that his self-representation in the text brings up important theoretical issues related to narrative reliability in history.

---

13. For detailed information on the manuscripts and editions of this work, see Hanke, "Bartolomé," xxxi–xlvi, and Adorno, "Censorship."

14. Keen, "Approaches to Bartolomé de las Casas," chapter 1 in *Essays*.

15. On the utopian vein in Las Casas's historical works, see especially Rabasa, "Historiografía colonial" and *Inventing America*, 164–79; Arias, *Retórica, historia y polémica*, 87–97; Pastor, *Jardín*, 219–62; and Keen, *Essays*, 60.

An Accusatory "I"

Critics have long noted Las Casas's animosity toward the previous historians, and in particular, toward Oviedo and Gómara (his "bêtes noires" for Bataillon).[16] Attention to this problem, however, has largely centered on discrepancies with respect to facts, and on ideological and political differences.[17] One aspect that critics have not noted is that Las Casas, in establishing his markedly antagonistic tone, borrows from the methodological and historiographical insights of Oviedo even as he battles them.[18] In his critique of Oviedo and others, Las Casas deftly exploits the *cronista real's* own strategies, turning the latter's discussion of hearsay, "fábulas," and "lies," as well as of the telltale artifice of a supernatural perspective in historical narrative, against Oviedo himself. In this regard, Las Casas's critical, argumentative, and justificatory discourse suggests a great deal about his own textual persona and range of vision. In attempting to discredit his adversary, the cleric invokes the humanist *topoi* on problems of coherence in narrative (which had been questioned by Oviedo) to characterize the *cronista's* work alternately as contradictory, epistemologically problematic, and akin in places to the "Greek" tradition, which, for humanist preceptors such as Vives, was emblematic of unreliable "poetic" distortion of historical fact. In doing so, Las Casas expands on the notion of coherence as pertaining to issues of probable cause and effect, and like Vives (and Augustine), insists that an account must reflect the Christian patterns of creation, fall, and redemption

16. Bataillon, "La idea del descubrimiento de América," in Bataillon and O'Gorman, *Dos concepciones,* 46.

17. The mutual acrimony between Oviedo and Las Casas has been the source of much historical debate, which Gerbi has summarized in *Nature in the New World* (353–59). See also Sánchez Alonso *Historiografía,* 2:98–99; Bataillon, *Estudios,* 157–64; and Hanke, *All Mankind,* 34–56, among others. On Las Casas's criticisms of Gómara, see Iglesia, *Cronistas,* 130–39. A number of scholars have also observed that the factual divergences are fewer than the heated rhetoric might suggest. Henríquez Ureña writes in *Corrientes* (24) that there was little in Las Casas's history that could not be inferred from other works of the period, and Saint-Lu, in "Prólogo" (xxxxvii), remarks that, while in many ways there is agreement about essential facts between the cleric's history and the major earlier works, one can perceive "la fuerte huella lascasiana . . . en la manera de relatarlos." Echoing Fabié, he describes Las Casas's style as "efectista." See also Salas, *Tres cronistas,* 128–46.

18. Given the editorial history of these two works, it is, of course, difficult to determine to what extent Las Casas had knowledge of Oviedo's writings. Las Casas cites the 1535 edition of the *Historia general y natural* and suggests familiarity with later sections, as when he charges that Gómara has copied parts of his history of Mexico from Oviedo, even though the relevant part of the latter's history would not be published until the nineteenth century. Oviedo in *HGN* (1:19) urges Las Casas to publish his own History so that eyewitnesses may respond to it; see also Hanke, *All Mankind,* 44.

in order to be credible. Las Casas couples the critique of factual, formal, and epistemological aspects of Oviedo's text with scathing attacks on the author. Questions of the moral character of the writer of history take on in Las Casas's text an importance and specificity not found in the earlier histories. Oviedo, for the most part, had refrained from naming names in his attacks on rival historians; Las Casas instead argues forcefully that the *cronista* in particular is guilty of grave crimes.

It is pertinent to note that while Las Casas's reproaches of Gómara broadly resemble those that Oviedo had waged at the humanists writing from Europe, his censorship of Oviedo hints at more serious implications. Oviedo's history, he suggests, shows signs of dissimulation not just in the sense of feigning or imaginatively conjecturing and rendering a plausible account, but in the sense of discrepancy between inner beliefs or knowledge and outer manifestation: in other words, representation that bears false testimony. In arguing that conscious misrepresentation in history is essentially a form of prevarication, Las Casas would appear to draw on the philosophical and theoretical traditions in sixteenth-century Spain censuring dissimulation and the doctrine of mental reservation.[19] If Oviedo is in fact as experienced an eyewitness as he claims to be (which he is not, according to Las Casas), then he should know better than to recount the history of the Indies as he does. Therefore, the Dominican argues, either he is a sinner whom God has blinded to the truth, or he must be speaking against his own mind, feigning as truthful an account he knows to be false. In this way Las Casas manipulates and intensifies the suggestions already present in Oviedo's history that falsehood in history constitutes active deceit.

Las Casas's prologue to the *Historia de las Indias* is connected to the direct attacks he makes on Oviedo's history and illustrates one of the most extreme directions taken by the debate over narrative credibility in the sixteenth century. In particular, he alludes to Oviedo's claims in his *proemio* that the history of the Indies is a supreme topic, one that not even Greek historians would have needed to embellish upon. He highlights the presence of multiple and often contradictory accounts of the same event in the *Historia general y natural* as a sign of unreliability, addresses problems related to the use of secondhand reports, and points to signs of "fiction" or fabrication related to epistemological questions. In drawing on the notion of an opposition

---

19. In *Ways of Lying*, Zagorin discusses the topic as it relates to the treatment of religious heterodoxy (153–85); see *The Catholic Encyclopedia*, s.v. "lying," "dissimulation," and "mental reservation."

between "true" history (revelation, prophecy) and unreliable conjecture (soothsaying), Las Casas points to a number of places where, he charges, Oviedo takes on the unnatural stance of an *adivino* that the *cronista real* had criticized in prior accounts. The careful exploitation of both the preceptive commonplaces and the vulnerabilities of his rival's text is closely connected, as we shall see, to Las Casas's construction of an authoritative "I."

Ann Rigney has described the processes by which historians address the context of an existing historical tradition, which "provides them with a pre-configured narrative schema and, to a certain extent, a vocabulary through which they can represent the . . . [data] and mark off their particular *prise de position* with respect to a master event." Although her study focuses on the historiography of the French Revolution, a number of her observations on the importance of *topoi* and their transformation by writers of history as a way of distinguishing what is both new and "truthful" about their visions of events are relevant to the works under study here. The "subversion of . . . commonplaces," Rigney notes, "points to both the societal nature of [the] discourse and to its didactic function in converting its public." By "meeting the readers' expectations" on a given topic, the historian is able to reconfigure the meaning of events and thus create a "didactic shift."[20] In other words, commonplaces would appear to fulfill an important function in historical narrative because they enable authors to simultaneously meet—and break—expectations. By subverting the commonplaces of earlier accounts, historians evoke an earlier version and contrast it with a "corrected" view. In the *Historia de las Indias,* the subversion of the *topoi* of prior accounts (such as the notion of New World history as marvelous) would appear to be one way in which Las Casas endeavors to make what is new or strange or idiosyncratic about his vision less doubtful, and thus would appear to be closely connected to the issue of reliability or credibility. Furthermore, the subversion of the meanings of prior accounts through the transformation of both biblical imagery and commonplaces of the humanist philological debates is linked in the *Historia de las Indias* to the notion of conversion and becomes a dominant strategy in the cleric's own effort to establish a credible version of events.

In the prologue, Las Casas puts forth a cogent statement of his own vision of the meaning of the clash between the New World and the Old, and this vision is intimately connected to his main reproaches of the other historians

20. Rigney, *Rhetoric,* 47.

of the conquest. Among the numerous authorities that Las Casas invokes in the prologue, Augustine weighs heavily in both the historiographical and autobiographical modes of his work, as Brading and others have noted.[21] In particular, the notion of coherence (in the sense of a representation that is coherent with Christian orthodoxy) as a sign of "truth" is taken from Augustine. For the latter, the sacred historian was part researcher and part prophet, and thus had access to both the fullness of historical knowledge and the grace of revelation. At the same time, the inability to distinguish truth amid divergent historical accounts is the sign of an ungodly reader for Augustine.[22] Las Casas claims that erudition is a crucial complement to his eyewitness experience and cites Flavius Josephus, who together with Augustine and Eusebius, appears not just as a source for the cleric's ideas on history, but as a figure to be emulated as well.[23] In structuring the prologue on a series of oppositions that seek to establish his own authority as rectifier of false and dangerous versions, Las Casas positions himself as a latter-day Josephus, who corrects earlier writers in much the same way as the Hebrew historian had claimed to rectify the misconceptions of Jewish history by Greek historians. Furthermore, Las Casas seeks to characterize the previous versions as indulging in the kinds of errors that humanists had perceived in the "Greek" tradition. Echoing the sorts of arguments employed by Vives, he highlights the problem of poetic distortion of historical fact in the Greek tradition to the extent that, he pointedly suggests, common criminals were represented, and came to be revered, as gods. Las Casas fulminates against the Greek historians as "verbose, eloquent, weighed down by words, and very concerned with their own reputations." This kind of chronicler, he adds, was intent on writing "not what he saw or experienced, but what he

21. Brading, "Two Cities"; Iglesia, in *Cronistas* (138), finds in the *Historia de las Indias* "el desarrollo vigoroso de una idea apriorística." On Augustinian theology as "grosso modo," the most important source for Las Casas's concept of history, see Bataillon, "Review," 220, and Pérez de Tudela Bueso, "Significado histórico," cx; on Las Casas's imitation of the *Confessions,* see Silva Tena, "Las Casas, biógrafo"; Pagden, *European Encounters,* 71–73; and Arias, "Autoescritura" and *Retórica, historia y polémica,* 18–24. Cortijo Ocaña, in "Creación," argues that Las Casas fashions himself as humanist, theologian, jurist, and writer of marvels.

22. Augustine, *City of God,* book 18, 406–8. See also Chapter 1, "Historical Representation in the Spanish Humanist Context" on Vives's interpretation of Augustine's ideas on history.

23. He cites Josephus on the differing goals that motivate historians to write: (1) the ambition to achieve fame and glory by writing eloquently; (2) the desire to serve a prince by commenting on his works and achievements, often in an adulatory fashion; (3) the obligation to rectify existing (false) histories by providing an eyewitness account; and (4) the mission of writers who are aware of the true spiritual meaning of events, and their willingness to uncover and make manifest their import for the common good. He then goes on to distinguish his own goals (3 and 4) from those of the other chroniclers of the Indies (1 and 2). *HI,* 1:3.

held as opinion, incorporating fables and erroneous fictions, so that each account differed from one another, with the result that both writers and readers were confused and deceived" (*HI*, 1:4).[24] In addition to the humanist commonplaces, Las Casas here echoes Augustine's opposition between sacred (coherent) and secular (contradictory) history, with the added spin that authors who write contradictory versions—based not on experience, but opinion—engage not in merely entertaining endeavors, but in active deceit. We see here a move away from the notion of "lying" histories as "fiction" to one in which falsehood in history is akin to that in everyday discourse. Charges of adulation and deception mingle with other, more insidious crimes. Like Josephus, and like Christian historians such as Augustine and Eusebius, who wrote to "cover the blasphemous mouths" of the Romans (*HI*, 1:10), Fray Bartolomé argues for a silencing of the existing record based on a deeply spiritual justification that suggests the need for drastic measures. He counsels the king not only to avoid blasphemous or sacrilegious books, but also to ban them from the kingdom.[25]

Amid Las Casas's torrent of references, instances of authors who have justly rebuked their contemporaries prevail, thus pointing to the target of his own attack. He writes that the contemporary writers on America "han escrito cosas vanas y falsas destas Indias, no menos corruptas que fingidas" ("have written vain and false things about these Indies, no less corrupt than made up") (*HI*, 1:17). In strategically lumping together a variety of registers that associate the rival histories with chivalric romance, Greek histories, and heretical material, Las Casas suggests in no uncertain terms that these works are dangerous enough to merit active revision and censure by the state. Of those writing in Latin, he continues, the only one worthy of mention is Peter Martyr d'Anghera, and he is to be considered reliable only on the subject of Columbus. Of those writing in Spanish, none are to be trusted.[26] Although Las Casas does not mention Oviedo here by name, he develops his critique of "Greek"-like exaggeration in the sections in the body of his work that are specifically directed at refuting the *Historia general y natural*. And, within the prologue, Las Casas recalls Oviedo's somewhat boastful

24. Collard, trans., *History*, 3.

25. "No siendo con verdad escritas, podrán ser causa como los otros defectuosos y nocivos libros, pública y privadamente, de hartos males, por ende no con menor solicitud deben ser vistas, escudriñadas y limadas, antes que consentidas salirse a publicar." *HI*, 1:5.

26. "Veo algunos haber en cosas destas Indias escrito, ya que no las que vieron, sino las que no bien oyeron (aunque no se jactan ellos así dello), y que con harto perjuicio de la verdad escriben, ocupados en la sequedad estéril e infructuosa de la superficie, sin penetrar lo que a la razón del hombre . . . nutriría y edificaría." *HI*, 1:11.

claim that to chronicle the Indies perforce requires outdoing the Greeks.[27] Las Casas implies, in one of his characteristic inversions, that Oviedo indeed has outdone the Greeks in his exaggerations and in the flattery accorded his patron. Throughout the *Historia de las Indias,* Las Casas cites Oviedo's work but transforms it to a contrary interpretation. There are numerous places where he invokes Oviedo's language, whether directly or indirectly, to present it as evidence of unreliability. The "intertextual antagonism" here, to recall Rigney's term, is much more direct and precise than that employed by Oviedo.[28] Las Casas mimics the *cronista*'s language in the *proemio* to book 1 of the *Historia general y natural* in a series of exclamations that echo and ironize Oviedo's panegyric introduction to the history of the Indies:

> ¡Cuántos daños, cuántas calamidades, cuántas jacturas, cuántas despoblaciones de reinos, cuántos cuentos de ánimas cuanto a esta vida y a la otra hayan perecido y con cuánta injusticia en aquestas Indias, cuántos y cuán inexpiables pecados se han cometido, cuánta ceguedad y tupimiento en las conciencias, y cuánto y cuán lamentable perjuicio haya resultado y cada día resulte, de todo lo que ahora he dicho, a los reinos de Castilla! Soy certísimo que nunca se podrán numerar, nunca ponderar ni estimar, nunca lamentar, según debería, hasta en el final y tremebundo día del justísimo y riguroso y divino juicio.

> [What damage, calamities, disruptions, decimations of kingdoms, what millions of souls lost to this life and the other in these Indies, how many unforgivable sins committed, what blindness and torpor of mind, what harms and evils past and present have been caused to the kingdoms of Castile by all that I have mentioned! I am certain that they cannot ever be enumerated, weighed, measured,

---

27. Las Casas's ironic treatment of the inexpressibility topos was already evident in the "Argumento del presente Epítome" of the *Brevísima relación de la destrucción de las indias* (69), where he writes: "Todas las cosas que han acaecido en las Indias, desde su maravilloso descubrimiento y del principio que a ellas fueron españoles para estar tiempo alguno, y después en el proceso adelante hasta los días de agora, han sido tan admirables y tan no creíbles en todo género a quien no las vio, que parece haber añublado y puesto silencio, y bastantes a poner olvido a todas cuantas, por hazañosas que fuesen, en los siglos pasados se vieron y oyeron en el mundo."

28. Rigney, *Rhetoric,* 47–51. Merrim, in "The First 50 Years" (60), describes this phenomenon in a different way, suggesting that the early writings on the New World make up a "textual family" or series in which the works "echo and fall back on each other."

and lamented enough from now until the final and fearful Day of
Judgment.] (*HI*, 1:11)[29]

In conjuring up Oviedo's famous preliminary ode to the innumerable and
unnarratable wonders of the New World, Las Casas inverts the language to
paint a picture of unpardonable sins and immeasurable catastrophes. Where
Oviedo had offered a hymn to nature as proof of the splendid fertility of
God's creation (Paradise found), Las Casas counters with a panorama of
irrevocable loss (expulsion from Eden). Likewise, Las Casas snubs Oviedo's
claim to a method of careful research and examination of witnesses: the
cronista is no less blind, Las Casas suggests, than the writers who never set
foot in the Indies. Oviedo and others who claim to have carefully listened
to and examined their sources have turned a deaf ear to the real meaning
of events, he suggests, putting forth an arid and idiosyncratic, even poisonous, partial view. The diatribe is juxtaposed to a promise of a different sort
of marvel, an account that will manifest "por diverso camino que otros
tuvieron, la grandeza y numerosidad de las admirables y prodigiosas obras
que nunca en los siglos ya olvidados haberse obrado creemos" ("in a different way from other versions, the grandeur and number of prodigiously
admirable works, which we do not believe have occurred in any previous,
forgotten centuries") (*HI*, 1:17).

The accusations of heresy are further developed in the prologue with
the imagery of sterility with which Las Casas endeavors to categorize
the earlier accounts. Once again, the language recalls Oviedo's praise
of the New World's fertility, a dominant theme in the first part of the
Historia general y natural.[30] Las Casas inverts the signs to portray accounts
such as that of Oviedo as not just useless, but dangerously un-Christian:
"Y porque sin arar el campo de la materia peligrosa que a tratar se
ponían con reja de cristiana discreción y prudencia, sembraron la simi-
ente árida, selvática, e infrutuosa de su humano y temporal sentimiento,
por ende ha brotado, producido y mucho crecido cizaña mortífera"
("And because they did not work the field of controversy with the plow

---

29. Collard, trans., *History*, 4–5 (slightly modified).

30. In the dedication to part 1 of the *Historia general y natural* (1:3), Oviedo expresses his wish
that his readers might raise "infinitas gracias y loores al Hacedor de tantas maravillas . . . oyendo
las cosas que aquí he escripto" so that he himself might not be "counted as a useless tree." In the
proemio of the first book, too, Oviedo elaborates on the "unnarratable multitude" of trees and fruits,
adding in book 19 that even barren territories in the Indies reveal hidden riches. He goes on to give
numerous examples of the hidden virtues of natural phenomena: even poisons and noxious things
often contain excellent medicinal properties. Oviedo, *HGN*, 2:187–88, book 19, pro.

of Christian discretion and prudence, they planted the arid, wild seed of their human and temporal feelings from which have sprung up and grown deadly weeds") (*HI*, 1:11–12).[31] To focus—as had Oviedo—on the prodigious natural exuberance of the Indies, Las Casas implies, is to miss the point that the New World was meant to be something more like a spiritual "garden," a theme to which he returns toward the end of book 1.[32] Rather than glorifying God's creation and its promise of fulfillment, Las Casas suggests, Oviedo and other writers who are complicit in the imperial project have produced histories that are not just inaccurate, but deadly dangerous and in bad faith, sowing poisonous seeds that have taken root and overrun what should have been a living "garden"—with noxious consequences for both the Church and society at large. By relying on partial views and "temporal" impressions, chroniclers such as Oviedo, he further claims, have ignored the essential truth that conquered peoples are rational beings; their misleading works have exacerbated both the violent extermination of natives and the colossal failure of the evangelical ideals in the New World. The image of a garden run wild clearly falls within the allusions to heresy ("materia peligrosa," "errónea ciencia," "perversa conciencia") ("dangerous material," "erroneous science," "perverse conscience") and he qualifies the damage done to the Crown and the Catholic Church by this kind of work as "irreparable" (*HI*, 1:12).

The tactic of painting his opponents as heretics is one that Las Casas repeats almost obsessively throughout the work. In arguing that Oviedo and others have misunderstood the providential meaning of the discovery and conquest, Las Casas contends that they have mistaken as "barbarians" what are in fact a "chosen" people.[33] This mistake is magnified, he adds, by an ignorance of ancient histories, which teach that all peoples have barbarous origins.[34] The transformation of topical imagery from the Hebrew Scriptures (found in Oviedo's Job-inspired *proemio*, and also in Juan Ginés de Sepúlveda's treatment of the indigenous population as sinful and requiring

---

31. Collard, trans., *History*, 5 (modified).

32. For Las Casas's discussion, in the context of Columbus's theories, of the likelihood that earthly paradise was located in the Western hemisphere, see *HI*, book 1, chaps. 140–46.

33. For a summary of the debate over the concept of the barbarian, see Pagden, *Caída*, 169–99.

34. As Gerbi has shown in *Nature in the New World* (266), Oviedo was likely the first to insist on the parallels between Greco-Roman antiquity and the peoples of the New World, an argument that would become "irresistible" for the advocates of the Indian cause.

Old Testament–style punishment),[35] into imagery that resonates with New Testament codes (e.g., the indigenous population as innocent victims who turn the other cheek) can be said to be his dominant strategy.

The harsh tone here is likely informed by what J. H. Elliot has called the "feverish climate" of fear over heterodox practices in Spain in the 1550s,[36] and indeed the strategy may well have started as a defensive one. While there is a certain amount of continuity in tone with the *Brevísima relación*, where Las Casas had ironized the topic of the Indies as marvelous in the "Argumento," and alluded briefly to the subject of heresy in his account of the German conquerors in the territory of Venezuela,[37] these brief traces expand in the *Historia* into an insistent claim that the crimes of the conquistadors extend to those who would chronicle them. In writing the prologue, Las Casas was fresh from the controversy at Valladolid (1550–51) with Juan Ginés de Sepúlveda, who had presented his main arguments in his *Democrates secundus* (written about 1543).[38] The topic of heresy figured prominently in the debate at Valladolid, and in a letter written after the controversy, Sepúlveda expands at some length on the grounds for considering Las Casas's ideas heretical.[39]

Las Casas repeats and magnifies the themes presented in the prologue in the sections of the history that attack Oviedo directly. He expends considerable energy contesting Oviedo's theory that the Indies were not a newly

35. Author of works of history, political and legal theory, and theology, Sepúlveda also held posts at the imperial court, such as *cronista oficial* for Charles V and Philip II, for whom he also acted as preceptor. He translated and commented on works of Aristotle, and participated in great debates of the period, not just at Valladolid against Las Casas in 1550, but against Luther as well. For biographical and bibliographical information, see Losada's introductory study to his translation of *Democrates secundus* (*Democrates segundo*). The juridical and theological polemic between Sepúlveda and Las Casas has been the subject of much study. The basic critical study in this regard is Hanke, *All Mankind*. See also Losada, *Fray Bartolomé*, and Pagden, who in *Caída* (167) examines Sepúlveda's use of Old Testament imagery.

36. Elliot, *Imperial Spain*, 209–29.

37. Las Casas, *Brevísima*, 148–51.

38. In this dialogue, Sepúlveda dramatizes the Just War debate, arguing that the Spanish conquest of the indigenous peoples is compatible with Christian beliefs. The interlocutors of the dialogue are Leopoldo, a German who is "somewhat contaminated by Lutheran errors" ("algo contagiado por los errores luteranos"), and Democrates, who manages to persuade the former that the conquest is not only just, but a religious duty of Catholic kings.

39. See Sepúlveda, "Proposiciones temerarias, escandalosas y heréticas que notó el doctor Sepúlveda en el libro de la conquista de Indias, que Fray Bartolomé de las Casas, Obispo que fue de Chiapa, hizo imprimir 'sin licencia' en Sevilla, año de 1552," in Fabié, *Vida y escritos*, 2:543–66; and Losada, *Fray Bartolomé*, 255–60. On the general panorama concerning questions of race and religion in Spain, see Elliot, *Imperial Spain*, esp. 209–29; on censorship and religious questions, see Adorno, "Censorship."

discovered territory, but the "forgotten" Hesperides. For Rigney this kind of extensive countering of previous assertions deemed false is a common historiographical practice.[40] Oviedo's theory, which he extracted from a number of "authorities," including passages from Pliny's *Natural History,* medieval traditions, and the forgeries (neither Oviedo nor Las Casas recognized them as such) of Annius of Viterbo, granted a mythological genealogy to the Spanish monarchy, dating its origins to a period before the Trojan war.[41] Recent historians have endeavored to explain Oviedo's adoption of such an untenable hypothesis in a variety of ways. The most generous view, put forth by Gerbi, suggests that this was just one more way in which "Oviedo was struggling to forge a mental link between the new lands and the Classical World." This kind of search for legendary roots from the Trojan period was fashionable, Gerbi adds, among other royal families in Europe at the time.[42] Bataillon documents more pragmatic and political considerations, to the effect that the notion of an ancient Spanish claim to the Indies was intended to bolster the Crown's legal dispute over the entitlements of the Columbus family, and Bolaños suggests that this passage may simply reflect Oviedo's early and excessive imitation of Pliny, a tendency that becomes more tempered in his later work.[43] One aspect that has escaped critical notice is that Oviedo clearly frames the passage in such a way as to emphasize its status as a personal opinion. "E para mí no dudo" ("I myself do not doubt"), he writes toward the beginning of this section, that the Indies were known to the ancients, and that Columbus "found" them through textual scrutiny (I:17, book 1, chap. 3). He ends his discussion of the Hesperides in a perspectivistic and even noncommital manner that seems to undercut or even disclaim his hypothesis:

> E por tanto, *yo creo que, conforme a estas auctoridades, o, por ventura a otras que, con ellas, Colom podría saber,* se puso en cuidado de buscar

---

40. Rigney, *Rhetoric,* 55.

41. Specifically, Oviedo had suggested that the Indies were discovered by the twelfth king of Spain, Hespero, and since, he tells us, it was common for lands to be named after their kings, it might therefore be inferred that the Indies had in fact been in the possession of the Spanish crown for more than 3,000 years.

42. Gerbi, *Nature in the New World,* 273–74. O'Gorman, in *Invention* (16–22), discusses this passage in Oviedo and Las Casas. For medieval traditions concerning the Trojan genealogy, and their creative use by imperial mythmakers, see Marie Tanner, *The Last Descendant of Aeneas;* Pierre Vidal-Naquet, in "Atlantis and the Nations," points to the continuing appeal of the Atlantis myth, from Plato's time to the twentieth century.

43. See Bataillon, "Historiografía," and Bolaños, "Historian."

lo que halló, como animoso experimentador de tan ciertos peligros y longuísimo camino. Sea ésta u otra la verdad de su motivo: que por cualquier consideración que él se moviese, emprendió lo que otro ninguno hizo antes dél en estas mares, *si las auctoridades ya dichas no hobiesen lugar.*

[And so *I think that, based on these authorities, or perhaps on others that Columbus might have known,* he began to search for what he found, as a courageous experimenter of such certain dangers and long road. Whatever his true motive, he undertook what no one before him had done in these seas, *even if we pay no heed to the authorities already mentioned.*] (Oviedo, *HGN*, 1:20, book 2, chap. 4, emphasis mine)

Whatever Oviedo's motivations for penning the Hesperides theory, it was an easy target for Las Casas, who suggests that the *cronista's* clever disclaimers were a self-serving dissimulation of his own views, a carefully worded pandering to the Crown. The cleric puts forth a barrage of geographical, historical, and philological arguments over a number of chapters to conclude that Oviedo's theory "is full of vanity and in no way credible" (*HI*, 1:91). While in many ways his objections to Oviedo's history resemble those summarized by Ferdinand Columbus in his biography of his father, Las Casas adds a characteristic twist, painting Oviedo's theory as a textbook case of the poetical exaggeration of historical fact so alarming to Vives and other humanists. As the "first inventor of this subtlety" (*HI*, 1:76, chap. 15), Oviedo is guilty, Las Casas reiterates, of leading the royal family into grave error.[44]

In his energetic rebuttal of Oviedo, Las Casas's argument follows divergent and often inconsistent paths, contending on the one hand that the famous Hesperides could not have referred to the Indies (but more likely to the Azores), while on the other summarizing several traditional authorities on the subject to find that "all that is proclaimed on these Hesperides is fabulous and incredible" (*HI*, 1:88, chap. 16). Fray Bartolomé relentlessly points to chronological inconsistencies, improbabilities ("Hespero" accomplished so much so quickly that the name must refer to several people), and incongruities (in some cases he is cited as son, in others as brother, of Atlas).

44. Las Casas claims that the Hesperides theory is an example of Oviedo's attitude "de nocivo lisonjero a nuestros ínclitos reyes, los cuales, como de su propia naturaleza real tengan los oídos y ánimos simplicísimos, creyendo que se les dice verdad, formarán conceptos dentro de sus pechos de que ni utilidad espiritual ni temporal servicio, ni provecho se les apegue." *HI*, 1:75, chap. 15.

He includes a heading to chapter 16 that highlights the entertaining or "agreeable" aspects of the Hesperides myth, as expressed in various authors. In ridiculing Oviedo's use of sources, he charges, as had Ferdinand Columbus, that Oviedo knew no Latin;[45] he identifies a passage to suggest that the *cronista* had misunderstood such elementary grammatical points as the usage of the preposition *ultra,* not to mention basic vocabulary: "It's one thing for poets to speak about the Gorgona women, and another about the Gorgona islands" (*HI,* 1:86, chap. 16). With apparent glee, Las Casas summarizes the efforts by earlier scholars to extract some kernel of historical truth from all the disparate myths and legends related to Atlantis, as from tales of nymphs, dragons, and superheroes. His sarcastic and polemical tone here contrasts with his far milder criticisms of Columbus for drawing on similar traditions, while at the same time exhibiting a clear critical distinction in his analysis between the fabulous mythological tales from the ancient world and the sort of material he finds appropriate to "true" history. In Las Casas's criticisms of Oviedo we find a clear and sustained effort to delineate the boundaries that separate the material of imperial mythmaking from that of history.[46] Indeed, one senses that his bitter debates over the forms of "truth" and invention in history were highly productive, and in this case fostered quite keen sensibilities concerning questions related to discursive boundaries.

Repeatedly in his critique of Oviedo's theory of the Hesperides, the cleric alludes to the notion of the unreliable historian as conjurer, writing caustically: "¡Hermosa, por cierto, sentencia y digna de tal probanza y de atribuirle tanta autoridad, y cuanta cual se suele atribuir a los sueños, o a las cosas que aún no son *in rerum natura* [sino que se] adivinan" ("A beautiful opinion, of course, and worthy of as much authority as is granted to dreams or to things that are divined but not within the natural world") (*HI,* 1:76, chap. 15). He further charges that, due to contradictions and illogical elements, Oviedo's theory should be "juzgada por adivinanza temeraria" ("judged as reckless guesswork") (*HI,* 1:78), reiterating that:

---

45. "Muchas y en muchas cosas Oviedo alega libros y autoridades que él nunca vió ni entendió, como él no sepa ni entienda latín, y así parece que hizo en ésta." *HI,* 1:86, chap. 16.

46. See, for example, Las Casas's rendering of Columbus's account of Amazons: "pienso que el Almirante no los entendía o ellos referían fábulas" (*HI,* 1:313, chap. 67). On the supposed lack of critical consciousness over distinctions between history and fiction in the period, see Wardropper, *"Don Quixote"*; Pastor, *Armature,* esp. 66–79; and more recently, David Boruchoff, "Poetry of History."

culpable adivinar es y lisonjear a España y vender a los reyes della las
cosas que nunca fueron, por haber sido, afirmar y boquear que en
los siglos pasados estas Indias o islas hubiesen a España pertenecido;
y así parece no ser cosa que en juicio de hombre discreto pueda
o deba caer opinión tan sola y singular, que sobre tan flacos fun-
damentos estriba. Y, por tanto, sólo debe quedar por improbable,
ficticia y frívola.

[(Oviedo) is guilty of soothsaying and flattering Spain and selling
to her kings things that never happened, by affirming that in past
centuries these Indies or islands belonged to Spain, and so it does
not seem that such a singular and unfounded opinion could fit in
the mind of a discreet man. It thus should be qualified as improbable, fictitious, and frivolous.] (*HI,* 1:82, chap. 15)

In arguing that Oviedo has based his theory on conjecture, Las Casas echoes
the idea of the unreliable historian as soothsayer in a somewhat different
way than had the *cronista real*. Oviedo had seen signs of imposture or conjecturing in those who, while relying on reported testimony, try to create an
impression in their narratives of events directly witnessed. Las Casas would
seem to imply a meaning similar to that which we saw in Pedro de Rhúa's
criticism of Antonio de Guevara, to the effect that flagrantly feigning facts
and fabricating historical sources to support them smacks of the task of the
poet-conjurer, not of the serious work of the historian-sage. The *adivino,* in
this view, conjures up facts and sources where they do not exist, as opposed
to the Christian wise man who is able to accurately decipher the hints of an
unfolding destiny before they are clearly manifest.

But elsewhere Las Casas echoes insights similar to those expressed by
Oviedo concerning the range of what historians can logically be said to
know. Specifically, in criticizing Oviedo's suggestion that native inhabitants
had brought disaster (slavery and extermination) upon themselves as punishment for their sinful conduct, Fray Bartolomé writes:

Cosa es maravillosa de ver el tupimiento que tuvo en su entendimiento aqueste Oviedo, que así pintase a todas estas gentes con
tan perversas cualidades y con tanta seguridad, para mostrar que
decía verdad, como si fuera una alhaja de su casa a la cual hobiera
dado mil vueltas por de dentro y por de fuera, no las habiendo
tractado sino cinco años, y éstos a solos los de la provincia del

Darién, . . . y no en otra cosa sino salteándolos y robándolos, matándolos y captivándolos.

[Oviedo's thick-headedness is truly astonishing. He paints all these peoples as having perverse qualities and writes with great assurance, so as to show that he is telling the truth, as if they were a trinket of his own that he could examine a thousand times inside and out. In reality he dealt with Indians for only five years, only in the province of Darien, and only to attack, rob, murder, and enslave them.] (*HI*, 3:536, chap. 146)

Las Casas charges Oviedo with narrating what cannot logically be known, namely, private qualities and customs of the indigenous peoples. He suggests that this kind of knowledge would require supernatural abilities, a capacity to examine someone else's habits as thoroughly as if he or she were a precious trinket, one "owned" by the historian, to be scrutinized at will (Las Casas's antislavery stance is apparent here, too). The kind of information provided by the *cronista* could not have been known "sino por revelación divina o por conjeturas de mucha conversación y de muchos tiempos con todas las gentes deste orbe habida" ("except by divine revelation or through conjectures based on much conversation over a great deal of time with all of the peoples of these regions") (*HI*, 3:533, chap. 145). Such liberties in imagining others' most private habits can be construed as a rather clumsy effort to justify otherwise impossible-to-document claims, Las Casas suggests, or conversely a level of intimacy that would imply complicity with, or participation in, the customs that Oviedo criticizes.

In many places, Las Casas's own portrayal of native inhabitants and Castilian conquerors clearly evokes Oviedo's account, even as he refutes it, and would seem to support a number of the theoretical insights under examination here. First of all, we find again a prevalence of descriptions of collective groups as opposed to individuals, which Rigney, as we saw in Chapter 2, finds to be a characteristic feature of historical accounts. Further, we also encounter a tendency to manipulate and subvert the *topoi* present in previous versions, which this critic highlights as central to the "societal" function of historiographical discourses. The sort of "didactic shift" that Rigney refers to is linked in Las Casas's *Historia de las Indias* to the metaphor of conversion and emerges, as we have seen, through a process of citation, whether through language that evokes but rebuts prior versions, as in the prologue, or through the kind of argumentative refutation, as in the case of the Hesperides, or through direct quoting and juxtaposition of contrary views, which is how he represents a collective portrait of native peoples.

Even twentieth-century defenders of Las Casas's talents as a historian would agree that his portrayal in the *Historia de las Indias* of indigenous peoples and their Castilian oppressors is simplistic.[47] Fray Bartolomé's evident erudition and the critical powers he displays in his juridical and theological treatises, or for that matter, in his major ethnographic work, the *Apologética historia sumaria,* might lead one to hope for a more nuanced treatment. Pérez de Tudela Bueso blames the lack of subtlety in this regard in the *Historia de las Indias* to "the closed system of his ideas"; several critics have pointed to the utopian cast of his work; and Franklin Knight reminds us that a great deal of Las Casas's information about native populations and geography is assumed to be inaccurate.[48] The outlines of Las Casas's representation in the *Historia de las Indias* of the native peoples as authentic "lambs" of God, and of the Castilians as predatory wolves or tyrants, are well known.[49] In presenting his rigorously simplistic portrayal as one that is orthodox both in terms of the Christian imagery and of the narrative patterns on which it draws, one suspects that Las Casas might have been seeking in part to provide a convincing alternative to what he viewed as the dangerous and contradictory fragments collected by Oviedo.

It is interesting to view Las Casas's critique of Oviedo in light of the lengthy sections in the *Apologética historia sumaria* that deal with divination. The *Apologética* has long been recognized as an important historical source for the study of pre-Columbian societies and an anthropological work in its own right. Once again, we find here an "intertextual antagonism" at work: Las Casas's defense of the Amerindian is framed within an account that in many ways demonizes the ancient civilizations of Europe and of the Middle East in terms similar to those that Sepúlveda had used to describe the

47. See, for example, Saint-Lu's description in "Prólogo" (xxxi–xxxii) of the "tragic monotony" of Las Casas's "schematic" treatment of the subject. Pérez de Tudela Bueso, in "Significado histórico" (xlvi), points to the "perfil casi angelical" of Las Casas's representation of indigenous peoples, as well as his tendency to extend the characteristics of the Antillean peoples as representative of all indigenous groups in the New World.

48. Pérez de Tudela Bueso, "Significado histórico," cx; Knight, "On the Poetry of History," 285. On the utopian cast of Las Casas's work, see Arias, *Retórica, historia, polémica,* 59–84; Pastor, *Jardín,* 219–62; and Rabasa, "Historiografía colonial."

49. See, for example, Hanke, *Bartolomé de las Casas: Pensador,* 100–101, and Huerga, *Vida y obras,* in *Obras completas,* 1:327–31. Pérez de Tudela Bueso studies the more nuanced treatment in the *Apologética* in his preliminary study to his edition of that work. See also Avalle-Arce, "Hipérboles," and Arias, *Retórica, historia y polémica,* chap. 5.

native Americans. Indeed, Las Casas prefaces his rather brief descriptions of Amerindian religious beliefs and customs with well over two hundred pages on the "superstitious," "abominable," and "bestial" practices of ancient Mediterranean and European peoples. Of particular interest to him is the figure of the soothsayer or *adivino*, whom in many Old World pre-Christian societies was revered as a divinity and whose "arte de ago-rería y de adevinar" ("art of soothsaying and divination") corresponds, in his view, to "el salir de seso y furor" ("being out of one's mind, and in a fury") of a demonic power.[50]

In commenting on the figure of the soothsayer in ancient Greek reli-gion, Las Casas highlights the deity Apollo, whom he characterizes as "un astutísimo y malvado demonio" ("an exceedingly astute and evil demon"). Apollo, he writes,

> declaraba más las cosas y agritaba más voces diciendo las cosas por venir . . . que otro ningún demonio, y tenía tanta industria y cautela que lo que no podía decir, o temía que le podían tomar en men-tira, por tales rodeos y tanta escuridad de palabras lo hablaba, que cuando saliese lo contrario de lo que preguntaban o pretendían, no le pudiesen redargüir de mentiroso, porque como el demonio sea disertísimo lógico . . . paralogizando engañaba a los hombres.

> [would declare more things and shout in more voices when tell-ing of things to come . . . than any other demon, and he was so cautious and full of industry that what he could not say, or when he feared he would be caught in a lie, he would speak in such a round-about way, and with so much obscurity in words, that when the opposite of what he had predicted occurred, they could not accuse him of lying. Since the devil is a dexterous logician, he would trick men with his paralogizing or fallacious arguments.][51]

Las Casas imagines the Greek god as a consummate liar and dissimula-tor, exceeding all other demons in evil and crediting him as the inventor of human sacrifice. Subsequent cults following the Apollonian tradition throughout Europe developed an astonishing range of divinatory prac-tices, according to Las Casas, who describes in detail such arcane forms

---

50. Las Casas, *Apologética*, 1:414 (my translation).
51. Ibid., 1:420 (my translation).

of divination as "geomancia," "aerimancia," "piromancia," "ornimancia," "pedoxomancia," "aurispicina," "nigromancia," "chiromancia," and "hidromancia"—to the point that the *Apologética* in recent scholarship has been considered an authoritative source on witchcraft in early modern Spain.[52] The cumulative effect of Las Casas's catalog of reproved practices and the inquisitorial tone that he adopts in this part of the *Apologética* make the Amerindian practices described in the following section seem benign by contrast.

Given that not all of the "demonic" practices Las Casas describes have been completely eradicated under Christianity, the *clérigo* extols the role of the inquisitor as a guardian of the faith. Immune to the deceptions of even the most Apollonian of demons, these "righteous judges" as he calls them, "tienen por fin de sus oficios la defensión y conservación de la fe católica, y los ejercitan en buscar, perseguir, castigar y extirpar los que en aquellas abusiones y supersticiones hallan inficionados" ("have as the aim of their duties the defense and conservation of the Catholic faith, and they exercise them in searching, persecuting, punishing, and exterminating those whom they find to be infected by those abuses and superstitions").[53] Inquisitors are God's "good angels" who defend the faith and ward off the power of evil. Las Casas even includes an account reported to him of an exorcism that took place during the Cumaná settlement.[54] In a concluding section in which he compares the pre-Christian religions of the Old World to those of the New, he argues that the presence of religious belief and practice is a clear proof of rationality among the Amerindians but, more important, that

> tuvieron muchas menos fealdades que otras afamadas y políticas naciones de las antiguas, y con menos heces de errores en su idolatría . . . en la elección de los dioses tuvieron más razón y discreción y honestidad que las más de todas cuantas naciones idólatras antiguamente hobo, bárbaros, griegos y romanos, y por consiguiente mostraron ser más que todos racionales.

52. Caro Baroja, *Inquisición*.

53. Las Casas, *Apologética*, 1:500 (my translation).

54. He recounts the story reported to him as follows: upon hearing of a demonic possession of a native, the Dominican Fray Pedro de Córdoba in Cumaná took the role of examiner and exorcist and was able to extract a confession from the demon (in indigenous language) that he was spiriting the souls of his followers to Hell. Las Casas, *HI*, 1: 520–21. Despite Las Casas's implication in this passage that this sort of inquisitorial technique is a viable one when dealing with Amerindian populations, in *Del unico vocationis modo* he argues that only nonviolent persuasion is a legitimate way of evangelizing natives.

[they had fewer ugly customs than the other famous and political nations of the ancients, and fewer base errors in their idolatry. . . . In choosing their gods they show more reason, discretion, and honesty than most of all the other idolatrous nations of antiquity, including barbarians, Greeks, and Romans, and therefore they have shown themselves to be more rational than the others.][55]

In the *Historia de las Indias,* Las Casas endeavors to undertake the role of inquisitorial examiner or "good angel," in this case to ferret out not the "ugly customs" and errors of native American peoples, but what he sees as the far more dangerous and "dexterous" works of the rival New World historians. The language of the reproof of superstitions provides him with both a critical discourse for addressing problems of truth and falsehood in history and also a tone of moral outrage in his attack on empire and its historians.

Las Casas on Oviedo

In book 3 of *Historia de las Indias* Las Casas singles out Oviedo's account as a particularly dangerous and blasphemous representation, and his portrayal of the *cronista* as "a capital enemy of the Indians" (*HI,* 3:523, chap. 142) makes the figure of Oviedo (as defamer of the indigenous peoples) a memorable aspect of the work. While a number of twentieth-century scholars who have studied Oviedo's works in depth have remarked on the latter's talents as ethnographer,[56] few would deny that his effort to depict the native peoples emerges from observations that range from outright bigotry to implicit admiration. He appears to have evolved in his appreciation of Amerindians, perhaps in part as a result of Las Casas's bitter denunciations of his work, but the sections of his history that reveal a more complex appreciation of natives tend to be in parts of his history that were not published until the nineteenth century. Nonetheless, there are passages in Oviedo's *Sumario* and part 1 of the *Historia general y natural* that do merit Las Casas's outrage. Fray Bartolomé quotes extensively (and renders notorious) some of Oviedo's most

---

55. Las Casas, *Apologética,* 1:663 (my translation).

56. See Salas, *Tres cronistas;* Ballesteros Gaibrois, "Fernández de Oviedo, etnólogo"; and Gerbi, who writes in *Nature and the New World* (348–49) that Oviedo's characterization of the indigenous peoples is the result of a "careful study" in which "the main features are perceived and rendered sympathetically," noting that his evaluation of the conquerors is, for the most part, harshly critical. Louise Bénat-Tachot in "Relato corto" and "Entrevue" (210) has illuminated a "fragmented and troubled" streak in Oviedo's representations of the indigenous peoples.

denigrating comments, such as the following one concerning the potential of the indigenous population for Christian conversion, taken from the *proemio* to book 5 of the *Historia general y natural:*

> Estos indios es gente muy desviada de querer entender la fe católica y es machacar hierro frío pensar que han de ser cristianos, y así se les ha parecido en las capas, o, mejor diciendo, en las cabezas, porque capas no las tenían, ni tampoco tenían las cabezas como otras gentes, sino de tan recios y gruesos cascos, que el principal aviso que los cristianos tienen, cuando con ellos pelean, es no darles cuchilladas en la cabeza, porque se rompen las espadas; y así como tienen el casco grueso, así tienen el entendimiento bestial y mal inclinado.

> [These Indians stubbornly refuse to understand the Catholic faith, and to think they will ever be Christianized is to beat a dead horse. So, they only wear Christianity on their sleeves, or rather, on their heads, because they have no clothes. They have no heads either for that matter, not like other people. They are so thick skulled that Christians hold as a basic principle never to hit them on the head in battle to avoid breaking their swords. As their skulls are thick, so is their intelligence bestial and ill disposed.] (Oviedo, *HGN,* 1:111, book 5, pro., as quoted by Las Casas, *HI,* 3:528, chap. 143)[57]

Las Casas does not fail to register the range of perspectives that Oviedo provides on the indigenous peoples and Castilians in *Sumario* and part 1 of the *Historia general.* Indeed, he highlights discrepancies and, like a skilled trial lawyer, points to them as evidence of falsehood. It is here that we can see Las Casas's critique not just of Oviedo's representation of the groups in conflict in the New World, but of the *cronista*'s entire perspectivist project.

In book 3, chapters 139 to 146, for example, Las Casas expends more ink criticizing Oviedo than putting forth a "corrected" descriptive image. Throughout, he points to contradictions as signs of "lies" or "fictions" that reveal, alternately, authorial stupidity or harmful intentions on the part of his rival. His criticisms range from those echoing the *cronista's* own criticism of earlier writers (a reliance on untrustworthy sources, such as "sailors or destroyers") (*HI,* 3:525, chap. 139) to others that imply more criminal errors. At times, he suggests, Oviedo's misrepresentations are not intentional,

---

57. Collard, trans., *History,* 274.

but rather a sign of blindness to evident facts: God permitted him "a que diese crédito a los que le referían mentiras y él también de suyo las dijese sin creer que las decía" ("to give credit to those who told him lies and to lie himself without believing that he himself was doing so") (*HI*, 3:526). But frequently, he insinuates that Oviedo has "lied" in a conscious fashion. In quoting some of Oviedo's criticisms of the Castilian conquerors, Las Casas argues that they make no sense in terms of the broader implications of the work, and thus present signs that he is speaking against his conscience: "Veis aquí que confiesa Oviedo, aunque le pese, convencido de las obras abominables manifestísimas de los españoles, los beneficios que los indios recibieron dellos, y argúyelos de serles ingratos" ("You can see here that Oviedo confesses, even though it grieves him, convinced as he is of the manifestly abominable deeds of the Spaniards, that the Indians received benefits from them, and he argues that they are ungrateful") (*HI*, 3:530). The contradictions in the *cronista*'s account, he suggests, are not just a sign of sloppy research or invention, but evidence of fawning hypocrisy, where the "sinful" *cronista* unwittingly manifests his guilt in perpetrating falsehoods. He recalls that Oviedo has given sworn testimony concerning indigenous peoples at the Council of the Indies, thus suggesting that he lied under oath.[58] Las Casas's schematic portrayal of groups in conflict would seem to stem in part from his strategy of rebuttal (correcting contradictions), as well as from an effort to adhere to the humanist historiographical ideal of coherence with Christian narrative patterns. One can also observe here his inquisitorial tone, as well as his legalistic tendency to present his evidence as if at criminal court, when he argues, for example, that Oviedo's historiographic errors constitute punishable crimes (defamation) with extensive liabilities (requiring financial restitution) (*HI*, 3:528, chap. 143).

Prophecy and the Portrayal of Character

As suggested earlier, Las Casas claims for himself a prophetic vision of New World history and characterizes the ability to correctly decipher providential signs as proof of good intentions and awareness of the divine will.[59] One way that Las Casas hints at his own visionary abilities is to revisit the notion of prophecy (as opposed to illicit soothsaying) as a model for historical

58. For more examples, see *HI*, 3:533–39.
59. As Pérez de Tudela Bueso notes in "Significado histórico" (cx), Las Casas was not alone in viewing the discovery as providential, but "lo que sí le distingue es la suprema seguridad con que se arroga el papel de hermeneuta sagrado del acontecer pretérito y pitia del porvenir."

inquiry. The topic emerges frequently in Las Casas's criticisms of Oviedo in book 1, and reveals a careful manipulation of the commonplaces on the subject. Las Casas's treatment recalls, as already suggested, the Augustinian view of the ongoing fulfillment of past prophecy in the present and the future as a sign of historical "truth." Divine Providence, Fray Bartolomé states flatly, does not permit things to occur without first announcing them (*HI, 1:58*, chap. 10), and thus a major role of the reliable historian is to retrospectively identify premonitions that have come to pass. Las Casas suggests that God reveals signs of important events through both Christian and infidel sources, and thus the notion of prophecy plays a privileged and pivotal role both in the course of human events and in the writing of history. Although pagan augury, in his view, often confirms Christian prophecy, the narrative stance of the *adivino* in historical writing is a telltale sign of unreliability or guesswork.

Las Casas's portrayal of Columbus has been the subject of much study,[60] and here I will just examine briefly some of the ways in which his treatment of this figure is framed by the providential cast of his work. Santa Arias has discussed the strategies used by Las Casas to present himself and the Admiral as heroic subjects with similar destinies.[61] One way in which Las Casas portrays Providence at work is at that moment when individuals freely make life-changing choices. Columbus's decision to embark on a western course is one such moment, as is Las Casas's own conversion. Las Casas presents Columbus in a somewhat equivocal fashion, as both a scholarly solver of riddles and a sort of bumbler who had to be deluged with divine hints and practically pushed on his way.[62] Oviedo's portrait of Columbus had already put forth a sort of puzzle as to whether the Admiral was inspired by careful study and initiative or by lucky coincidence. Although Oviedo privileges the image of an erudite Columbus who found the new lands "written" in ancient texts (*HGN, 1:17*, book 2, chap. 3), his inclusion of the rumors concerning the anonymous pilot as first discoverer evokes an alternative perspective or possibility to the image that he deems most likely. Las Casas, as we shall see, disparages Oviedo's source on Columbus's early explorations

---

60. See Zamora, *Reading Columbus;* Rabasa, "Historiografía colonial"; Arias, *Retórica, historia y polémica,* 33–57.

61. Arias, *Retórica, historia, polémica,* 57–58, 118.

62. See O'Gorman, *Invention,* 13–22, on Las Casas's and Oviedo's treatment of the subject; Pagden, *European Encounters,* 96–98, for a description of the changing portrayals of Columbus in the early sixteenth century; Zamora, *Reading Columbus,* 63–94, on Las Casas's treatment of the admiral.

(the *cronista*'s information came from a sailor, Hernán Pérez, "whom he cites at times like his evangelist") (*HI,* 3:526, chap. 143). But the cleric does not discard the elements derived from such an overrated source (historiographical practice dictates that he deal with them). Rather, Las Casas incorporates the disparate versions into his own account, inscribing them into a providential framework that, while preserving the discrepancies, makes them irrelevant.

In stressing what he views as the providential plan embodied in Columbus, Las Casas also expands on the portrait included in Ferdinand Columbus's biography of his father.[63] The Admiral himself had insisted on the idea that his own proper name was a cipher for his destiny, and Las Casas provides a brief etymological study as a gloss on this interpretation of the name Christopher ("bringer or carrier of Christ") (*HI,* 1:26, chap. 2).[64] Las Casas emphasizes not so much Columbus's navigational skills as those of a learned reader able to decipher both ancient and modern intimations of the existence of the "new" world. He compares the Hebrew and pagan prophecies of the birth of Christ to the hints about unknown territories that, he supposes, Columbus must have read in ancient canonic texts.[65] Likewise, he suggests, the Admiral would have found clues in contemporary cartographers and modern authorities such as Pierre d'Ailly, the Christian philosopher and astrologer, whose *Imago mundi* Columbus had carefully perused and annotated.[66] In addition to the copious learned ancient and modern premonitions of the New World, God also sent Columbus signs in the form of observations by "idiots," "como echándoselas delante para que en ellas tropezase" ("as if throwing them in his way so that he might trip over them") (*HI,* 1:68, chap. 13). He identifies the sources of this kind of unstudied proof by name: sailors such as Martín Vicente, who found pieces of carved wood in an eastward-flowing current, and Pero Correa, who

63. Las Casas acknowledges his debts to F. Columbus; Fabié in *Vida y escritos* (363–73) has made clear the extent of the borrowing in chapters 2, 3, and 5 of the *Historia de las Indias.* See also Arias, *Retórica, historia y polémica,* 38.

64. On Columbus's use of this signature after 1502, see Varela, "Introducción," lxxi–lxxii.

65. He cites Augustine and Eusebius to the effect that divine providence sends prophecies through sacred as well as diabolical sources: "permitiendo que los teólogos y hechiceros y adivinos, y los mismos demonios, respondiendo en sus oráculos a los idólatras, den de las causas por venir adversas o prósperas, ciertos responsos." *HI,* 1:58, chap. 10. Las Casas further suggests, in *HI* (1:59–60, chap.10), that the discovery of the Indies was foretold by Seneca (*Medea*), Virgil (*Eclogue* 4), Ovid, and St. Ambrose.

66. Pierre D'Ailly (Pedro de Aliaco) was, according to Las Casas, "en filosofía, astrología y cosmografía doctísimo . . . y este doctor creo cierto que a Cristóbal Colón más entre los pasados movió a su negocio." *HI,* 1:61.

reported seeing thick canes in the ocean. Columbus, Las Casas writes, was able to decode the meaning of this fragmentary evidence in an erudite fashion, conjecturing, based on a passage from Ptolemy, for instance, that the canes were a species from the East Indies, and that the carvings pointed to the presence of human societies (*HI,* 1:67, chap. 13). In short, Las Casas suggests, the signs as to Columbus's sure success in his endeavor were so many and so varied that "parece que Dios lo movía con empellones" ("it appears that God pushed and shoved him") (*HI,* 1:71, chap. 13). The providential overtones here coexist with the suggestion that Columbus was slow to act, a somewhat reluctant (and later, even unworthy) candidate to fulfill such an important mission.[67]

In addressing the rumors of an earlier discovery by an anonymous pilot as pivotal to Columbus's decision to embark, Las Casas, like Oviedo, emphasizes the oral—and thus unverifiable—nature of the information ("díjose," "se decía," "dizque") (*HI,* 1:72, chap. 14), but extracts a contrary conclusion as to its reliability. Las Casas tells us that he himself had believed such common rumors when he first traveled to the Indies, as did most of the early colonists, and provides details as to why such speculation falls within the realm of the probable.[68] He further registers a variety of possible scenarios to explain why the nameless and moribund pilot might have revealed such a secret to Columbus: either the two were already acquainted, or Columbus showed himself to be "curious and solicitous," or the pilot was perhaps returning a kindness to a host. In any case, writes Fray Bartolomé, the truth or falsehood of these rumors is of little consequence, given the multitude and variety of the divine instructions that were showered on Columbus:

> Bien podemos pasar por esto y creerlo o dejarlo de creer, puesto que pudo ser que nuestro Señor lo uno y lo otro le trajese a las manos, como para efectuar obra tan soberana . . . por medio dél. . . . Esto, al menos, me parece que sin alguna duda podemos creer: que, o por esta ocasión, o por las otras, o por parte dellas, o por todas juntas, cuando él se determinó, tan cierto iba de descubrir lo

---

67. See Zamora, *Reading Columbus,* 93, on Las Casas's critical attitude toward Columbus, whose story appears in the *HI* less as a "biography of an individual" than "as the reconstitution of an exemplary life to serve as an admonishment for others."

68. He cites the following arguments to support this "vulgar opinion": the circumstance that it was accepted as fact among early colonists, the presence of oral traditions among indigenous peoples about the appearance of white, bearded men before the Spaniards, and the likelihood that a storm or strong currents might have obscured the pilot's perception of the distance traveled. *HI,* 1:72, chap. 14.

que descubrió y hallar lo que halló, como si dentro de una cámara, con su propia llave lo tuviera.

[Well may we pass over this and either believe it or not, as it could have been that our Lord brought these signs to his hands so as to achieve through him such a sovereign deed. . . . This, at least, I think we can believe without doubt: that for this reason, or for the others, or for some of them, or for all of them together, when he took his decision, he was so sure of discovering what he discovered and to find what he found as if he had locked it in a chamber with his own key.] (*HI*, 1:74, chap. 14)

One senses here a restriction on the part of the author-narrator as to Columbus's ultimate inspiration or motivation, which recalls Oviedo's own reticence to speculate on the inner workings of the minds of others. However, Las Casas's hesitance to guess at the thoughts of the Admiral would appear to be based on the evidence of a divine plan, perceived in retrospect, which makes the inward beliefs of others somehow irrelevant. Regardless of what Columbus might have thought or known, Las Casas suggests, he was chosen by God to fulfill his mission and, thus, possessed as much certainty as to his future findings as if he held the key to a lock. This sort of restriction concerning a historical figure's inner perceptions, which Dorrit Cohn has highlighted as a borderline separating historical from fictional discourse, prevails despite the markedly providential cast that Las Casas gives to the Columbus material, and points to his tone of careful consideration here.

One finds a similar optic in the portrayal of Montezuma. The following narrative sketch of the Aztec ruler at a critical juncture, for example, exhibits a number of parallels with that of Columbus (although not nearly so much source material to work on). In relating Montezuma's fateful decision to greet Cortés's invading army with gifts, Las Casas takes greater liberties in guessing at his subject's inner motivations. He writes:

Diose prisa Montezuma en enviar respuesta y aquellos dones a los españoles, mandando a su gobernador que les dijese que se fuesen, creyendo que eran niños que fácilmente se contentaban, porque se tornasen a su tierra y saliesen de la suya; y teníalo mal pensado, porque cuánto más oro les enviara, como después les envió, siempre diciéndoles que se fuesen, fuera como fue mayor cebo para que fueran, como fueron, a sacárselo de las entrañas. Desta prisa de echarlos era la causa porque tenía por cierto, según sus profetas o agoreros le habían certificado, que su estado y riqueza y prosperidad había de perecer dentro de los pocos años por cierta gente que había de venir en sus días, que de su felicidad lo derrocase; y por esto vivía siempre con temor y en tristeza y sobresaltado, y asi lo significaba su nombre, porque Montezuma quiere decir en aquella lengua hombre triste y enojado. También significa hombre grave y de grande autoridad, y que es temido, todo lo cual en él se hallaba.

[Montezuma hurried to send an answer and those presents to the Spaniards, ordering his governor to tell them that they should go away, believing that they were children who were easily mollified, so that they would go back to their lands and leave his; and he made a mistake, because the more gold he sent them each time he told them to leave, it was as if he baited them more to go, as they did, to tear more out from under him. This urgency for throwing them out was caused by his belief, certified to him by his prophets and soothsayers, that his reign and wealth and prosperity would be finished in a few years due to some people who would come in his time, who would topple him from his happiness. That is why he was always fearful and sad and nervous, and that is what his name means because "Montezuma" in that language means an angry and sad man. It also means a grave man of great authority, who is feared, all of which was found in him.] (*HI,* 3:443, chap. 121)

What might appear to be a series of strategic miscalculations are in fact just an anxious awaiting of a set destiny, one that Las Casas finds confirmed by the outcome of conduct and events, as well as by the presence of parallel auguries and, once again, a proper name that encapsulates and announces a historic fate.

The Cleric's Apology: "Mis ojos corporales mortales"

Las Casas's acute critical sense about the discursive norms of historical writing, so evident in his forceful attacks on rival texts, coexists with a sense of uncertainty in some of the narrative and descriptive passages that rely on his own eyewitness information and present himself as historical actor. Indeed, in the sections of his work in which he describes his own recollections of encounters between Castilians and indigenous peoples, one finds in places doubts regarding his abilities and perceptive skills as eyewitness. Las Casas's sharply polemical tone vis à vis the texts and actions of others contrasts with the hesitancy concerning his memories of some of the events in which he himself participated or witnessed in the past. For example, he describes a memory of the extreme cruelty inflicted by the Castilian conquerors on innocent natives in characteristically graphic terms:

> Hacían una horca luenga y baja, que las puntas de los pies llegasen al suelo, porque no se ahogasen, y ahorcaban trece juntos, en honor y reverencia de Cristo, Nuestro Redentor, y de sus doce Apóstoles; y así, ahorcados y vivos, probaban en ellos sus brazos y sus espadas.

> [They built a long gibbet, low enough for the toes to touch the ground and prevent strangling, and hanged thirteen of them at a time in honor of Christ our Savior and the twelve Apostles. When the Indians were thus still alive and hanging, the Spaniards tested their strength and their blades against them.] (*HI*, 2:71, chap. 17)[69]

This passage displays a patent mediation of Christian concepts and imagery that invoke an image of perverted sacrifice, and yet, at the same time, the narrator suggests an element of doubt as to the exactitude of his own memory: "Todas estas obras y otras, extrañas de toda naturaleza humana, vieron mis ojos, y ahora temo decirlas, no creyéndome a mí mismo, si quizá no las haya soñado. Pero en verdad, como otras tales y peores y muy más crueles y sin número se hayan perpetuado en infinitas partes destas Indias, no creo que de aquéstas me he olvidado") ("My eyes have seen these and other acts so foreign to human nature, and now I fear to say them, not believing myself, and I wonder whether I might have dreamed them. But truly, since an innumerable number of even more cruel crimes have happened in infinite parts of the Indies, I do not think I have forgotten these") (*HI*, 2:71, chap. 17). On the one hand, Las Casas's suggestion that this memory was a dream or vision points to its value as a symbolic "truth." But on the other, the prophetic vision here coexists with a hint of incredulity concerning his own recollection—in itself an ironic treatment of the history of the conquest of the Indies as a "marvelous" and

---

69. Collard, trans., *History*, 121.

inexpressible topic.[70] At the end of this same chapter, he reiterates the sense of fallibility as regards his own perspective: "Todo esto yo lo vi con mis ojos corporales mortales" ("All this I saw with my bodily mortal eyes") (*HI,* 2:72). The author's restricted vision here highlights the sense that the historian is necessarily limited to a "mortal" or partial point of view.

Pagden, in addressing the autobiographical aspect of the *Historia de las Indias,* has noted that, like the bishop of Hippo, Las Casas casts the narrative of his own conversion as an act of reading.[71] Fray Bartolomé relates the account of this event in the third person, beginning in chapter 79 of book 3 with a description of "the cleric Bartolomé de Las Casas," who finds time—amid managing the mining and agricultural tasks of natives on his *repartimiento*—to prepare an Easter sermon. In reviewing his materials, he notes, his former self "comenzó a considerar consigo mismo sobre algunas autoridades de la Sagrada Escritura, y, si no me he olvidado" ("started to consider in his mind some of the authorities of the Scriptures, and if I have not forgotten"). He goes on to quote from the passage of Ecclesiastes that inspired him and then continues: "He started, I say, to consider the misery and servitude that these people had suffered" (*HI,* 3:282–83, chap. 79). The hesitation in grammatical person with which he describes this event is telling. The third person, characteristic, as Pagden notes, of his "pre-conversion" state,[72] alternates with the "I" of the backward-looking historian who adopts a posture of modest self-scrutiny toward his own record. The hint of forgetfulness on the part of the I-historian concerning crucial events in his past has parallels in other scenes, such as the following, in which we find him describing a beating he witnessed in Puerto Rico: "Oyó los azotes el clérigo, porque pasaba por allí; fue allá luego, y con vehemente compasión y autoridad, increpa al cruel visitador la injusticia que hacía, el cual todo confuso ninguna cosa le osó decir; pero quitado el clérigo de allí, creo, si no me he olvidado, que tornó a azotar al indio" ("The cleric heard the blows because he was passing by, then he went there and with vehement compassion and authority he rebukes the cruel inspector for the injustice he was committing. In his confusion, the latter dared say nothing, but once the cleric had left, I think, if I have not forgotten, he went back to beating the Indian") (*HI,* 3:332, chap. 91). Of course, the different pronouns refer rather transparently to the same authorial voice, but the alternation in grammatical person when referring

70. See Greenblatt, *Marvelous Possessions,* 52–85, on the topic of the marvelous as it relates to the early accounts of the New World.

71. Pagden, *European Encounters,* 71–73.

72. Ibid., 72.

to the author's self suggests a strange multiplicity on the part of his narrative persona, one who endeavors to preserve within the text both an image of his past self as "another" and that of a writer who constantly interjects his "present," authoritative voice onto the narrative of his own past deeds.

Silva Tena, who examines Las Casas's use of pronouns throughout the *Historia,* notes a clear and consistent pattern of separating his roles as author and as participant. He uses the "I" to testify to what he has heard or seen about the actions of historical figures, and to state his own opinions and critiques of others, as well as to give a few personal details about himself. Las Casas uses "we" to include himself in the collective Spanish consciousness, usually to express a sense of personal atonement for his own participation in the broader sins of the conquest. The "he" refers to "the cleric Las Casas," seen as a historical actor or participant.[73] The last case, while ostensibly a transparent instance of an autobiography in the third person, is complicated by the fact that the author frequently appears as an eyewitness (*yo*) within the same scenes where we find him as a third-person character: "Todo esto pasó allí, estando yo presente" ("All this happened in this way, when I was there") (*HI,* 3:548, chap. 149). Las Casas's third-person conversion narrative (the self as another) coexists with his "I," which appears alternately as a simple bystander able to vouch for the deeds of the cleric ("yo lo vi") and as a backward-looking and authoritative priestly chronicler who, while expressing doubts about his own memory, claims to expose the innermost intentions of others based on his erudition and perceptive abilities. This effort to fashion a biography of himself from a variety of perspectives appears aimed at creating a more credible or "objective" view of his controversial record.[74] When faced with the dilemma of choosing the appropriate perspective from which to narrate (eyewitness versus distant sage)—a dilemma that was addressed, but not resolved, as we saw, in the rhetorical treatises—Las Casas chooses not to limit his options.

The use of multiple pronouns can be observed in book 3, chapter 129. Here, Las Casas begins by recalling (in the first-person singular) how he witnessed the first *trapiche,* or sugar mill, to appear in Santo Domingo and the significant technological advance that it represented in terms of both the quantity and quality of output: "I saw it" ("yo lo vi"). However, the mills took a heavy toll on the laborers assigned to them, and Las Casas, utilizing the third-person singular, narrates his own efforts to obtain permission to

73. Silva Tena, "Las Casas, biógrafo," 526–27.

74. Recently Zamora, in "Transatlantic Humanism," has aptly described this facet of the text as the author's "dialogue" with himself.

trade for African slaves to alleviate the lot of the natives, as if to suggest a more distanced perception of his role. He includes his subsequent recognition, also in the third-person singular, of his grave error in this regard, as well as his own doubts as to whether he would be forgiven:

> Después se halló arrepiso, juzgándose culpado por inadvertente, porque como después vio y averiguó . . . ser tan injusto el cautiverio de los negros como el de los indios, no fue discreto remedio el que aconsejó que se trajesen negros para que se libertasen los indios, aunque él suponía que eran justamente cautivos, aunque no estuvo cierto que la ignorancia que en esto tuvo y buena voluntad lo excusase delante el juicio divino.

> [The clergyman soon repented and judged himself guilty of ignorance, because as he later saw and confirmed . . . black slavery was as unjust as Indian slavery. The unwise practice, which he earlier had recommended, of bringing over blacks so that the Indians could be freed—even though he thought (the blacks) had been justly captured—was no remedy. He was not sure that his ignorance and good faith on this point would excuse him in the eyes of God.]

The cleric's retrospective acceptance of responsibility for his own mistakes is followed by a description of the plagues inflicted upon the Castilians in punishment for their cruelty. Las Casas ends on an expiatory note with another shift in pronoun: "Esta isla la hallamos llenísima de gentes que matamos y extirpamos de la haz de la tierra y henchímosla de perros y bestias" ("We found the island full of people whom we killed and erased from the face of the earth, filling it with dogs and beasts") (*HI*, 3:473–75, chap. 129). "I," "he," "we": the multiple pronouns respond, clearly, to various roles he fulfills as retrospective writer who narrates and evaluates events in which he participated.

While this particular episode is unproblematic, the multiple narrative roles Las Casas assigns to himself taken as a whole bring up interesting questions of reliability, because they problematize the logic of the narrative situation in his history. Santa Arias notes that in combining the forms of secular biography and religious autobiography, Las Casas produces a break with traditional forms in which the exemplary narrative of a spiritual life fuses with the kind of self-justification more common to legal defense.[75] Arias aptly describes the range of situations in which the author presents this distant figure of himself: we find him alternately characterized as "liberator" of indigenous peoples, expert counsel in courtlike battles in the Consejo de Indias and at the imperial court, and the reader is presented with positive evaluations of his deeds and character in direct speech from eminent figures. Although this critic notes tensions between some of these different roles, she emphasizes the author's qualities of exemplarity and self-lessness as transcending the motivations of economic or political self-interest that she finds characteristic of other New World chroniclers.[76]

However, the effort to adopt a posture of modest exemplarity regarding his own abilities and memory would seem to have consequences unintended by the author when he presents himself, for example, as artful, if persecuted, negotiator in his dealings at the Council of the Indies and at the imperial court: "Esta fue una de las señaladas cosas que acaecieron en España: que un clérigo harto pobre y sin renta y persona que le ayudase y ningún favor adquirido por industria humana, sino sólo el que Dios le quiso dar, antes perseguido y abominado de todo el mundo . . . hubiese tanto lugar con el Rey" ("This was one of the most outstanding events that occurred in Spain: that a poor clergyman with no estate and no outside help other than God's, persecuted and hated by everybody . . . should come to have such influence on a king") (HI, 3:509, chap. 138).[77] Often, the authorial I, as witness to the cleric's political successes, intuits divine assistance (of which the character is not aware), as in chapter 139. At times, there are notes of self-congratulation that are quite discordant with the sober piety of the prologue (not to mention the humble and forgetful mind behind those "corporal and mortal eyes") as, for example, when he cannot resist demonstrating his dexterity in the adversarial atmosphere of the Council of the Indies: "Era cosa de ver cómo [el clérigo] a cada uno y a todos respondía y satisfacía, siempre volviendo por sí y defendiendo los indios y culpando las injusticias y daños irreparables que se les hacían" ("It was a sight to be seen how the clergyman answered and satisfied everyone, always standing up for himself, defending the Indians, denouncing the injustice and irreparable damage done to them" (HI, 3:514, chap. 139).[78]

It would seem that, in arriving at these odd and innovative narrative solutions in a work that aspires to be both history and apology, Las Casas

75. Arias, "Autoescritura"; Retórica, historia y polémica, 15–18.
76. Arias, "Autoescritura," 18.
77. Collard, trans., History, 264.
78. Ibid., History, 268 (modified).

appears to have transgressed a discursive boundary, which may explain the difficulties that critics have had in reading the autobiographical sections in which he presents himself as a character. Indeed, Menéndez Pidal used passages such as these to bolster his interpretation of Las Casas as paranoiac, finding his "presumptuous vanity" to be a sign of a "pathological disposition that clouds the moral sense of this cleric who aspires to very high virtues but is dominated by the fantastic vanity of an imaginative child."[79] But until recently most historians have paid little attention to his multiple narrative personae. Saint-Lu, while recognizing the tendency toward self-exaltation, suggests that this should not be read as "incompatible with the sincerity of the historian."[80] A number of critics have sought to compare him to a character in a work of fiction (Don Quijote).[81] Both Arias and Pagden have perceived this distancing effect as an effort to emphasize a breach between the vision of the (converted) narrator and that of his earlier, sinning self.[82] The imagery of confession and atonement is clear in the chapters that follow his account of the Cumaná fiasco,[83] and culminate in the characterization of the *clérigo*'s religious profession in terms of death (and anticipated "resurrection") (*HI*, 3:591, chap. 160). But the tone of spiritual exemplarity imposed by the retrospective narrator strikes a discordant note with the moments of unrepentant self-glorification and with the intensely personal attacks that he wages on his rivals, thus leading one to question the judgment of the historian as much as that of his character, the "*clérigo* Las Casas." While it is possible that, as Arias seems to suggest, Las Casas was trying to hint in these self-exalting passages at both his own successes at court and, simultaneously, the errors in judgment that led to the Cumaná fiasco, the absence of narratorial commentary—present elsewhere on decisions and actions that he would later come to regret, such as that on African slavery—leave one little guidance for judging either Las Casas as actor or as subsequent redactor. Since the work ends shortly after the account of the Cumaná episode, there

---

79. Menéndez Pidal, *El padre Las Casas*, 33.

80. Saint-Lu, "Prólogo," xlii.

81. In this context, see in particular Silva Tena, "Las Casas, biógrafo," and Menéndez Pidal, *El padre Las Casas*, as well as Juana Gil-Bermejo García, "Fray Bartolomé de las Casas y el 'Quijote,'" in *Estudios Lascasianos*, 351–61. See also Avalle Arce, "Hipérboles," 42.

82. Pagden, *European Encounters*, 72; Arias, "Autoescritura."

83. Oviedo's account of the Cumaná fiasco in *HGN*, 1:199–201, book 19, chap. 5, has been much commented on by historians. Gerbi summarizes the criticism in *Nature and the New World* (355–59); for earlier treatments of the subject see Bataillon, *Estudios*, 157–77; Fabié, *Vida y escritos*, 107–22; Losada, "Fray Bartolomé," 125–58; and Keen, "Approaches," in Friede and Keen, eds., *Bartolomé de las Casas in History*, 3–5.

is no insight as to the cleric's evaluation of his own performance in the wake of such a transformative experience.

My point here is not to scold such an eminent figure as Las Casas on subtle points of his self-presentation nearly 450 years after the fact, but rather to examine issues of reliability and the logical status of historical narrative that these autobiographical passages bring up. In a work of fiction one could attribute this sort of gap in perception on the part of the narrator vis-à-vis his characters to a conscious effort by the author to represent his creatures as either unreliable or errant or blind. But in a work of history or autobiography, where the author takes responsibility for the words of the narrator as his own, such distancing makes no sense. In her study of the distinctions between fictional and factual life stories, Dorrit Cohn describes "narratives that center on a life plot as the generic region where factual and fictional narratives come into closest proximity, the territory that presents the greatest potential for overlap."[84] Las Casas's life story does indeed present a fascinating borderline case. Although the cleric's work does not fit into the categories described by Cohn, who presents a four-part model of first- versus third-person regimes as narrated in either historical or fictional lives, one might transpose some of her arguments to illuminate the problems at work in this text. On the one hand, it seems significant that Las Casas inserts his third-person autobiographical account within a first-person historiographical one. The dominant speaker in the text is the retrospective historian, and the cleric's other textual personae or "characters" are subsumed within the dominant vision associated with this voice. There is stability in the origin of the speaker's voice, if not in his various textual manifestations. Most readers take the exhibitionism of some of the autobiographical sections with a grain of salt, keeping in mind Lejeune's insight that in autobiography we expect self-representation to involve distortion.[85] And yet, as Cohn notes in referring to signs of "impaired vision" in (autobiographical) confessional texts, "the critical reader has no choice but to refer all of the telltale evidence of self-deception to [the author] himself, thereby subverting authorial intentions, his authority as self-narrator."[86]

According to Martínez Bonati, the origin of the narrator's voice is a key site for distinguishing between the logic of fiction and of other types of narratives. In his *Fictive Discourse and the Structures of Literature,* this critic

84. Cohn, *Distinction,* 18.
85. Lejeune, *On Autobiography,* 14.
86. Cohn, *Distinction,* 33.

points to the distinctive qualities of fiction that emerge from the logical fact of its being purely imaginary discourse emanating not from the author but from an imaginary narrator. In a work of fiction, what Martínez calls the "mimetic" (narrative-descriptive) sentences of the basic narrator are taken as "true" by the reader in a way that those of the characters are not. This ironic "suspension of disbelief" is unique to the experience of reading fiction, wherein the fictive quality of the narrator results in an absolute freedom from referentiality. For Martínez Bonati, an unreliable narrator presents a variation on this model, and tends to be constructed either by the introduction of a secondary character whose "mimetic" assertions deviate from those of the basic narrator, or by creating a perceptible difference between the components of a basic narrator's "mimetic" and "nonmimetic" discourse (discourse related to judgments or feelings).[87] The basic credibility accorded to the fictive narrator contrasts with the more cautious ways in which we tend to approach nonfictional narrative: "The narrations of presumed fact that we hear or read every day are limited throughout in credibility, and we project from them an unstable objectivity. In real life, speakers are primarily fallible and never absolutely accurate and truthful."[88] In a specifically historical narrative, moreover, the credibility of an account is more often than not measured by elements that are not internal to the text, but by external factors—not the least of which are the preexisting historiographical tradition, and the way in which the historian's evidence is proven against subsequent historical events and developments. Thus, to return to Las Casas, while one can wonder at the strange narratorial multiplicity and even the occasional exhibitionism in his self-presentation, and even dispute many of his facts (as historians have done), few today would dispute *grosso modo* the value of the polemical way in which he attacks the premises and consequences of empire, thus allowing for a certain reliability in the spirit, if not always in the letter, of his analysis of the catastrophic legacy for indigenous peoples of conquest and colonization. To put it another way, the reader adopts quite different standards when evaluating reliability in a work of fiction and in one of history.

Las Casas is remarkably consistent in his endeavor to sort out and differentiate the numerous roles that give him authority to write: eyewitness, prominent actor in events, guilty chorus of the colonial conscience, wise prophet-historian, and jurist. And yet his carefully constructed effort

87. Martínez Bonati, *Fictive Discourse*, 34–36.
88. Ibid., 118.

to distinguish these roles points to an odd coexistence in his work of insight into epistemological concerns about the writing of history and a measure of blindness as to his own perceptive abilities. If Las Casas understood Oviedo's proposal of seeking historiographical verisimilitude through the uses of multiple perspectives and styles, the cleric did not agree with it. His own text would suggest that a truly Christian view of events would not present contradictions. There is little room here for variance in perspective, no apparent leeway for differences in eyewitness accounts given in good faith.

In juxtaposing the works of these historians, I have endeavored to show the keen sensibilities as to the textual signs of "truth" and "lies" that emerged from an otherwise cumbersome and ideologically motivated debate. Amid the acrimonious climate and evident crisis between the competing concepts of history and the norms for narrating it, one can glimpse in the works of Oviedo and Las Casas efforts to define discursive boundaries as well as innovative solutions to the monumental task of recording the history of the New World. These efforts were informed both by the debate over the qualities of "truthful" versus "lying" histories (as it was expressed in the humanist preceptive works) and by a historical context preoccupied by questions of religious dissimulation. One senses in these works a self-consciousness about the different kinds of imagination or fabrication that go into history, and thus a level of conceptual precision perhaps greater than the limited available descriptive lexicon ("historia," "novela," "mentira," and so on) would suggest. Thus, though bitter, their debate was productive. By engaging this debate in such an energetic fashion, Oviedo and Las Casas can be said finally to have founded the critical tradition that continues to inquire about the status of these early colonial texts.

4

HISTORY AND MEMORY: NARRATIVE PERSPECTIVE IN BERNAL
DÍAZ DEL CASTILLO'S *HISTORIA VERDADERA DE LA CONQUISTA
DE LA NUEVA ESPAÑA*

IN THIS CHAPTER I EXAMINE the *Historia verdadera de la conquista de la Nueva
España* by Bernal Díaz del Castillo (ca. 1495–1584) with an eye to problems
of narrative temporality, distance, and perspective and what they might suggest about the question of narrative reliability in his work. I hope to show
that a study of some of the salient textual properties of the *Historia verdadera*
brings further into focus a number of the problems specific to the writing of
history, such as the representation of historical figures and the treatment of
the historical tradition, which I highlighted in the works of Oviedo and Las
Casas. Furthermore, by stressing some of Bernal Díaz's narrative transgressions, I will show the manner in which his work invites one to contemplate discursive boundaries in historiography. A narratological approach that
keeps in mind the context in which Bernal Díaz wrote his history enables
one to describe with greater specificity the narrative strategies he adopts, as
well as to better understand the textual codes that have enabled works such
as the *Historia verdadera de la conquista de la Nueva España* to be so readily read
as "literary" or even "novelistic."

Bernal Díaz is not always the most reliable source on the events of his
own life, as Wagner has shown.[1] Born in Medina del Campo, Extremadura,
Bernal Díaz is listed as a passenger to the Indies in October 1514, not, as
he tells us, in Pedrarias Dávila's expedition that sailed earlier that year.[2] He
claims to have participated in early expeditions in the Gulf of Mexico: that
of Francisco Hernández de Córdoba (1517) and of Juan de Grijalva (1518),
although Wagner casts doubt on the latter. After accompanying Cortés's
campaign in 1519, he later participated in the expeditions to Chiapas (1523)
and Honduras (1524–26), and would eventually settle on an *encomienda* in

---

1. See Wagner, "Bernal Díaz" and "Notes on Writings by and about Bernal Díaz" for a careful study of the chronology of the *encomendero's* life and writings, as well as "The Family of Bernal
Díaz" for a reconstruction of the complexities of the *cronista's* family life. Sáenz de Santa María's
findings complement Wagner's in the "Suplemento" to his critical edition of the *Historia verdadera*
(60–61) and also his *Introducción crítica* (43–78).
2. Wagner, "Bernal Díaz," 157.

Guatemala. He began to write his history after 1551, and would send a completed copy to Madrid after 1568. This version ended up in the hands of the Mercedarian friar Alonso de Remón, who added extensive interpolations to the text about Bartolomé de Olmedo, a fellow Mercedarian and participant in Cortés's expedition. The Remón copy was published in Madrid in 1632. Bernal Díaz appears to have continued working on the Guatemala manuscript until late in life.[3] He died in Guatemala in 1584.

Critical Perspectives: Postmodernism and the Spanish-American Literary Tradition

Unlike the histories of Oviedo and Las Casas, which—despite the self-conscious stances and bitter allegations of their authors—have been quite consistently read as "historical" texts, the *Historia verdadera* has had an uneven fate in terms of critical reception. Verónica Cortínez, in her book *Memoria original de Bernal Díaz,* has summarized the changing fortunes of the old *encomendero*'s work, which, prized in the nineteenth century as the most accurate and detailed historical account of the conquest of Mexico, in the twentieth has paradoxically come to be considered by many as a work of Spanish American "literature." As Cortínez writes: "Las mismas páginas que antes se valorizaban por la cantidad de detalles históricos que contenían, hoy se resaltan por la minuciosa belleza con la que describen un mundo asombroso" ("The same pages that were once valued for the quantity of historical details they contained are appreciated today for the careful beauty with which they describe an astonishing world").[4] This shift in perception of Bernal Díaz's history can be traced through a number of small but significant changes in critical emphasis. In the 1940s Iglesia criticized the "dehumanization" of history, noting that "mientras un texto filosófico o literario se estudiaba procurando verlo

3. For a description and history of the existing manuscripts and editions of Bernal Díaz's work, see the indispensable preliminary study in Sáenz de Santa María's critical edition (ix–xxxvii). Sáenz presents the text of the Remón manuscript, reconstructed from the first edition of the work (Madrid, 1632), which Sáenz considers to be the closest to Bernal Díaz's original, juxtaposed in a parallel column to the Guatemala manuscript. In the "Suplemento" to the critical edition, he includes the prologues prepared by Bernal Díaz's son, Francisco, which were preserved in the Guatemala and Alegría manuscripts, as well as the modifications of the former and the Mercedarian interpolations to the Remón text. All citations are from Sáenz de Santa María's rendering of the Remón text, hereafter given as *HV*, with page and chapter, except where noted. English translations are my own.
4. Cortínez, *Memoria*, 90.

en su integridad . . . el texto histórico [era] tratado de modo inverso: se acudía a él en busca de determinados datos, de 'citas'" ("while a philosophical or literary text was studied in an effort to see it as a whole . . . the historical text [was] treated in an inverse way; it was read in search of particular facts, of 'quotes'").[5] O'Gorman, too, argued against the positivist practice of reading the *crónicas* not as integral works but as sources of empirical historical facts to be analyzed and agglomerated into an "objective" account of past events.[6] At about the same time that Iglesia and O'Gorman were reexamining the intellectual legacy of their predecessors, other scholars explored the more "literary" aspects of these texts. Most prominently, Leonard hypothesized that chivalric romances such as the *Amadís de Gaula* were an active inspiration to the conquistadors, a kind of "unconscious" prism through which they perceived, acted, and, in the case of Bernal Díaz, later wrote.[7] Ida Rodríguez Prampolini, and later Steven Gilman, among others, sought to establish more direct textual parallels in terms of literary reference, while Rudolfo Schevill argued against any such clear links.[8] In subsequent decades, the "literary" qualities of Bernal Díaz's work received increasing critical attention. As Cortínez has aptly described it, "la incertidumbre entre historia y literatura marca no sólo el texto de Bernal, sino también la construcción del sistema literario por parte de críticos y escritores" ("the uncertainty between history and literature does not just mark the text of Bernal, but also the construction of the

5. Iglesia, *Cronistas*, 11.

6. O'Gorman, *Cuatro historiadores*, 168.

7. In researching the sixteenth-century book trade between Spain and America, Leonard documented in *Books of the Brave* that, despite legal prohibitions, novels of chivalry and other literary works, including the *Quijote*, circulated within the Spanish colonies: "Light literature . . . was unconsciously helping to shape historic events, and it assuredly played an important, if a subjective and impalpable, role in this first act of the drama of expanding Western civilization. Moreover, the Conquistador's addiction to fiction brought the habit of secular reading to the remotest portions of the earth at the very moment that Occidental institutions and laws were transplanted there." Leonard, *Books of the Brave*, 315.

8. More recently, Adorno has also criticized Leonard's view, suggesting that the chivalric novels were less an inspiration to soldiers than a reference point for explaining the experience of the conquest to Europeans. The problem presented by writing about the discovery of America and the conquest of its indigenous peoples was not formal, but semantic and eminently political, she argues, noting that in writing about native Americans, the *cronistas de Indias* exploited chivalric romance to both "celebrate the military values of medieval *caballería* and extol over things unheard of and unseen," and to "reject the idea of the fictional romance, not because their own representations were immoral, but because, unlike the romances, they were true." See Adorno, "Literary Production," 17–18, and also her excellent summary of scholarship on this question in her introduction to the 1992 edition of Leonard's *Books of the Brave*.

[Spanish American] literary system by critics and writers").[9] As I will suggest, the techniques of narratology may assist in clarifying the nature of this uncertainty in Bernal Díaz's text.

Roberto González Echevarría and Walter Mignolo have made important strides in sorting out the general nature and sources of the paradoxes inherent in contemporary readings of colonial texts. González Echevarría criticizes the "literary" approaches to the *crónicas* that focus exclusively on the "imaginative" interpolations, and suggests that, while many of the insights from this sort of approach have been important, they are restricted to a partial view of the works, as had been the positivist historical analyses of the past. González Echevarría further notes that interest in the imaginative aspects of the *crónicas de Indias* has been fostered by the embracing of these texts by many contemporary Spanish-American writers as a "chosen origin" for the novel. One critical proposal that he puts forth is to adopt a "bifocal" approach to these texts, one that accounts for both the sixteenth-century norms for writing history and the properties that have earned them modern "literary" recognition.[10]

Mignolo, addressing a similar concern from a different angle, suggests that the presence of such historiographical works within the Spanish American literary "canon" is emblematic of a broader intellectual trend, in which there has been

> un cambio epistemológico en el cual se consolidan la historia literaria y la historia de la historiografía y se recuperan, del pasado, aquellos textos que "muestran" desde la perspectiva de la *recepción,* ciertas propiedades o historiográficas o literarias, aunque estas propiedades no sean características en la *producción* de tales discursos.

> [an epistemological change in which literary history and history of historiography are consolidated, and those texts from the past that "show" from the perspective of *reception* certain historiographic or literary properties are recuperated, although these properties may not be characteristic of the *production* of such discourses themselves.][11]

---

9. Cortínez, *Memoria,* 22. See chapter 4 of this book for a review of the reception by contemporary novelists and writers of the *Historia verdadera* as a foundational work in the Spanish American tradition.

10. González Echevarría, "Humanismo."

11. Mignolo, "Cartas," 59 (emphasis in original).

Margarita Zamora, too, highlights the blurring of boundaries as one that critics tend to "avoid or ignore."[12] While Mignolo's and Zamora's distinctions between the time of production and that of reception have helped to sharpen contemporary critical sensibilities toward colonial texts, especially as regards the recognition of rhetorical and historiographical conventions, their analyses hint at, but do not ultimately address, the assumptions underlying (nor the difficulties following from) the "epistemological" shift to which they allude, that is, the broader question of the ways in which the recuperation of the *crónicas de Indias* as "literary" texts has coincided with (or perhaps even anticipated) the larger poststructuralist questioning of what constitutes "history."

To be precise, the recovery of the chronicles of the Indies has coincided with—and thus to some degree been colored by—not just the sort of aesthetic or cultural project hinted at by González Echevarría, but also the contemporary critique of the value and method of historical studies.[13] Certainly one can say that under the umbrella of postmodernism, history as a discipline—and not just the study of the early historiographical accounts of the Spanish Indies—can be said to find itself at a point of reversal vis-à-vis the status envisioned for it by the sixteenth-century humanists. What for Vives and other preceptors was the supreme discipline, one that was both preserved in and embodied by narrative discourses that aspired to truth, has in recent decades become relegated by some to the category of "verbal fictions,"[14] to borrow Hayden White's phrase, and thus, as legitimate a subject for literary as for historical study. In its most extreme form, as Carlo Ginzburg notes, this approach has resulted in the reduction of history to rhetoric.[15] While the postmodern critique of the traditional claims to truth, accuracy, and reliability in history, and the resulting emphasis on the narrative aspects of the practice, has prompted a great deal of debate among historians, the increasing inclusion of historical texts as objects for literary study (and, consequently, the free application of techniques of literary or

---

12. Zamora, "Historicity," 334.

13. On this topic, see Zagorin, "Historiography," 193–205; Lorenz, "Historical Knowledge"; and Cohn, "Focus on Fiction," in *Distinction*, 1–17.

14. The phrase comes from White's article "The Historical Text as Literary Artifact" in *Tropics,* 82; see also "The Fictions of Factual Representation" in the same volume. Although White modifies this notion in later works, he continues to argue, in *Figural Realism* (6), that literary and historical discourse "are more similar than different since both operate language in such a way that any clear distinction between their discursive form and their interpretative content remains impossible."

15. Ginzburg, *History,* 38.

rhetorical analysis to works of historiography) has only more recently begun to receive in-depth critical consideration by literary critics.

Carlos Fuentes's essay on the *Historia verdadera*, titled "La épica vacilante de Bernal Díaz del Castillo" and included in his book of essays, *Valiente mundo nuevo*, seems to be an example of a reading that freely adopts such a postmodern perspective in the sense that it would appear to assume no difference between historical and fictional texts. About Bernal Díaz, Fuentes writes:

> Tiene un pie en Europa y otro en América y llena el vacío dramático entre los dos mundos de una manera literaria y peculiarmente moderna. Hace, en efecto, lo que Marcel Proust hizo recordando el pasado. . . . Busca el tiempo perdido: es nuestro primer novelista. . . . Bernal, como Proust, ha vivido *ya* lo que va a contar, pero debe dar la impresión de que *lo que cuenta* está ocurriendo al ser escrito.
>
> [He has one foot in Europe and another in America and he fills the dramatic vacuum between the two worlds in a manner that is literary and peculiarly modern. He does, in effect, what Marcel Proust did in remembering the past. . . . He searches for lost time: he is our first novelist. . . . Bernal, like Proust, has *already* lived what he is going to tell, but he must give the impression that *what he is telling* is happening as he writes.][16]

The elements that, according to Fuentes, make the *Historia verdadera* akin to a novel include Bernal's effort to "make the past become present," his technique of characterization, which makes the figures he represents "concrete individuals, not allegorical warriors," and a taste for details and for gossip.[17] Certainly one can perceive in Fuentes's description what Cortínez has called an "act of will," a willful stretching of traditional categories in order to fit this work into a "literary" tradition.[18] On the one hand, this sort of

---

16. Fuentes, *Valiente,* 73–74 (emphasis in original).

17. Ibid., 74–80. Cascardi, in "Chronicle" (199–201), expands on the notion of the *Historia verdadera* as possessing a novel-like quality, and Cortínez, who summarizes in "Yo, Bernal Díaz" (59–69) the diverse critical efforts to define the genre of the *Historia verdadera*, specifies that the originality of the work abides in the temporal distance and discordance between the young hero and the aging narrator, a distance that earns the narrative a modern quality.

18. Cortínez, *Memoria,* 20.

reading suggests an evident lack of sensibility for conventional expectations of historiography. Leaving aside the terminological imprecisions here (they aim perhaps toward impressionistic rather than technical accuracy), one can only guess whether this reading reflects a skepticism concerning the idea of history as a discipline capable of inquiring into the "truth" about the past, or simply a wish for an account of the discovery and conquest that would grant an experience akin to that of reading fiction.[19] After all, if one accepts Martínez Bonati's formulation, the basic logic of fiction—and that which distinguishes it from other types of narratives, such as those of historiography—is one in which the narrator's statements of singular detail are taken by the reader as unconditionally true.[20]

On the other hand, Fuentes's characterization of the *Historia verdadera* as a "novel"—and he is not alone in his appreciation[21]—brings up a number of thorny questions. Significantly, some of the aspects that Fuentes highlights as "novelistic" in Bernal Díaz's text coincide in many ways with the humanist hopes for historical narrative. (And it is precisely to this sort of reading that González Echevarría and Mignolo, as well as Zamora, address their critiques.) As seen in the previous chapters, by the time Bernal Díaz was composing his work, the rhetorical notions of history were under dispute; the methodological self-consciousness of Fernández de Oviedo, in particular, points to an active engagement and critique of the humanist historiographical doctrines, rather than a slavish following of them. And as I hope to show in this chapter, despite Bernal Díaz's claims that he is an "unstudied idiot" ("un idiota sin letras" (*HV*, 650, chap. 212), the *Historia verdadera* in some paradoxical ways fulfills the humanist precepts. The text, it is true, exhibits in places the sort of epistemological transgressions more

19. For a study of the role of the *Historia verdadera* within Fuentes's larger literary project, see Cortínez, *Memoria original* (esp. chapter 5).

20. "The basic logical structure of fiction can be considered derivative and as emerging, through negation, from real and ordinary narrative, since the narrations of presumed facts that we hear or read every day are limited throughout in credibility, and we project from them an unstable objectivity. In real life, speakers are primarily fallible and never absolutely accurate and truthful. A speech intimating unrestricted truth of singular detail is in reality extremely atypical. In literature, the primary teller is the one who never errs on a point of singular circumstances; the derivative and atypical basic narrator is the one who becomes, in this respect, unreliable." Martínez Bonati, *Fictive Discourse*, 118.

21. See also Cascardi, who writes in "Chronicle" that the *Historia verdadera* has "striking novelistic tendencies" (212) and that Bernal Díaz is "able to superimpose the past on the present as if nothing had ever dissociated the two" (203). Durán, in "Bernal Díaz" (799), suggests that the *cronista* aims at achieving "una reconstrucción total del pasado, con todos los pormenores necesarios para que el lector pudiera volver a vivir los acontecimientos de la conquista como si en ellos estuviera tomando parte."

common to fiction than to history, but this sort of transgression is not a consistent feature of Bernal Díaz's work; in most respects his text follows the aspects that I have been highlighting as reflecting the logic and characteristics of historical writing.

The Past Made Present

I will start with the temporal question alluded to by Fuentes, that of Bernal Díaz's making the past appear to be present as a sign of the "novelistic" quality of the work. Although a number of critics have highlighted this feature as a notable one in the *Historia verdadera,* to my knowledge there has been no study of the precise ways in which Bernal Díaz uses verbal tense—and most particularly, the present tense—as one way to achieve this effect. But first it should be noted that Fuentes's equation of the effort to make the past seem present with a "novelistic" quality would seem to reflect, on the surface, a curious critical oversight, given that to conjure up an image of the past as present, to narrate in such a way as to re-create for the reader the impression of a direct perception of events, is the traditional explanation for the use of the "historical present" as a stylistic device, one that signals an effort on the part of the narrator to link in a figurative fashion the time of the writing and the time of events. Lausberg characterizes the historical present as a conventional rhetorical technique for narrating events in such a way as to make them appear to be more "manifest" and "credible" by re-creating the perspective of the eyewitness.[22] One is reminded of Vives's notion of representing the past as if a spectacle before the reader's eyes. In this regard, it is perhaps important to recall that, despite Bernal Díaz's claims to the contrary, he had some awareness of the rhetorical commonplaces concerning the writing of history, and of the practical critique of them popularized by writers such as Fernández de Oviedo.[23] But this critical consciousness about metahistorical notions echoes but faintly in the *Historia verdadera,* and the author often fails to adhere to the norms that he evokes. Like the notes of style and literary reference recognized by Gilman, the humanist views on the writing of history are less a direct influence than a

---

22. Lausberg, in *Handbook,* § 810–14, cites as sources, among others, Quintilian's *Institutio oratoria,* IV.2.123–24 and IX.2.41–42.

23. For a contrary point of view, see Julio Caillet-Bois, who writes in "Bernal Díaz" that no other work of the period shows "un desdén más explícito por las conveniencias [sic] del género histórico, ni hay otra que más desenfadadamente se desentienda de ellas" (228).

sort of "tenuous reminiscence" in the *Historia verdadera*.[24] On the one hand, Bernal Díaz insists, like Oviedo and Las Casas before him, on his authority as eyewitness, on the superiority of things seen directly over secondhand reports, as well as the notion that contradictions are a clear sign of unreliability. On the other, his allusions to norms are often perplexing, even equivocal. He writes, for example, in the prologue:

> Digo y afirmo que lo que en este libro se contiene es muy verdadero, que como testigo de vista me hallé en todas las batallas y reencuentros de guerra; y no son cuentos viejos, ni Historias de Romanos de más de setecientos años, porque a manera de decir, ayer pasó lo que verán en mi historia, y cómo y cuándo y de qué manera.

> [I say and affirm that what is contained in this book is very true, that as an eyewitness I found myself in the battles and skirmishes of war; and these are not old stories, nor Histories of Romans from seven hundred years ago, because it is as if what you will see in my history happened yesterday, and how and where and in what manner.] (*HV*, 3)

Yet in telling of how he planted the first orange trees in New Spain, the author proceeds to refer to his own account as an "old story" ("cuento viejo"): "Well I know that people will say that these old stories do not fit in my account, and I will leave them" ("Bien sé que dirán que no hace al propósito de mi relación estos cuentos viejos, y dejarlos he" (*HV*, 32, chap. 16). Like Oviedo, Bernal Díaz frequently disparages the artful histories of those such as Gómara, who wrote from hearsay ("de oídas") (*HV*, 35, chap. 18) and followed the humanistic models, which emphasized the need for a rhetorically elegant presentation of history. And yet he also voices his own wish to leave a sort of written monument to his fellow soldiers in terms that would seem to echo Vives's hopes for a vivid historiography:

---

24. Gilman, "Bernal Díaz," 102. In chapter 18, for example, where Bernal Díaz criticizes Francisco López de Gómara's "historia de buen estilo," the old conquistador echoes both the commonplaces of the humanists and the sorts of critiques made by Oviedo: "tan grande y santa empresa salió de nuestras manos, pues ella misma da fe muy verdadera; y no son cuentos de naciones extrañas, ni sueños ni porfías, que ayer pasó a manera de decir, si no vean toda la Nueva-España qué cosa es. Y lo que sobre ello escriben, diremos lo que en aquellos tiempos nos hallamos ser verdad, como testigos de vista, e no estaremos hablando las contrariedades y falsas relaciones (como decimos) de los que escribieron de oídas, pues sabemos que la verdad es cosa sagrada." Bernal Díaz, *HV*, 35.

Y más digo, que, como ahora los tengo en la mente y sentido y memoria, supiera pintar y esculpir sus cuerpos y figuras y talles y meneos, y rostros y facciones, como hacía aquel gran pintor y muy nombrado Apeles, e los pintores de nuestros tiempos Berruguete, e Micael Angel, o el muy afamado burgalés, que dicen que es otro Apeles, dibujara a todos los que dicho tengo al natural, y aun según cada uno entraba en las batallas y el ánimo que mostraba.

[And I say further that, as I now have them in my mind and senses and memory, I wish I knew how to paint and sculpt their bodies and figures and gestures and faces and features, just as that great and very famous painter Apelles used to do, and the painters of our times Berruguete and Michael Angelo, or the very famous man from Burgos, of whom it is said that he is another Apelles, so as to draw all those I have mentioned in a natural fashion, and the way in which each entered into battles and the spirit demonstrated by each.] (*HV*, 644, chap. 206)

Here, Bernal Díaz unabashedly declares his hope that his own work would seem to bring figures and events to life, thus echoing the humanist ideal of achieving in historical narrative a vividness that might be comparable to the visual illusions of the best of the Renaissance masters. As we shall see, the narrator's efforts to comply, however vaguely, with the historiographic commonplaces, as well as his frequent falterings in this regard, lend his text some highly idiosyncratic qualities.

Returning now to Fuentes's observation that the treatment of time in the *Historia verdadera* points to a "novelistic" quality in the work: it clearly raises important theoretical questions, such as whether verbal tense has the same function in historical as opposed to fictional works. The topic, it turns out, is not a new one. Käte Hamburger, for one, discusses the historical present as an illustration of her argument for a radically different logic in historical versus fictional works, distinguishing between first-person narration, in which the narrator can be said to be telling his tale as if he were reliving it, and third-person narration. The latter, for Hamburger, involves a sort of "dramatic visualization" that points to the "fictionalizing function of the historical present" in a third-person ("objective," for Hamburger) historical account.[25] Weinrich, who in his study of time in narrative is less concerned with discursive distinctions than is Hamburger, finds the

---

25. Hamburger, *Logic*, 102.

historical present to embody a "temporal metaphor" that creates a tension in the narrative by crossing the logical frontier between time of the events and time of the narration.[26] I will now examine Bernal Díaz's resourceful use of the present tense in the *Historia verdadera* in this light, and the ways in which it points to crucial questions of narrative perspective in his history.

One finds the sort of first-person "presentification" described by Hamburger in places where Bernal Díaz discusses the topics of history and memory, as in "me parece que ahora que lo estoy escribiendo, se me representa por estos ojos pecadores toda la guerra, según y de la manera que allí pasamos" ("it seems to me that now as I am writing, all of the war, and the manner in which we were there, is represented before my sinful eyes") (*HV*, 64, chap. 34); or, "muchas veces, ahora que soy viejo, me paro a considerar las cosas heroicas que en aquel tiempo pasamos, que me parece que las veo presentes" ("oftentimes, now that I am old, I stop to consider the heroic things that we did back then, and it seems to me that I see them as present") (*HV*, 205, chap. 95). Clearly, for the author-narrator, the process of writing is connected, to some extent, to reliving events through memory. This sort of autobiographical "presentification" is readily understandable, given the narrative situation of the author, who began to compose his work in the 1550s, long after the battles that he describes. The *Historia verdadera* also exhibits in places a related phenomenon, one like that described by Weinrich as evoking a "tension" in which the narrator "participates" in the drama of the events, as in the following: "Y andando en estas batallas, nos cercan por todas partes" ("And marching in these battles, they surround us on all sides") (*HV*, 120, chap. 63), or: "Así como llegaron a nosotros, como eran grandes escuadrones, que todas las sabanas cubrían, se vienen como perros rabiosos e nos cercan por todas partes, e tiran tanta de flecha e vara e piedra, que de la primera arremetida hirieron más de setenta de los nuestros" ("Just as they came upon us, since they had large squadrons that covered all the savannahs, they come upon us like mad dogs and surround us on all sides, and fire so many arrows and spears and stones that on their first attack they wounded more than seventy of our men") (*HV*, 62, chap. 34). The reader does not understand the present tense in these examples literally, but as one way in which the narrator "relives" events to heighten dramatic effect. (And, in general, the *Historia verdadera* does display the sort of constant crossing of frontiers between the time of events and that of the narrative that Weinrich finds to be characteristic of historiographic discourse.)

26. Weinrich, *Estructura*, 162.

However, Bernal Díaz would seem to use the present tense in ways that are not merely temporal, that is, geared toward linking past events and the narrative that captures them. One of the most consistent uses of the present tense in the *Historia verdadera* is to signal a change in narrative distance. In relating the words of others, Bernal Díaz, like Oviedo, privileges the use of indirect over direct representation of speech. But whereas Bernal Díaz usually begins by recounting the speech of others in indirect discourse, introducing the quoted language with a verb such as *decir* and a relative pronoun and transposing it to the imperfect (Genette refers to this as "transposed speech"),[27] he often switches midsentence to the present tense, thus creating an impression, albeit incomplete, of direct discourse. This facet of Bernal Díaz's prose can be seen in innumerable passages such as the following, wherein Cortés receives gifts of women from the *Cacique Gordo:*

> Cortés las recibió con alegre semblante, y les dijo que se lo tenían en merced; mas para tomarlas, *como dice que seamos hermanos, que hay necesidad que no tengan aquellos ídolos en que creen y adoran, que los traen engañados y que como él vea aquellas cosas malísimas en el suelo y que no sacrifiquen, que luego tendrán con nosotros muy más fija la hermandad; y que aquellas mujeres se volverán cristianas primero que las recibamos,* y que también habían de ser limpias de sodomías porque tenían muchachos vestidos en hábito de mujeres.

> [Cortés received them with a joyful countenance, and told them that he was grateful, but that before they could take them (the gift of women), *as if to say let's be brothers, it is necessary that they do not have those idols that they believe in and adore, that (the idols) are deceiving them, and that once he sees that those bad things are on the ground, and that they do not sacrifice, then they will have with us a much stronger brotherhood; and that those women must become Christian before we receive them,* and that they must also be clean of sodomy because they had boys dressed in women's clothing.] (*HV,* 97, chap. 51, my emphasis)

---

27. Genette, in *Narrative Discourse* (170–72), finds three ways in which speech can be represented in narrative: (1) mimetic, or direct speech; (2) transposed speech, in which the narrator inserts the words of another into his own discourse; and (3) narrativized speech, in which spoken words become another event.

The present tense suggests a hesitation or switch in narrative distance (from indirect to direct recording of speech) that points to a mixing of the perspective of the narrator and that of the character whose words he represents (the verb tense hints at a direct quotation of Cortés's words, but the personal pronouns maintain the narrator's indirect stance). The switch in verb tense, as in the example above, would seem to be aimed at making this transposed scene more vivid, at highlighting key points of Cortés's speech. One sees a similar phenomenon in the following passage, in which the Aztec chief, addressing Cortés, requests a chance to explain to his people the reasons for his "imprisonment":

> Montezuma dijo a Cortés que quería salir e ir a sus templos a hacer sacrificios e cumplir sus devociones, así para lo que a sus dioses era obligado como para que conozcan sus capitanes e principales, *especial ciertos sobrinos suyos que cada día le vienen a decir que le quieren soltar y darnos guerra, y que él les da por respuesta que él se huelga de estar con nosotros: porque crean que es como se lo han dicho,* porque así se lo mandó su dios Huichilobos.

> [Montezuma told Cortés that he wanted to leave and go to his temples to make sacrifices and fulfill his devotions, as he was obliged to do by his gods and to see his captains and noble leaders, *especially some of his nephews who each day come to tell him that they want to free him and make war on us, and that he gives as his answer that he is happy to be with us so that they believe it is as they have been told,* because that is what their god Huichilobos ordered.] (*HV*, 210, chap. 98, my emphasis)

Here too, the present tense signals the inclusion of a character's spoken words within the narrator's discourse, in this case emphasizing what will become one of the most dramatic episodes in the work (more on this later). An even more audacious variation—in epistemological terms—can be seen in the following, wherein Bernal Díaz hints at the direct quoting of the warnings of Aztec idols:

> Parece ser que los Huichilobos y el Tezcatepuca hablaron con los papas, y les dijeron que se querían ir de sus provincias, pues tan mal tratados eran de los teules, e que *adonde están aquellas figuras y cruz que no quieren estar,* e que ellos no estarían allí si no nos mataban,

e que aquello les daban por respuesta, e que no curasen de tener otra; e que se lo dijesen a Montezuma y a todos sus capitanes, que luego comenzasen la guerra y nos matasen; y les dijo el ídolo que mirasen que todo el oro que solían tener para honrarles lo había-mos deshecho y hecho ladrillos, e que mirasen que nos íbamos señoreando de la tierra.

[It seems that Huichilobos and the Tezcatepuca spoke with the *papas* and told them that they wanted to leave their provinces, because they were so badly treated by the *teules,* and that (the gods) *do not want to be near those figures and cross,* and that they would not stay unless we were killed, and that that was their answer, and that they should not wait for another; and that they should tell Montezuma and all his captains that they should wage war immediately and kill us. The idol told them to see that all the gold with which they were once honored had been destroyed by us and made into bricks, and to look out that we were taking over the land.] (*HV,* 231, my emphasis)

Although in most cases this sort of usage of the present tense refers to spoken language, in places it indicates a quoting of written language, as when Bernal Díaz quotes from memory a letter sent from Cortés to the troops accompanying Pánfilo de Nárvaez (*HV,* 239, chap. 112). The use of the present tense to hint at a direct recording of speech can also be seen where Bernal Díaz refers to it specifically as a "dialogue," that is, in his well-known exchange with "Fame":

Y quiero proponer una cuestión a modo de diálogo: y es, que habiendo visto la buena e ilustre fama que suena en el mundo de nuestros muchos y buenos y notables servicios que hemos hecho a Dios y a su majestad y a toda la cristiandad, da grandes voces y dice que fuera justicia y razón que tuviéramos buenas rentas, y más aventajadas que tienen otras personas que no han servido en estas conquistas ni en otras partes a su majestad; y asimismo pregunta que dónde estan nuestros palacios y moradas, y qué blasones tenemos en ellas diferenciadas de las demás; y si están en ellas esculpidos y puestos por memoria nuestros heroicos hechos y armas.

[And I want to propose something in the manner of a dialogue: and it is that, upon seeing the good and illustrious news that resonates in the world of the many and good and notable services that we have done for God and for your majesty and all Christianity, Fame cries out and says that it would be just and reasonable that we should have good incomes, and better ones than those of others who have not served your majesty either in these conquests or in other parts; and (Fame) asks: Where are our palaces and dwellings, and what heraldry do we display to distinguish them from others, and whether upon them are sculpted and engraved for memory our heroic deeds and coats of arms?] (*HV,* 652, chap. 210)

This case is somewhat different from the others, however, because Bernal Díaz's "dialogue" here refers not to a remembered exchange from the time of events, but to a clearly invented one that corresponds to the time of his writing. Nonetheless, this example underlines the present tense as a signal in the *Historia verdadera* not just of the temporal duality implicit in any narrative rendering of past events, but as a suggestion of the inclusion within the narrator's discourse of the words of a character, which points to the markedly "oral" quality of his prose.[28] This use of the present tense is not really problematic (recent studies suggest that it is a common feature of spoken language)[29]—but does point to a consistent effort on the part of the narrator to highlight or emphasize certain elements of the quoted discourse, and in places may indicate (as in the quoting of the words of idols) questions concerning the narrator's sense of distance toward the story he tells.

In this regard, it is interesting to find the specter of the narrative stance of the *adivino,* so maligned by Oviedo and Las Casas as a sign of unreliable reporting of events not observed, as a notable characteristic of Bernal Díaz's "eyewitness" account and, perhaps, as an aspect that has justly

---

28. A number of critics have pointed to the evident orality in Bernal Díaz's prose. See, for example, Caillet-Bois, who writes in "Bernal Díaz" (228) that the *Historia verdadera* is "ese alegato donde parece oírse la voz de todos," and Cortínez's discussion in *Memoria* (125) of the orality in Bernal Díaz's work as evidenced by his frequent referral to his text in terms that denote spoken language (e.g., *plática,* a term that suggests "un tipo de discurso donde la belleza formal se supedita no al concepto de la verdad, sino al acto de decirla").

29. I am indebted to Cohn's succinct summary of theoretical work on the historical present in "The Deviance of Simultaneous Narration" in *Distinction* (96–108). A number of recent studies point to the function of tense in terms of narrative perspective: see Martínez Bonati, "El sistema del discurso y la evolución de las formas narrativas," in *La ficción narrativa,* as well as Bellos, "The Narrative Absolute Tense," on literary usage, and Wolfson, "Tense-Switching," on conversational usage.

earned him literary fame. Indeed, in a crucial part of his narrative—that of
the capture of the Aztec lord—Bernal Díaz not only achieves the effect of
presenting the past as if in the process of being witnessed, but conjures up
a sort of inside view into the thoughts of Montezuma quite uncharacter-
istic of works—whether fictive or historiographical—of his time. While
Cortínez has observed that the author of the *Historia verdadera* is not "loyal"
to any one perspective, noting in particular the temporal division in the
author's narrative "I,"[30] to my knowledge, critics have not recognized the
old conquistador's even more problematic narrative shifts when recounting
the experiences of others, as he does in the following passage about Montezuma, caught in Cortés's trap:

> Y si antes estaba temeroso, entonces estuvo mucho más; y después
> de quemados [los prisoneros] fue nuestro Cortés . . . y él mismo le
> quitó los grillos, y tales palabras le dijo, que no solamente lo tenía
> por hermano, sino en mucho más, e como es señor y rey de tantos
> pueblos y provincias, que si él podía, el tiempo andando le haría
> que fuese señor de más tierras . . . ; y que si quiere ir a sus palacios,
> que le da licencia para ello; y decírselo Cortés con nuestras lenguas,
> y cuando se lo estaba diciendo Cortés, parecía que le saltaban las
> lágrimas de los ojos al Montezuma; y respondió con gran cortesía
> que se lo tenía en merced. *Porque bien entendió Montezuma que todo*
> *eran palabras las de Cortés; e que ahora al presente que convenía estar allí*
> *preso, porque por ventura, como sus principales son muchos; y sus sobrinos*
> *e parientes le vienen cada día a decir que será bien darnos guerra y sacarlo de*
> *prisión, que cuando lo vean fuera que le atraerán a ello, e que no quería ver*
> *en su ciudad revueltas, e que si no hace su voluntad, por ventura querrán*
> *alzar a otro señor; y que él les quitaba de aquellos pensamientos con decirles*
> *que su dios Huichilobos se lo ha enviado a decir que esté preso.*

> [If he had been afraid before, then he became even more so; and
> after (the prisoners) were burned, our Cortés went . . . and himself
> took off (Montezuma's) shackles, and said such words to him, that
> he not only considered him a brother, but much more, and as he
> is the lord and king over so many towns and provinces, that if he
> could, later he would make him lord over more lands . . . , and that
> if he wants to go to his palaces, that he has permission to do so; and

30. Cortínez, "Yo, Bernal Díaz."

Cortés says all this to him with our translators, and when Cortés was telling him this, it seemed that tears were jumping from the eyes of Montezuma; and he answered with great courtesy that he was grateful. *Because Montezuma well understood that all these were just words on the part of Cortés; and that now it was necessary to remain there as prisoner, because perhaps, since his chiefs are many and his nephews and kin come every day to say that it will be good to wage war on us and take him out of prison, that when they see him outside they will draw him in to (this plan) and that he didn't want to see any uprisings in his city, and if he does not follow their wishes, perhaps they will want to raise up another lord; and that he tried to keep them from these thoughts by telling them that their god Huichilobos had sent to say that he should remain in prison.]* (*HV*, 204, my emphasis)[31]

In switching into the present and future tenses, Bernal Díaz appears to shift from the time of his narration to the time of the conquest, even momentarily accessing the Aztec lord's thoughts. These temporal changes in recounting the inner perceptions of Montezuma are epistemologically more problematic in terms of perspective than either his recording of his own experience or his transposing the words of others, because they seem to represent the immediacy of the events as perceived by another figure.[32] In this sense, they disturb the narrative situation, bringing into high relief the instability of Bernal Díaz's narrative stance, which in places like this one would seem to move from a remembered eyewitness (first-person) perspective to one that is focalized through the consciousness of another, making this section of the narrative quite unnatural or improbable in logical terms.[33] This passage recalls Hamburger's distinction between first- and third-person narration using the historical present, in which the latter

31. I have slightly modified the punctuation represented in Sáenz's rendition of the Remón manuscript, so that it more closely follows the sense of the passage in the Guatemala manuscript, *HV*, 204, chap. 95.

32. For the challenges that this type of narrative posture presents for verisimilitude, see Martínez Bonati, *Ficción*, 82.

33. For a differing point of view, see Pellicer: "Como [Bernal Díaz] es testigo de vista no es un narrador omnisciente, de ahí que a menudo alude a la falta de información sobre un suceso determinado, o al olvido. Este tipo de narración, más o menos pura, hace que se recurra en muy pocas ocasiones al diálogo. Dejando a un lado la vigorosa personalidad de nuestro autor, está claro que el texto gana en veracidad y persuasión al ser narrado desde la primera persona." Pellicer, "La organización narrativa," 85.

shows signs of "fictionalization."[34] This sort of disruption in the narrative situation points to a clear transgression in the narrative pact on which Bernal Díaz claims his reliability and would seem to indicate a borderline regarding what is legitimate for historiographic—as opposed to fictive—discourse. It is this sort of transgression, it seems to me, more than the inclusion of seemingly irrelevant details, that points to textual properties more logically attributed to fictive than to historical writing. In works of fiction, Martínez Bonati has written, the fact that the basic narrator has absolute credibility means that types of discourse that would ordinarily be "epistemologically invalid or doubtful" can be taken to be true without restrictions.[35] In a work of history, however, such liberties can be taken only as shortcomings, as a suspension or breach in the author's promise of an account that does not overstep his own "natural" limitations. Needless to say, Bernal Díaz's failure (in historiographic terms) here marks a literary achievement, one that contributes to perhaps the most remarkable representation of Montezuma in all of the early Spanish chronicles of the Indies.[36]

In this regard, it is perhaps pertinent to remember that, aside from broad similarities such as the episodic structure (common to both historical and fictional narratives) and the limited literary references, noted by Gilman and others, Bernal Díaz's narrative acrobatics do not present a consistently articulated (artistic) pattern in his work and, for that matter, have little in common with the fictional works of his day. As Kaiser has noted, characterization in the novel of the period is usually structured around behavior, as described directly by the narrator and as verified through a character's words and gestures.[37] Martínez Bonati observes that the ability to narrate the immediacy of another's experience requires an inverisimilar narrative stance more characteristic of modern novels than of major fictional works of the sixteenth and seventeenth centuries.[38] And the sort of fusion between the words of a narrator and those of a character is also more characteristic

---

34. Hamburger, in *Logic* (107), goes so far as to suggest that the historical present has a very different function in historical as opposed to fictional texts. In historical texts, she maintains, the present tense has a truly temporal function and marks an imaginative effort on the part of the author at "presentification"; whereas in fictional works the present tense is "not functionally different" from the past tense.

35. Martínez Bonati, *Ficción*, 81.

36. For the ways in which Bernal Díaz draws on existing models of descriptive portraits, see Rose-Fuggle, "Era el gran Montezuma."

37. Kayser, "Origen," 9.

38. Martínez Bonati, in *Ficción* (82): "Porque el narrador no parece pretender estar dando cuenta inmediata de los hechos, la manera de narrar, la epistemología del discurso, del *Amadís* es más verosímil que la del *Quijote* y mucho más verosímil que la de la novela realista moderna."

of modern works than of those of Bernal Díaz's time.[39] In this sense, Bernal Díaz's narrative choices, which create momentary effects like those we have come to associate with modern works of fiction, are quite idiosyncratic in formal terms when compared to the discursive practices of his day.

Narrative Perspective: "Yo, Bernal Díaz"

The sort of "focalization" of the narrative perspective through the consciousness of Montezuma just examined is not a dominant narrative strategy in the *Historia verdadera,* but, like the mixing of the narrator's and the characters' words in the indirect representation of speech, it complicates Bernal Díaz's repeated claims of maintaining a clear-cut eyewitness point of view. As we shall see, the author engages in other noteworthy narrative audacities as well.

It would seem that for Bernal Díaz, as for Oviedo and Las Casas, the notion of reliability is inextricably bound up in problems of narrative perspective. Bernal Díaz insists repeatedly on the integrity of his point of view, which he defines as limited by his natural range of vision. He professes in the prologue, as we have seen, to have witnessed everything he relates, and frequently evidences an awareness of the epistemological constraints on such an outlook, clarifying, for example, that "porque yo no fui en esta entrada, digo en esta relación que 'dicen que pasó lo que he dicho'" ("because I did not go on this campaign, I write that 'they say that it happened as I have said'") (*HV,* 303, chap. 132). In deflating Gómara's report that one of the apostles had appeared to assist the Castilians in a battle in Tabasco, for example, he writes: "Y pudiera ser que los que dice el Gómara fueran los gloriosos apóstoles señor Santiago o señor san Pedro, e yo, como pecador, no fuese digno de verles; lo que entonces vi y conocí fue a Francisco de Morla en un caballo castaño, que venía juntamente con Cortés" ("And it might be that those whom Gómara mentions were the glorious apostles Sir Saint James and Sir Saint Peter, and I, as a sinner, was not worthy of seeing them; what I then saw and recognized was Francisco de Morla on a chestnut horse. He was riding together with Cortés") (*HV,* 63–64, chap. 34). In this twist, worthy of Las Casas in its deftness, Bernal evokes Gómara's earlier version and discredits it with a nonmiraculous (and rather more mundane) narrative image. But in relating a secondhand indigenous report of a

---

39. On this topic, see Rojas, "Tipología del discurso del personaje."

supernatural apparition, he adopts a much less critical attitude. Here we find Montezuma interrogating his allies about the battle in Almería:

> Preguntó el Montezuma que, siendo ellos muchos millares de guerreros, que cómo no vencieron a tan pocos teules. Y respondieron que no aprovechaban nada sus varas y flechas ni buen pelear; que no les pudieron hacer retraer, porque una gran tecleciguata de Castilla venía delante dellos, y que aquella señora ponía a los mexicanos temor, y decía palabras a sus teules que los esforzaba; y el Montezuma entonces creyó que aquella gran señora que era Santa María. . . . Y porque esto yo no lo vi, porque estaba en México, sino que lo dijeron ciertos conquistadores que se hallaron en ello y plugiese a Dios que así fuese!

> [Montezuma asked why, with so many thousands of warriors, were they unable to vanquish so few *teules*. And they answered that their spears and arrows and good fighting were useless; that they could not make them go back, because a great *tecleciguata* of Castile came before them and that that lady made the Mexicans afraid, and said words to the *teules* that gave them strength; and Montezuma then thought that that great lady was Saint Mary. . . . And because I didn't see this as I was in Mexico at the time, but rather it was told to me by certain conquistadors who were there, and please God that it might be so!] (*HV*, 200–201, chap. 95)

The account of such a miracle, witnessed by anonymous indigenous warriors, interpreted by Montezuma, and later passed on by unnamed conquistadors, points to the rather endearing way in which Bernal Díaz often waffles on his own stated principles. The promise of a direct, unembellished point of view becomes visibly complicated as well in the following passage, in which he endeavors to account for the ingredients in Montezuma's supper:

> Oí decir que le solían guisar carnes de muchachos de poca edad; y como tenía tantas diversidades de guisados y de tantas cosas, no le echábamos de ver si era de carne humana y de otras cosas, porque cotidianamente le guisaban gallinas, gallos . . . , faisanes, perdices de la tierra . . . y así, no miramos en ello. Lo que yo sé es, que desque

nuestro capitán le reprendió el sacrificio de comer carne humana, que desde entonces mandó que no le guisasen tal manjar.

[I heard tell that they used to stew the flesh of young boys; and since he had so many kinds of stews and so many things, we didn't look to see if it was human flesh or something else, because daily they cooked up hens, roosters..., pheasants, local partridges..., and so we didn't look carefully. What I know is that, after our captain admonished him for sacrificing and eating human flesh, (Montezuma) ordered that such a delicacy no longer be prepared for him.] (*HV*, 184, chap. 91)

In practice, even for the eyewitness, the difficulty of separating "things heard" from "things seen" is one that is dramatized over and over again in his history, and as the narrative progresses, he increasingly claims credibility based both on his own (unique) eyewitness experience and on his ability to speak for his fellow soldiers who have no voice:

Por esto digo yo en mi relación: "Fueron y esto hicieron y tal les acaeció," y no digo: "Hicimos ni hice, ni en ello me hallé," mas todo lo que escribo acerca dello pasó al pie de la letra; porque luego se sabe en el real de la manera que en las entradas acaece; y ansí, no se puede quitar ni alargar más de lo que pasó.

[That's why I say in my account: "They went and they did this and such and such happened to them," and I don't say "we did nor I did, nor I was there," but all that I write about happened just so, because one always finds out later at camp what happened on the battlefield, and so it is not possible to take away or to add to what happened.] (*HV*, 339–40, chap. 142)

He emphasizes this aspect of his account again in relating his efforts to defend his work against the criticisms of the two *licenciados* who review his manuscript and question how anyone could remember so many names and events in such great detail:

A esto respondo y digo que no es mucho que se me acuerde ahora sus nombres: pues éramos quinientos y cincuenta compañeros que siempre conversábamos juntos, así en las entradas como en las velas, y en las batallas y encuentros de guerras, e los que mataban de nosotros en las tales peleas e cómo los unos con los otros, en especial cuando salíamos de algunas muy sangrientas e dudosas batallas, echábamos menos los que allá quedaban muertos, e a esta causa los pongo en esta relación.

[To this I answer and say that it's not surprising that I should remember their names now: we were five hundred and fifty companions who always conversed with one another, whether we were attacking or standing watch, or in the battles and encounters of war. And, in talking to each other we would miss those who had died on the field, especially when we got out of some very difficult and bloody fights, which is why I mention them in my account.] (*HV*, 644, chap. 206).

The notion of the *Historia verdadera* as both a firsthand view and a collective register of the base-camp accounts of others fits in with Bernal Díaz's tendency to mix his own words with the speech of the historical actors he represents, and points to the complex scope of his project.

As it happens, one finds remarkable variations in what the narrator is able to perceive in the *Historia verdadera*. In places, as we have seen, Bernal Díaz as narrator betrays a fantastic ability to decipher the thoughts of Montezuma. However, elsewhere in the account of the dramatic triumphs and reversals of the Castilians in Tenochtitlán, he maintains a steadfastly limited view, one that appears restricted even when compared to that of other historical figures portrayed. Indeed, aside from the momentary inside views, Bernal Díaz's account of the encirclement and ultimate defeat of the Aztec prince is notable for the backseat role taken by the teller, who highlights the amusements provided for the imprisoned leader, the gifts and pleasantries exchanged between the great Montezuma and his captors, and the (often deficient) manners of those charged with guarding him. Bernal Díaz at first presents Montezuma as happily integrated within the Castilian company: we find him enjoying a boating trip to his hunting grounds in the company of his captors and ordering his hunters to capture a hawk that has caught the fancy of one of the Spanish captains. The progressive entanglement of Montezuma in Cortés's snare is achieved with considerable distance. As tensions mount among Montezuma's allies, Bernal Díaz portrays the lord of Tenochtitlán's increasing submission to Cortés through his interactions with the Spaniards and his conflicts with his upstart nephew,

Cacamatzin. The gravity of the situation is clear from the way in which Montezuma is seen as lying to his own allies (he explains his imprisonment as voluntary and sanctioned by his idols), and yet Bernal Díaz limits his own comments to statements such as: "Montezuma era cuerdo y no quería ver su ciudad puesta en armas" ("Montezuma was wise and did not want to see an uprising in his city") (*HV*, 214, chap. 100). In noting the contrast between the Aztec prince's fragility at the hands of Cortés and his continued ability to command obedience from his own subjects, Bernal Díaz writes: "Miren qué gran señor era, que estando preso así era tan obedecido" ("See what a great lord he was, that though a prisoner he was still obeyed in this way") (*HV*, 217, chap. 100). Indeed, the most accurate insight on the situation—that which most faithfully reflects the developments as recounted from beginning to end—is voiced not by the narrator, but by Cacamatzin, Montezuma's nephew,[40] who threatens impending disaster, calls his uncle a "hen" ("gallina"), and sorely chastizes him for handing over his empire to the Castilians. The sort of suppression of the narrator's explicit vision and commentary on events here, and the presentation of a more exact evaluation in the words of the "enemy" suggests an element of perspectivism in this scene and highlights the range of narrative techniques that Bernal Díaz employs in endeavoring to capture in finest detail the enigmatic figure of Montezuma.

Narrative Voice and the Portrayal of Historical Figures

Bernal Díaz's liberties in narrative perspective, however, coexist within the vast sweep of the *Historia verdadera* with techniques of portraying characters that are consistent with what Rigney has described as characteristically historiographic, which I have discussed in Chapter 1. The figures that Bernal Díaz preserves for memory, himself included, are often sketched in broad and contradictory lines, recorded in many cases with a succinct epithet aimed more, it would seem, at identification than characterization. In describing his own role as a young soldier—as critics have often noted—Bernal Díaz emphasizes on the one hand that he was a figure of some importance in the conquest, frequently consulted by Cortés, conversant with Montezuma and privy both to his captain's strategies and even

---

40. Bernal Díaz writes that Cacamatzin "entendió que había muchos días que estaba preso su tío Montezuma, e que en todo lo que nosotros podíamos nos íbamos señoreando." *HV*, 213, chap. 100.

to "secret" communications between indigenous leaders. On the other, he recognizes that he, like the vast bulk of the soldiers taking part in the conquest, is unlikely to be remembered by history. Posterity might easily find someone such as himself to be indistinguishable from others in his company: "En la capitanía de Sandoval había tres soldados que tenían por renombre Castillos: el uno dellos era muy galán, y preciábase dello en aquel sazón, que era yo, y a esta su causa me llamaban Castillo, el galán" ("Under Sandoval's captainship there were three soldiers who went by the name Castillo: one of them was a very fine-looking fellow, and knew so himself at the time; and that was me, and because of this I was called Castillo, the gallant") (*HV,* 435, chap. 160). The reference to himself here in the third person—in addition to being a moment of vanity—hints at an awareness that the role that Bernal Díaz highlights for himself in his own work cannot be taken for granted by the reader, and that outside of his own *Historia verdadera,* he is likely, if remembered at all, to be indistinguishable from others with the same family name. While this effort at clarifying the who's who among the soldiers may well be related to the old soldier's subsequent aspirations to *hidalgo* status,[41] it also alludes to a problem common to the representation of historical figures.

The sort of disjunction between the portrayal of himself as an important actor at decisive moments and at the same time as rather unremarkable has parallels in other ambiguities of his self-representation. Bernal Díaz's construction of a narrative "I" has been the subject of much critical study, although perhaps never so succinctly stated as by one of his earliest readers, Antonio de Solís, who wrote, somewhat unkindly, in his own *Historia de la conquista de México* (1684), that Bernal Díaz's "particular" (private) history, as he calls it,

> pasa hoy por historia verdadera ayudándose del mismo desaliño y poco adorno de su estilo para parecerse a la verdad y acreditar con algunos la sinceridad del escritor: pero aunque le asiste la circunstancia de haber visto lo que escribió, se conoce de su misma obra que no tuvo la vista libre de pasiones, para que fuese bien gobernada la pluma: muéstrase tan satisfecho de su ingenuidad como quexoso de su fortuna: andan entre sus renglones muy descubiertas la envidia y la ambición.

41. Wagner, in "Bernal Díaz," notes that the *cronista*'s name rarely appears in other accounts of the period; Sáenz de Santa María observes that for most of his life, the author went by the name "Bernal Díaz," and suggests that he probably adopted the "del Castillo" in the 1560s. See his *Introducción crítica,* 44, and his "Suplemento" to the critical edition, 61.

[passes today as a true history. The very same carelessness and lack of adornment of his style helps create the appearance of truth and convinces some of the writer's sincerity. But though he is assisted by the circumstance of having witnessed what he wrote, his work itself reveals that the author's vision was not free from passion so as to govern well his pen. He shows himself to be as satisfied with his own cleverness as he is dissatisfied with his fortune. Envy and ambition wrangle openly between his lines.][42]

Modern critics have delineated in greater detail the protagonism of his "I," as well as the author's petulance, egotism, and the undeniable *simpatía* of his narrative persona, not to mention his likely pragmatic and legal aims in writing the work.[43] Many have commented on the strong presence of Bernal Díaz's "I," the best-known passage being that included in another part of his "dialogue" with Fame:

> Y entre los fuertes conquistadores mis compañeros, puesto que los hubo muy esforzados, a mí me tenían en la cuenta dellos, y el más antiguo de todos; y digo otra vez que yo, yo, yo lo digo tantas veces, que yo soy el más antiguo y he servido como muy buen soldado a su majestad y dígolo con tristeza de mi corazón, porque me veo pobre y muy viejo, una hija por casar, y los hijos varones ya grandes y con barbas.

> [And among my companions the strong conquistadors—for some of them were very valiant—I was counted as one of them, and as the one who had been there first. And I repeat that I, I, I say it so many times that I am the first to have gone and I have served his majesty as a good soldier and I say it with sorrow in my heart, because I am poor and very old, with a daughter to be married and my sons already grown and bearded.] (*HV*, 652, chap. 210)

---

42. Solís, *Historia*, 1:2, 27.

43. The most thorough studies of Bernal Díaz's narrative "I" are by Rose de Fuggle, "El narrador fidedigno," and Cortínez, whose book comprises the most complete description to date of Bernal Díaz as narrator. See Cortínez, *Memoria,* chapter 2, and also "Yo, Bernal Díaz." On legal battles, see Iglesia, "Introducción al estudio," which also addresses questions of Bernal's self-presentation, and Adorno, "Discursive Encounter." Others who have studied Bernal as a narrator include González Echevarría, "Humanismo," and Loesberg, "Narratives of Authority."

Yet while readers have invariably noted the forcefulness with which this "I" demands to be heard, they have not agreed on what sort of a "character" his self-portrait might add up to. Cortínez has described the complexity of Bernal Díaz's construction of himself in his work, wherein he takes on the roles of author, character, and reader.[44] One finds hints as to Bernal Díaz's historical being, but no real answers within the text; one can only guess at the measure of sincerity or accurate self-representation in his discourse about himself, particularly in the final chapters, in which lofty providential overtones coexist with (and are eroded by) the narrator's incessant complaints. He suggests, for example, that his history has been divinely inspired to preserve the memory of all of the glorious foot soldiers who took part in the conquest: "Gracias a Dios y a su bendita madre nuestra señora, que me escapó de no ser sacrificado a los ídolos, e me libró de otros muchos peligros y trances, para que haga ahora esta memoria" ("Thank God and his blessed mother our lady, that I escaped being sacrificed to the idols, and was freed from many other dangers and bad situations so that I now may write this memory") (*HV*, 644, chap. 206). But this sort of note often mingles with a more petulant one, as when he writes:

> Mas, si bien se quiere notar, después de Dios, a nosotros los verdaderos conquistadore [*sic*] que los descubrimos y conquistamos, y desde el principio les quitamos sus ídolos y les dimos a entender la santa doctrina, se nos debe el premio y galardón de todo ello, primero que a otras personas, aunque [s]ean religiosos; porque cuando el principio es bueno, el medio y el cabo todo es digno de policía y cristiandad y justicia que les mostramos en la Nueva-España.

> [After God it is to us, the true conquerors who discovered and conquered (the natives), and from the beginning we took away their idols and we gave them to understand the sacred doctrine—it is to us before any others that the prize and reward is due, even before the clergy, because when the beginning is good, the middle and the end are all worthy of the order and Christianity and justice that we showed them in New Spain.] (*HV*, 647, chap. 208)

In places, he drops all claims to piety, arguing that the long-hoped-for royal recognition and rewards "se me deben bien debidas" ("are very much owed

44. Cortínez, *Memoria*, 135.

to me") (*HV,* 652, chap. 210). As in the case of Las Casas's portrayal of himself, this mixing of registers suggests problems of narratorial reliability, but here, too, one has no choice but to attribute these conflicting signals to the author himself. It is quite impossible to unravel a precise image of the "character" of the author from the narrative *persona* that he creates, which provides many clues, but few answers, as to his true motivations.

In his treatment of other historical actors, Bernal Díaz employs a range of techniques, some involving extensive descriptive and narrative portrayal, and others consisting of quick, formulaic descriptions and even lists. In the latter, there seems to be an abyss between Bernal Díaz's stated aim of "sculpting" the figures of his fellow soldiers and his actual practice. The multiplicity of experiences of a large collective body of soldiers does not conform to a coherent narrative, but spills over and must be accommodated into catalog-like chapters, such as the sections on Montezuma's palace and the market of Tlatelolco. The more rhetorically elaborate portraits of chapter 206 are, as María Luisa Fischer has noted, less lifelike representations than "undifferentiated portraits, indistinguishable if not for the name or the written inscription," and would appear to be based on the models of Pérez de Guzmán and Fernando del Pulgar, while the lists in chapters 205, 211, and 212 appear to aim at creating a sense of documentary exactitude.[45] Cortínez has discussed the ways in which Bernal Díaz makes constant and recurring reference to figures of all social rank,[46] and I would add that this aspect of his history, together with the litany of "my dead companions," points to the "social" character (to borrow Rigney's phrase) of his history, which endeavors in a typically historiographic fashion to record traces of a vast number of figures, many of whom reappear erratically, if at all, in the work. Amid the vast sweep of his prodigious memory, which claims to record the masses of fallen soldiers, a few characters, such as Cortés and Montezuma, and a number of others, stand out.

In what follows, I will contrast briefly the different approaches Bernal Díaz takes in sketching the two most important figures of his history. Cortínez has written the most complete description of the ways in which Bernal Díaz portrays Cortés, emphasizing the fairness with which the old soldier seems to both celebrate his captain's talents and to criticize his shortcomings.[47] Indeed, in Bernal Díaz's account, Cortés's astuteness throughout the

45. Fischer, in "Bernal Díaz," 50. See also Gilman, "Bernal Díaz," and Rose-Fuggle, "Era el gran Montezuma," on the possible influences of Pérez de Guzmán and Fernando del Pulgar.
46. Cortínez, *Memoria,* 58–69.
47. Ibid., 39–58.

Aztec campaign is matched only by his disastrous blunderings in all of his subsequent dealings with the Castilian imperial bureaucracy. The narrator refrains from presenting us the sort of inside vision we see of Montezuma, insisting instead on the restricted objectivity of his own point of view. In recalling the captain's brilliant leadership, he highlights his own changing perception of events over time:

> Una cosa que he pensado despúes acá, que jamás nos dijo tengo tal concierto en el real hecho, ni fulano ni zutano es en nuestro favor, ni cosa ninguna destas, sino que peleásemos como varones; y esto de no decirnos que tenía amigos en el real de Narváez fue muy de cuerdo capitán, que por aquel efecto no dejásemos de batallar como esforzados, y no tuviésemos esperanza en ellos, sino, después de Dios, en nuestros grandes ánimos.

> [One thing I have since thought is that he never told us I have such an agreement in (Narváez's) camp, nor that so and so is in our favor, nor anything like that, but just that we should fight like men: and not to tell us that he had friends in Narváez's camp was a sign that he was a very prudent captain, so that we would fight harder because we had no hope in anyone except, after God, our own great valor.] (*HV*, 262, chap. 122)

In his summary description following the account of Cortés's death, for example, Bernal Díaz emphasizes what could be observed or inferred from Cortés's conduct: "No era nada regalado ni se le daba nada por comer manjares delicados" ("He was not at all fancy nor used to eating elaborate dishes"), "Era muy afable con todos nuestros capitanes y compañeros" ("He was very affable with all of our captains and companions"), "Cuando estaba muy enojado se le hinchaba una vena de la garganta y otra de la frente" ("When he was very angry one vein would swell on his throat and another on his forehead"); and he is careful to distinguish this sort of direct observation from others he has heard secondhand: "Oí decir que cuando mancebo . . . fue algo travieso con las mujeres" ("I heard tell that in his youth . . . he was a bit dissolute with women"), "Oí decir que era bachiller en leyes" ("I heard tell that he had a bachelor's degree in law") (*HV*, 622, chap. 204). In commenting on Cortés's testament, for example, he writes: "No lo sé bien, mas tengo en mí que, como sabio, lo haría bien, . . . y como era viejo, que lo haría con mucha cordura y mandaría descargar su conciencia" ("I am not sure, but for myself think that, as a wise man, he would do it well, and because he was old, that he would do it with prudence and to have a clear conscience") (*HV,* 621). In general, he limits himself to the sort of observations that can reasonably be inferred about those one spends time with, that is, the sorts of observations that a historian can legitimately record about real people. In places, however, he does hint at psychological insights in other ways. An important passage in this regard appears in chapter 54, where he describes how, at the time Cortés sent his first *relación* to the emperor, the *cabildo* of soldiers who supported the renegade captain sent a separate letter to the king. Bernal Díaz describes the encounter that followed:

> Nos rogó que se la mostrásemos, y como vio la relación tan ver-dadera y los grandes loores que dél dábamos, hubo mucho placer y dijo que nos lo tenía en merced, con grandes ofrecimientos que nos hizo; empero no quisiera que dijéramos en ella ni mentáramos del quinto del oro que le prometimos, ni que declaráramos quiénes fueron los primeros descubridores; porque, según entendimos, no hacía en su carta relación de Francisco Hernández de Córdoba ni del Grijalva, sino a él sólo se atribuía el descubrimiento y la honra y honor de todo . . . y no faltó quien le dijo que a nuestro rey y señor no se le ha dejar de decir todo lo que pasa.

> [He begged us that we show it to him, and when he saw the account to be so true and full of the praise that we gave him, he was very pleased and said that he was grateful to us and offered us great gifts. But he did not want us to tell about the fifth of the gold that we promised him, nor that we should declare who were the first conquistadors, because, as we understood, he did not mention Francisco Hernández de Córdoba or Grijalva in his letter, but instead attributed to himself alone the discovery and the honor and the glory. . . . And there were those who told him that one must not refrain from telling our king and lord everything that happens.] (*HV,* 103–4, chap. 54)

Bernal Díaz returns to the topic of Cortés's apparent omissions and distortions in chapter 205, in which he lists the "valorous" captains and soldiers who participated in the conquest whom, he writes, received only belated recognition by the *marqués,* recognition that came far too late to be translated into tangible rewards from the emperor: "E quedábamos en blanco hasta ya a la postre" ("And we were left empty-handed until the very end") (*HV,* 626, chap. 205). As in the lies of Montezuma to his followers, which Bernal Díaz portrays as a self-interested attempt on the part of the prince to survive the political upheaval brought on by the Castilians in Mexico—one that would cost him the sovereignty of an empire—Cortés's failure to fully disclose the "truth" here likewise reveals a weakness in character, an evident gap between the remarkable qualities that enable him to both manipulate and lead and the personal ambition that induces him to forget those who helped him succeed.

Treatment of the Historical Tradition

The element of perspectivism, or the use of multiple perspectives, that Bernal Díaz achieves in parts of the *Historia verdadera* is perhaps related to other divide-and-conquer techniques in his work, most specifically to his stance vis-à-vis the historical tradition. Indeed, one point on which both Fernández de Oviedo and Las Casas largely concur has to do with their representation of the vast majority of foot soldiers of the conquest as a brutal, greedy lot, driven by their desire for gold. Even Francisco López de Gómara, whose *Historia de la Conquista de México* (Zaragosa, 1552) is generally more favorable to the conquest project, depicts the illusions of the common conquerors with biting irony. While Bernal Díaz's direct criticisms of López de Gómara are a patent and often-commented-upon aspect of his work, one topic that has received less attention is the indirect manner in which he addresses the historical tradition as it reveals itself in the account of Cortés's chaplain. In this regard, it is worthwhile to briefly compare a few key passages so as to point to one aspect in which the old *encomendero* takes issue, not so much with his rival's failure to fairly apportion the "glory" of the conquest, but with his clear suggestions that many of the soldiers in Cortés's company bordered on the witless. In a passage that merits quoting at length, from "El recibimiento que hicieron a Cortés en Cempoallan" (chapter 32), for example, Gómara emphasizes the meeting of Old- and New-World peoples as one of profound misperceptions:

> Salieron de la ciudad muchos hombres y mujeres, como en recibimiento, a ver aquellos nuevos y más que hombres. Y dábanles con alegre semblante muchas flores y muchas frutas muy diversas de las que los nuestros conocían; y aun entraban sin miedo entre la ordenanza del escuadrón; y de esta manera, y con regocijo y fiesta,

entraron en la ciudad, que todo era un vergel, y con tan grandes y altos árboles, que apenas se parecían las casas. A la puerta salieron muchas personas de lustre, a manera de cabildo, a los recebir, hablar y ofrecer. Seis españoles de caballo, que iban adelante un buen pedazo, como descubridores, tornaron atrás muy maravillados, ya que el escuadrón entraba por la puerta de la ciudad, y dijeron a Cortés que habían visto un patio de una gran casa chapado todo de plata. El les mandó volver, y que no hiciesen muestra ni milagros por ello, ni de cosa que viesen. Toda la calle por donde iban estaba llena de gente, abobada de ver caballos, tiros y hombres tan extraños. Pasando por una muy gran plaza, vieron a mano derecha un gran cercado de cal y canto, con sus almenas, y muy blanqueado de yeso de espejuela y muy bien bruñido; que con el sol relucía mucho y parecía plata; y esto era lo que aquellos españoles pensaron que era plata chapada por las paredes. Creo que con la imaginación que llevaban y buenos deseos, todo se les antojaba plata y oro lo que relucía.

[Many men and women went out from the city as if in welcome, to see those new and larger-than-life men. And with happy countenance they gave them many flowers and many fruits that were different from the ones known by our men: and at this time they still mixed with the squadron without fear. And in this way, with rejoicing and festivity, they entered the city, which was all a garden, and with such great and tall trees that the houses could barely be seen. At the gate, many illustrious persons came out, in the manner of a council, to receive them, speak, and make offerings. Six Spaniards on horseback, who had gone a bit ahead, like discoverers, turned back astonished, now that the squadron was entering through the city gate, and told Cortés that they had seen the patio of a great house that was all covered with silver. He ordered them to go back and not to make a fuss over that or anything else they saw. The whole street through which they passed was full of people, who were dumbfounded at the sight of such strange horses, weapons, and men. As they passed by a very grand plaza, they saw to their right a strong fenced-in area with parapets, and very white from plaster, and very well finished, that, with the sun, shined very much and looked like silver; and this is what those Spaniards thought was silver plate on the walls. I think that with the imagination and good wishes that they had, they fancied everything that shone to be silver and gold.][48]

This grandiose entry into Cempoal, in which López de Gómara accentuates the superior strength of the conquering force (and the naive welcoming of a pacific people), is undercut in his account by the Castilian vanguard's mistaking of whitewash on the walls of a house for silver. The mistaken impression has a parallel in what Gómara describes as the bewildered gaze of the natives. Bernal Díaz, while preserving some descriptive elements (the town was "hecho un verjel" and crowded with onlookers), decisively counteracts the notion of the Spanish soldiers as somehow suffering from collective delusion:

> Nuestros corredores del campo, que iban a caballo, parece ser llega-
> ron a la gran plaza y patios donde estaban los aposentos, y de pocos
> días, según pareció, teníanlos muy encalados y relucientes, que lo
> saben muy bien hacer, y pareció al uno de los que iba a caballo
> que era aquello blanco que relucía plata, y vuelve a rienda suelta a
> decir a Cortés cómo tenían las paredes de plata. Y doña Marina e
> Aguilar dijeron que sería yeso o cal, y tuvimos bien que reír de su
> plata y frenesí.

> [Our scouts, who were on horseback, seem to have arrived at the
> great plaza and patios where the rooms were, and which had appar-
> ently been whitewashed recently, which they know how to do
> well, and it seemed to one of these horsemen that the white color
> shined like silver, and he turned around swiftly to tell Cortés that
> the walls were of silver. And Doña Marina and Aguilar said that
> that must be plaster or whitewash, and we had a good laugh about
> their silver and frenzy.] (*HV*, 85–86, chap. 45)

As in his deflation of Gómara's report of the appearance of Saints James and Peter on the battlefield, Bernal Díaz carefully counters the image of the conquerors as blinded by the frenzy for riches. The joke, here, is on a single soldier, and the mistaken judgment corrected by the interpreters as soon as it is uttered.

48. López de Gómara, *Historia*, 56–57.

Gómara develops the theme of misplaced illusions in chapter 110, "How Cortés Fled Mexico," where he expands on some of the tragic consequences of the Castilians' stubborn preoccupation with riches. In recounting the panicked flight of Cortés's troops from the Aztec capital, Gómara writes:

> Si esta cosa fuera de día, por ventura no murieran tantos ni hubiera tanto ruido; mas, como pasó de noche oscura y con niebla, fue de muchos gritos, llantos, alaridos y espanto, que los indios, como vencedores, voceaban victoria, invocaban sus dioses, ultrajaban los caídos y mataban los que en pie se defendían. Los nuestros, como vencidos, maldecían su desastrada suerte, la hora y quién allí los trajo. Unos llamaban a Dios, otros a santa María, otros decían: "Ayuda, ayuda; que me ahogo." No sabría decir si murieron tantos en agua como en tierra, por querer echarse a nado o saltar las quebradas y ojos de la calzada, y porque los arrojaban a ella los indios, no pudiendo apear con ellos de otra manera; y dicen que en cayendo el español en agua, era con él el indio, y como nadan bien, los llevaban a las barcas y donde querían, o los desbarrigaban. También andaban muchos *acalles* a raíz de la calzada, que se derribaban unos a otros en agua y a tierra; y así, ellos se hicieron a sí mismos más daño que los nuestros, y si no se detuvieran en despojar los españoles caídos, pocos o ninguno dejaran vivos. De los nuestros tanto más morían, cuanto más cargados iban de ropa y de oro y de joyas, porque no se salvaron sino los que menos oro llevaban y los que fueron delante o sin miedo; por manera que los mató el oro y murieron ricos.

> [Had this happened in daylight, perhaps not so many would have died nor would there have been so much noise; but since it happened in the dark of a foggy night, there was great shouting, cries, howls, and fear. The Indians, as winners, shouted victory, invoked their gods, committed outrages on the fallen, and killed those who still defended themselves on foot. Our soldiers, as the defeated, cursed their disastrous luck, the hour, and he who had brought them there. Some called to God, others to Saint Mary, others said: "Help, help; I am drowning." I could not say whether as many died on land as in the water, for trying to swim away or to jump over the streams and bays of the causeways. Unable to bring them down any other way, the Indians threw them into the water, and

they say that in falling into the water, the Spaniard went down
with the Indian, and since the latter are good swimmers, they
took the Spaniards to the boats or wherever they wanted, or they
ripped open their bellies. Many *acalles* were also walking close to
the causeway and they knocked each other down both on land and
in the water, and so, they did more damage to themselves than our
men did to them, and if they had not stopped to despoil the fallen,
few or none of the Spaniards would have been left. In terms of our
men, the more they were loaded down with clothing and jewels,
the more of them died. The only ones who saved themselves were
those who carried the least gold and those who went ahead or
without fear, so that one could say that they were killed by gold
and died rich.][49]

Within Gómara's masterful representation of this terrifying scene, with its
cacophony of voices, I would like just to emphasize a particularly vivid
instance of his ironic depiction of the Castilian soldiers as not just deluded
but ultimately destroyed by their blind greed for riches.

Bernal Díaz chips away, constantly, if indirectly, at this negative image
common to the other accounts, freely admitting that the desire for wealth
was a powerful motivation, while at the same time quoting the resentment
of foot soldiers at the barely concealed looting of Montezuma's treasure by
Cortés and others.[50] At the same time, he also highlights moments when
his own modest concern for holding on to a bit of treasure was crucial to
his survival. After the flight from Tenochtitlán, for example, he tells us
that his own small store of gold saved him from death and starvation by
enabling him to purchase assistance from the indigenous allies: "Si no se lo
pagábamos con algunas piecezuelas de oro y chalchihuites que llevábamos
algunos de nosotros, no nos lo daban de balde" ("If we had not paid for it
with a few tiny pieces of gold and chalchihuites that a few of us carried,
they would not have given it for free") (*HV,* 290, chap. 128). Later, it is
Cortés's gifts of money, jewels, and lavish entertainment that finally obtain
royal payment and recognition for the captain. Once again, his account
does not refute Gómara's version outright, but incorporates the negative
image of conquistadors by attributing it instead to Narváez's men. Indeed,
within the collective homage that Bernal Díaz pays to the common soldiers

49. Ibid., 174.
50. See in particular the discourse of Cárdenas to this effect, *HV,* 226–27, chap. 105.

who made possible the conquest, and in his view, subsequent benefits for the social fabric of New Spain, Narváez's men are initially singled out to be as ignominious and destructive as those portrayed by, say, Las Casas. They are greedy and violent, stealing from Cortés's camp and alienating the hard-won alliances. Narváez's crew carries the smallpox infection that would decimate the indigenous population, and much like Gómara's deluded riders, they are at a loss to decipher the realities of this new land, mistaking, for example, fireflies for the tinder (*mechas*) of firearms. Bernal Díaz's tacit refutation of the larger picture contrasts with his direct criticisms of Gómara, which, as Iglesia and Lewis have shown, are often either unfair or focus on seemingly irrelevant details in the narrative.[51] The careful consideration of the historical record that one senses in these passages is similar to that one finds in episodes such as that of Cholula,[52] wherein there are clear signs that Bernal Díaz's work is in many ways conditioned by the texts on which he bases his history and to which he responds.

Enrique Pupo-Walker once observed that the *Historia verdadera* is a complex work that is "nutrida de otras lecturas y en [la] que se destacan episodios de singular amplitud imaginativa" ("nourished by other readings and in which a few episodes of particularly imaginative amplitude stand out").[53] On the one hand, one finds in parts of the *Historia verdadera* what appears to be a careful consideration of the historical record, that is, not just an imaginative reconstruction or an effort to address pragmatic concerns or legal battles, but clear signs of a mindful exploitation of the narrative configurations contained in prior historical accounts, and a narrative that in many ways exhibits traits that adhere to the logic of writing history. On the other, one finds the sort of fascinating (and problematic, for historiographical discourse) audacities that Bernal Díaz takes in narrative perspective and the treatment of some of his historical actors. Although parts of the *Historia verdadera* can be read as constructing a world that seems imaginary at times because of Bernal Díaz's re-creation of past events as present, the importance of the work lies in that it captures the author's lived experience. While the reader does not

51. See Iglesia, who suggests in "Las críticas de Bernal Díaz del Castillo" (35) that, contrary to the old *encomendero's* claims, "Gómara no sólo estimuló a Bernal Díaz sino que le sirvió de pauta en su relato"; and Lewis, "Retórica y verdad" (47), who finds Bernal Díaz's criticisms and characterization of Gómara's account to be unfair.

52. On this episode, see Marcus, "La conquête de Cholula"; Adorno, "Discourses"; and Beckjord, "Con sal y ají."

53. Pupo-Walker, "Creatividad," 33.

grant the author absolute credibility concerning his version of the conquest, the historicity of the events broadly defined is essential to the significance of his text. The *Historia verdadera* is truly a work of historiographical art, one that exhibits properties of history as well as the telltale transgressions of memory.

CONCLUSIONS

THE REFLECTIONS CONCERNING the relationship between language and truth in history in the context of empire neither began nor ended with the early Spanish chroniclers of America. One could trace the intellectual lineage of this topic as far back as Thucydides, who links the imperial power struggles of Athens to a breakdown in language and, ultimately, to a tragic collapse of law and order. Or, in the more immediate Iberian context, one could look to Antonio de Nebrija, who, in his prologue to the first grammar of the Castilian language, *Gramática de la lengua,* famously wrote that language has always been the "companion" of empire. Great powers begin, grow, and flourish together with their respective languages, he explains, and together they will inevitably become corrupted and fall. At the time Nebrija published his *Gramática* in 1492, he was unaware of Columbus's discoveries to the west. Yet, in congratulating the Catholic queen on her recent military successes and consolidation of power in the Iberian Peninsula, he impresses upon her the need to have her own deeds recorded in Castilian, so that the memory of her reign will be preserved in a native "home" and not be left to wander at the mercy of the tongues of foreigners.[1]

While the discussions on the writing of history that emerged in the context of the Spanish colonial expansion into New World territories can be understood to a great extent as a response to the pressures of empire on questions of language and discourse in the tradition of Thucydides and Nebrija, they still resonate today on many levels. The humanists were deeply concerned with issues of style in historical writing, in part because of the connection they perceived between narrative and the social or pedagogical functions of history. In the rhetorical treatises of Vives we find a consideration of historical writing in the context of a broader program of teaching aimed at preparing students and citizens for the considerable challenges of his times. At the core of his treatment is the concern for keeping history

---

1. Nebrija, "Prólogo," 97–101.

alive and meaningful by adopting if necessary the techniques of fiction to present the "truth" about the past as if perceived. Epistemological questions related to the concepts of verisimilitude and probability such as those brought up by Vives were put to the test in the early historiography of the Indies, which was written in an atmosphere of extreme political, moral, and religious controversy. The intellectual challenges posed by the crisis in humanistic thinking on the writing of history, the pressures of representing New World cultures and events according to Old World standards, and the moral controversies spawned by Spain's imperial expansion brought new exigencies as well as insights into old debates. Charges of what today we might call "spin" abounded on all sides, and in critiquing the humanist rhetorical model for history, Fernández de Oviedo, Las Casas, and Díaz del Castillo all sought ingenious ways of countering opposing views while at the same time arguing for their own credibility.

Gonzalo Fernández de Oviedo inscribes his *Historia general y natural* both within, and in contrast to, the humanist tradition, and undertakes in particular a critique of the notion of the reliable historian as a distant sage. Those who have no experience in the New World employ an unnatural narrative point of view that Oviedo equates with fraudulent invention or superstitious practices. In general, he highlights the limitations of his own vision and, by extension, that of any historian in chronicling events not witnessed. In asserting the importance of experience as well as erudition, he arrives at the insight that reliability in historiography is connected to narrative perspective. His stated refusal to mix his own words or point of view with those of the figures he seeks to represent affects the structure (or lack thereof) in his work, as well as his hesitant portrayal of historical actors and the ambiguous notion of exemplarity in his work. If the historian's authority is necessarily constrained to his natural range of vision, then he operates under considerable restrictions concerning what he can or cannot know and assert about the individuals and events he represents. At the same time, Oviedo engages different historiographical traditions within his voluminous history, combining multiple styles and also at times adopting imaginative ways of putting forth his own authorial views on events he has not seen directly.

Like Oviedo, Bartolomé de Las Casas takes an adversarial approach toward the existing historiographical tradition and, like the *cronista real,* arrives at productive insights through his otherwise bitter polemics. Amid the strident criticisms that Las Casas wages at his rivals, one senses an effort to gain lexical precision and to separate the material of "myth" from that of "history." Unlike merely entertaining "fictions," he further suggests, "lies" in history belong to a more insidious sort of deception, and hint at a discrepancy between external utterance and inner belief. Las Casas indeed devotes much of his history to exposing the "heresies" of his rivals, and in this accusatory mode he presents himself as able to detect through textual evidence the inner betrayals of others. In keeping with his goal of writing an orthodox version of New World history, he presents his narrating self as a sort of inquisitor-sage who is able to decipher a divine plan. At the same time, however, his prophetic vision vis-à-vis historical developments and the actions of others coexists with an often restricted view of his own role in events, as evidenced by his curious use of multiple pronouns to refer to himself as a participant. The wildly varying range of what Las Casas as historian and as actor can perceive in the *Historia de las Indias* lends his work a peculiar shape and indicates that narrative reliability works in different ways in historical as opposed to fictional texts. Were the *Historia de las Indias* a work of fiction, one might interpret such disparate self-presentations as a sign of narrative unreliability. However, in this case, the multiple versions of the self all refer to the author. As in all historical texts, the credibility of the account is measured not just by internal evidence but also by factors completely external to the text—such as the preexisting historiographical tradition and the way in which the historian's evidence is proven against subsequent historical events and developments. Thus, while one can wonder at Las Casas's multiple textual presences, few today would dispute the general validity of his polemical critique of empire and its catastrophic impact on indigenous peoples.

Last but not least, the *Historia verdadera* of Bernal Díaz del Castillo, although written at the margins of the humanist historiographical debates, presents similar narrative dilemmas. To a far greater degree than the histories of Oviedo or Las Casas, the *Historia verdadera* emits ambiguous signals as to its own discursive character, and here the techniques of narratology make it possible to describe textual codes that have enabled his work to so readily be read as "novelistic." At the same time, one finds that, for the most part, his treatment of character and his concern for addressing the narrative configurations of the existing historical tradition give evidence of a complex and properly historiographical project.

Given that the greater part of Oviedo's and Las Casas's histories were not published until the nineteenth century, one might well ask whether their debates on the writing of history had an impact upon their contemporaries or whether they simply gathered dust in the archives. The dilemma of whether the historian should adopt a limited or far-reaching point of view reappears in a number of subsequent early modern Spanish works. A notable treatment of the problem can be found in the work of Luis Cabrera de Córdoba (1559–1623), whose treatise *De la historia: Para entenderla y escribirla* (1611) I quoted at the beginning of Chapter 1. His discussion of the writing of history is striking for the way in which it recasts the traditions concerning the chronicler of history as an inspired visionary, while at the same time categorically distinguishing between works of history and fiction. Although Cabrera frames his discussion of history in Aristotelian terms—eschewing any mention of the Spanish historians of the Indies, whose books were for the most part banned during Philip II's reign—one finds that insights similar to those of Oviedo and Las Casas survive in his work alongside the more traditional humanistic *topoi*. He draws both on Vives's treatment and on the other major sixteenth-century rhetorical discussion of history in the Spanish context, namely, Sebastián Fox Morcillo's *De Historiae Institutione Dialogus* (1557), but departs from them by starkly distinguishing historical writing from poetic fiction. He notes that, unlike works of fiction, in which the order or sequence of events is clear because the actions are fulfilled within the text, in historical narratives, very basic questions concerning cause and effect are often in doubt and cannot necessarily be determined by the historian with accuracy. More often than not, disruptions in "natural" temporal order may not be apparent within the text itself, but must be identified through comparative analysis with other texts (in which the actions may lack direct causal connections) or against a horizon ("nature" or "reality") that is far more vast and elusive. Thus problems of order are far more difficult to resolve in historical than in fictional texts simply because they are less likely to be part of a clearly elaborated artistic design.

Cabrera further argues that, unlike poetic fictions, historiography must stick to real events and to the words and deeds of actual people, and notes that the depiction of individuals in the two kinds of narrative would seem to obey different rules. The historian need not (and, indeed, cannot) comply with Aristotle's notion that the depiction of fictive characters should be "consistent and the same throughout."[2] In portraying individuals, Cabrera suggests, the historian lacks the knowledge or understanding possessed by the writer of imaginative works concerning his creations and necessarily must derive his vision of the (real) figures he treats from incomplete or contradictory data: "El historiador, como halla los hombres los establece, o varía, mudables, o constantes, buenos o malos, según los tiempos"

2. Aristotle, *Poetics*, 2327; §15.

("The historian represents men as he finds them, variable or constant, good or bad, according to the times").[3] The representation of historical figures thus lacks the artistic function within the work as a whole possessed by fictive beings. Furthermore, in commenting on Aristotle's statement that poetry deals with universal truths, and history with particular ones, Cabrera suggests that the opposite is also true. While poetry may be concerned with the particular (he cites, for example, elegies and love poems), historiography often captures the fortunes of collective groups. Finally, the moral lessons embedded within history grant it a universal quality not envisioned by Aristotle: "Su fin es enseñar universalmente a bien vivir con los exemplos . . . enseña a dezir y hazer . . . con más prudencia que dan los preceptos de los filósofos" ("[History's] goal is to teach universally how to live well by example . . . it teaches how to speak and act . . . with more prudence than can be gleaned from the precepts of the philosophers).[4] Cabrera emphasizes the social function of history, while echoing the notion of the superior status accorded history within the humanist program. Yet Cabrera amplifies this *topos* to new heights. The reading of history brings remarkable benefits to just about any reader, whether the prince, the "simply curious," or even "idiots" in need of instruction.[5] With considerable flourish, Cabrera de Córdoba exalts the discipline over all the other liberal arts: "El que la aborrece no es hombre" ("He who abhors it is not a man").[6]

At the same time, Cabrera is reluctant to relinquish the notion of the humanist historian as inspired authority. The author of a "legitimate and perfect" history must be a sage able both to glean the truth of important matters and to deliver it in a narrative package appropriate for royalty and "idiots" alike. Cabrera's portrait of the ideal writer nearly crumbles under the weight of its own hyperbole: the historian must be "erudito, elocuente, grave, entero, severo, urbano, diligente, medido, estudioso, de gran seso, bondad y justicia" ("erudite, eloquent, grave, having integrity, severe, urbane, diligent, balanced, studious, and of great intelligence, goodness, and justice").[7] Further, there is a perceptible shift from Vives's idea of objectivity as a self-evident textual property in narrative (congruent with the perceivable order in reality and with Christian values) to a focus on the figure of the historian as guarantor of the truth. There are, of course, echoes

3. Cabrera de Córdoba, *De historia*, 25–26.
4. Ibid., 25.
5. Ibid., 35.
6. Ibid., 40.
7. Ibid., 30–31.

of Vives's humanist sage here, but Cabrera (who envisions a court historian, chosen by and dependent upon the prince) aspires less to a self-evidently objective record of the facts than to a clear conscience on the part of the author regarding his account. Cabrera again marks an important distinction from Vives's treatment: historical discourse represents not a mirror image of reality, but rather the historian's view of events.

Despite his praise for history as the supreme discipline, Cabrera nonetheless recognizes that a "perfect" and "legitimate" work is difficult to capture in practice, simply because the author must rely on the narratives of others. The historian faces a dilemma in terms of defining the scope of his work: the eyewitness's limited vision, for Cabrera, jeopardizes history's unique claim to truth. The distant stance of the *sabio* is a measure of his independence from partial views and, thus, of his reliability. And yet, by treating a subject beyond his experience, the historian faces challenges in terms of epistemology because he must rely on the works of others and often guess at the credibility in differing accounts on the basis of probability. Where Vives's ideal of history breaks down on the slippery slope of language, in Cabrera's treatise it is the irreducibility of compelling and contradictory accounts that stumps even the best-trained sage.

One suspects that the debates over the range of the historian's vision that appear in the early historiography of the Indies and are resurrected in Cabrera's treatise were not lost on Miguel de Cervantes. The figure of the fictional historian in part 2 of the *Quijote* as a "sabio encantador" (wise enchanter) in many ways reflects a playful and ironic rendering of the humanist discussions of the writing of history I have been outlining here. The specter of the historian as wise sage also survives in the treatise of Jerónimo de San José, *Genio de la historia* (1651). San José reconstructs the inquirer as a prophet, who like a latter-day Ezequiel, gathers together scattered and forgotten fragments, conjuring up and molding them into a narrative "body" before finally "breathing" life into the text with vivid detail.[8]

If—as San José's discussion of the writing of history suggests—the insights of Oviedo and Las Casas had already become obscured by the mid-seventeenth century in Spain, they are surprisingly relevant to recent theoretical discussions. For theorists such as Martínez Bonati, Rigney, Cohn, and Genette, the concepts of narrative voice and perspective are critical for distinguishing between historical and fictive narrative. The fact that the historian narrates in a voice assumed to be his or her own

8. San José, *Genio de la historia*, 360.

has important logical consequences, making the phenomenon of narrative perspective in history much less flexible than in works of fiction. As a textual analog of the author, the historical narrator tells his tale under notable restrictions and is limited to the sorts of perceptions that mortal minds are able to see and understand about those around them. At the same time, one is struck by the often multifaceted quality of the historical narrator, whose voice frequently reflects a variety of (at times incompatible) roles (participant, retrospective commentator, judge of the testimonies of others). When adopting the narrative perspective of another "character" or agent in the events he or she recounts, the writer of history faces epistemological questions that would be largely irrelevant in a work of fiction. The necessarily restricted stance of the narrator of history brings up distinctive challenges in the portrayal of individual figures and groups in history. Further, the social function of historical narrative may explain its tendency to exploit commonplaces as a way of both manipulating the historical tradition and of establishing a competing claim to credibility.

Finally, recent events remind us that the inquiry into problems of language and truth in history remains pertinent in our own times. As one ponders the consequences of the U.S. invasion of Iraq, one is reminded that questions of evidence and truth in public discourse are far from settled in the context of twenty-first-century imperialism. In this regard, it might be well to recall the link that sixteenth-century Spanish humanists made in their discussions of history between issues of style and pedagogy. Although one suspects that the proposals for a return to the "rhetorical" study of history of the 1970s put forth by cultural critics such as Hayden White may well have been intended to signal the dangers of ideological misuses of history, one might question the premises of an approach that teaches that the narrative or ideological aspects of history are just like those of "fiction." Perhaps a better way to guard against the excesses of ideology and "spin" in public discourse is to not to ignore boundaries between historical and fictional discourse, but rather to attempt to better understand, distinguish, and qualify the sorts of imagination that legitimately can go into the writing of history.

BIBLIOGRAPHY

Abellán, José Luis. *El erasmismo español.* 1976. Reprint, Madrid: Austral, 1982.

Adorno, Rolena. "Censorship and Its Evasion: Jerónimo Román and Bartolomé de las Casas." *Hispania* 75, no. 4 (1992): 812–27.

———. "Discourses on Colonialism: Bernal Díaz, Las Casas, and the Twentieth-Century Reader." *MLN* 103, no. 2 (1988): 239–58.

———. "The Discursive Encounter of Spain and America: The Authority of Eyewitness Testimony in the Writing of History." *William and Mary Quarterly* 3rd ser., 49 (April 1992): 210–28.

———. *The Intellectual Life of Bartolomé de Las Casas.* New Orleans: Graduate School of Tulane University, 1992.

———. "Introduction." In *The Books of the Brave, Being an Account of Books and of Men in the Spanish Conquest and Settlement of the Sixteenth-Century New World,* by Irving Leonard, ix–xl. Berkeley: University of California Press, 1992.

———. "Literary Production and Suppression: Reading and Writing about Amerindians in Colonial Spanish America." *Dispositio* 11, nos. 28–29 (1986): 1–25.

Álvarez López, Enrique. "La historia natural en Fernández de Oviedo." *Revista de Indias* 17, nos. 69–70 (1957): 541–601.

Arendt, Hannah. "The Concept of History." In *Between Past and Future,* 41–90. New York: Penguin, 1977.

Arias, Santa. "Autoescritura y ejemplaridad en la escritura de la historia de Bartolomé de las Casas." *Texto crítico* 16, nos. 42–43 (1990): 5–20.

———. "Empowerment Through the Writing of History: Bartolomé de las Casas's Representation of the Other(s)." In *Early Images of the Americas: Transfer and Invention,* edited by J. M. Williams and R. E. Lewis, 163–79. Tucson: University of Arizona Press, 1993.

———. "La *Historia de las Indias* de Bartolomé de las Casas: Estrategias de poder y persuasión." *Confluencia: Revista Hispánica de cultura y literatura* 7, no. 1 (1991): 31–42.

———. "Retórica e ideología en la *Historia de Indias* de Bartolomé de las Casas." Ph.D. diss., University of Wisconsin, Madison, 1990.

———. *Retórica, historia y polémica: Bartolomé de las Casas y la tradición intelectual renacentista.* Lanham, Md.: University Press of America, 2001.

Aristotle. "Poetics." Translated by I. Bywater. In *The Complete Works of Aristotle,* edited by J. Barnes. Vol. 2, 2316–40. Princeton: Princeton University Press, 1984.

Asensio, Eugenio. "El erasmismo y las corrientes espirituales afines: Conversos, franciscanos, italianizantes." *Revista de Filología Española* 36 (1952): 31–99.

Augustine. *City of God.* Translated by Gerald G. Walsh et al. New York: Doubleday, 1958.

Avalle-Arce, Juan Bautista. "Las hipérboles del padre Las Casas." *Revista de la facultad de humanidades* 2, no. 1 (1960): 33–55.

———. "Introducción." In *Memorias de Gonzalo Fernández de Oviedo,* edited by Juan Bautista Avalle-Arce. Selections from *Quincuágenas.* North Carolina Studies in the Romance Languages and Literatures. Vol. 1, 9–15. Chapel Hill: University of North Carolina Department of Romance Languages, 1974.

Ballesteros Gaibrois, Manuel. "Fernández de Oviedo, etnólogo." *Revista de Indias* 17, no. 69–70 (1957): 445–67.

———. *Gonzalo Fernández de Oviedo.* Madrid: Fundación Universitaria, 1981.

Barnes, Harry E. *A History of Historical Writing.* Norman: University of Oklahoma Press, 1937.

Bataillon, Marcel. *Érasme et L'Espagne.* New ed. 3 vols. Edited by Daniel Devoto. Vol. 1. Paris: Droz, 1991.

———. *Estudios sobre Bartolomé de las Casas.* Barcelona: Peninsula, 1965.

———. "Historiografía oficial de Colón de Pedro Mártir a Oviedo y Gómara." *Imago Mundi* 1, no. 5 (1954): 23–39.

———. Review of Millares' edition of *Historia de las Indias. Bulletin Hispanique* 54, no. 2 (1952): 215–21.

Bataillon, Marcel, and O'Gorman, Edmundo. *Dos concepciones de la tarea historiográfica con motivo de la idea del "descubrimiento de América."* Mexico City: Imprenta universitaria, 1955.

Beckjord, Sarah H. "Con sal y ají y tomates: Las redes textuales de Bernal Díaz en el caso de Cholula." *Revista iberoamericana* 61, nos. 170–71 (1995): 147–60.

Bellos, David. "The Narrative Absolute Tense." *Language and Style* 13, no. 1 (1980): 77–84.

Bénat-Tachot, Louise. "Entrevue avec le cacique Agateite: Un temps fort de l'etnographie dans la *Historia general y natural de las Indias* de Gonzalo Fernández de Oviedo." In *Relations entre identités culturelles dans l'espace iberique et inbero-américain.* Vol. 2. *Elites et masses,* edited by Augustin Redondo. Paris: Presses de la Sorbonne Nouvelle, 1997.

———. "El relato corto en la *Historia General y Natural* de Gonzalo Fernández de Oviedo." In *La formación de la cultural virreinal,* edited by Karl Kohut and Sonia Rose. Vol. 1, 103–23. Madrid: Iberoamericana, 2000.

Black, Robert. "The New Laws of History." *Renaissance Studies* 1, no. 1 (1987): 126–56.

Bonilla, Adolfo. *Luis Vives y la filosofía del renacimiento.* 3 vols. Madrid: L. Rubio, 1929.

Bolaños, Álvaro Félix. "La crónica de Indias de Fernández de Oviedo: ¿Historia de lo general y natural, u obra didáctica?" *Revista de Estudios Hispánicos* 25, no. 3 (1991): 15–33.

———. "The Historian and the Hesperides: Fernández de Oviedo and the Limitations of Imitation." *Bulletin of Hispanic Studies* 72, no. 3. (1995): 273–88.

———. "El líder ideal en el libro de caballerías y la crónica de indias de Gonzalo Fernández de Oviedo." Ph.D. diss., University of Kentucky, 1988.

———. "Milagro, Peregrinación y Paraíso: Narración de naufragios del cronista Fernández de Oviedo." *Revista de estudios hispánicos* (Río Piedras) 9 (1992): 163–78.

———. "Panegírico y libel del primer cronista de Indias Gonzalo Fernández de Oviedo." *Thesaurus* 45, no. 3 (1990): 577–649.

———. "El primer cronista de Indias frente al 'mare magno' de la crítica." *Cuadernos Americanos* 4, no. 2 (1990): 42–61.

Boruchoff, David. "The Poetry of History." *Colonial Latin American Review* 13, no. 2 (December 2004): 275–82.

Brading, D. A. *The First America: The Spanish Monarchy, Creole Patriots, and the Liberal State, 1492–1867*. Cambridge: Cambridge University Press, 1991.

———. "The Two Cities: St. Augustine and the Spanish Conquest of America." *Revista portuguesa de filosofía* 44, no. 1 (1988): 99–126.

Brody, Robert. "Bernal's Strategies." *Hispanic Review* 55, no. 3 (1987): 323–36.

Cabrera de Córdoba, Luis. *De historia: Para entenderla y escribirla*. 1611. Edited with a preliminary study by Santiago Montero Díaz. Madrid: Instituto de Estudios Políticos, 1948.

Caillet-Bois, Julio. "Bernal Díaz del Castillo, o de la Verdad en la Historia." *Revista iberoamericana* 25 (1960): 199–228.

Campbell, Mary B. *The Witness and the Other World: Exotic European Travel Writing, 400–1600*. Ithaca: Cornell University Press, 1988.

Campion, Nicholas. *The Great Year: Astrology, Millenarism and History in the Western Tradition*. London: Penguin, 1994.

Cañizares Esguerra, Jorge. *How to Write the History of the New World: Histories, Epistemologies, and Identities in the Eighteenth-Century Atlantic World*. Stanford: Stanford University Press, 2001.

Carbia, Rómulo. *La crónica oficial de las indias occidentales: Estudio histórico y crítico acerca de la historiografía mayor de Hispanoamérica en los siglos XVI a XVIII*. La Plata: Biblioteca Humanidades, 1934.

Carilla, Jesús, ed. *Oviedo on Columbus*. Translated by Diana Avalle-Arce. Preface by Anthony Pagden. Turhout, Belgium: Brepols, 2000.

Caro Baroja, Julio. *Inquisición, brujería y criptojudaismo*. 3rd ed. Barcelona: Ariel, 1974.

Carruthers, Mary. *The Book of Memory*. Cambridge: Cambridge University Press, 1990.

Cascardi, Anthony J. "Chronicle Toward Novel: Bernal Díaz' History of the Conquest of Mexico." *Novel: A Forum on Fiction* 15, no. 3 (1982): 197–212.

Castillero, R. Ernesto J. "Gonzalo Fernández de Oviedo y Valdés, veedor de Tierra Firme." *Revista de Indias* 17, nos. 69–70 (1957): 521–40.

Certeau, Michel de. "L'histoire, science et fiction." In *La philosophie de l'Histoire et la pratique historienne d'aujourd'hui*, edited by D. Carr et al., 19–39. Ottawa: University of Ottawa Press, 1982.

———. *The Writing of History*. Translated by Tom Conley. New York: Columbia University Press, 1988.

Cervantes Saavedra, Miguel de. *El ingenioso hidalgo don Quijote de la Mancha*. Edited with an introduction and notes by Luis A. Murillo. Madrid: Castalia, 1991.

Cicero. *De oratore*. Translated by E. W. Sutton. Rev. ed. Loeb Classical Library. Vol. 1. Cambridge: Harvard University Press, 1942.

Ciruelo, Pedro. *Reprovacion de las supersticiones y hechizerías*. 1538. Edited with an introduction by Alva V. Ebersole. Valencia: Albatros, 1978.

Cochrane, Eric. *Historians and Historiography in the Italian Renaissance*. Chicago: University of Chicago Press, 1981.

Cohn, Dorrit. *The Distinction of Fiction*. Baltimore: Johns Hopkins University Press, 1999.

Collard, Andrée, trans. *History of the Indies*. New York: Harper &; Row, 1971.

Colón, Cristóbal. *Textos y documentos completos*. 2nd ed. Edited with an introduction by Consuelo Varela. Madrid: Alianza, 1989.

Colón, Fernando. *Life of the Admiral Christopher Columbus by His Son, Ferdinand*. New Brunswick: Rutgers University Press, 1959.

Cortijo Ocaña, Antonio. "Creación de una voz de autoridad en Bartolomé de las Casas: Estudio del prólogo de la *Historia de las indias*." *Revista iberoamericana* 61, nos. 170–71 (1995): 219–29.

———. "Introducción." In *Teoría de la historia y teoría política en el siglo XVI. De historiae institutione dialogus*, by Sebastián Fox Morcillo. 1557. Edited and translated by Antonio Cortijo Ocaña. Alacalá: Universidad de Alcalá, 2002.

Cortínez, Verónica. "Crónica, épica y novela: La *Historia verdadera de la Conquista de la Nueva España* y 'El mundo nuevo' de *Terra nostra*." *Revista chilena de literatura* 38 (1991): 59–72.

———. *Memoria original de Bernal Díaz del Castillo*. Huixquilucan, Mexico: Oak Editorial, 2000.

———. "'Yo, Bernal Díaz del Castillo': ¿Soldado de a pie o idiota sin letras?" *Revista chilena de literatura* 41 (1993): 59–69.

Cuccorese, Juan Horacio. "Juan Luis Vives y la concepción de la historiografía integral." *Revista de la Universidad* (La Plata) 16 (1962): 109–31.

Curtius, Ernst Robert. *European Literature and the Latin Middle Ages*. Translated by W. R. Trask. Princeton: Princeton University Press, 1990.

Daston, Lorraine. "Historical Epistemology." In *Questions of Evidence: Proof, Practice, and Persuasion across the Disciplines*, edited by J. Chandler et al., 282–89. Chicago: University of Chicago Press, 1994.

———. "Marvelous Facts and Miraculous Evidence in Early Modern Europe." *Questions of Evidence: Proof, Practice, and Persuasion across the Disciplines*, edited by J. Chandler et al., 243–74. Chicago: University of Chicago Press, 1994.

Díaz del Castillo, Bernal. *Historia verdadera de la conquista de la Nueva España*. Critical edition and supplement by Carmelo Saénz de Santa María. 2 vols. Madrid: Instituto "Gonzalo Fernández de Oviedo" CSIC, 1982.

Diccionario de autoridades. 3 vols. Madrid: Gredos, 1969.

Durán, Manuel, "Bernal Díaz del Castillo: Crónica, historia, mito." *Hispania* 75, no. 4 (1992): 795–804.

Dussel, Enrique. *The Invention of the Americas: Eclipse of the "Other" and the Myth of Modernity*. Translated by Michael D. Barber. New York: Continuum, 1995.

Ebersole, Alva V. "Introducción." In *Reprovación de las supersticiones y hechizerías*, by Pedro Ciruelo. Valencia: Albatros, 1978.

Eisenberg, Daniel. *Romances of Chivalry in the Spanish Golden Age*. Newark: Juan de la Cuesta, 1982.

Elliot, J. H. *Imperial Spain 1469–1716*. 1963. Reprint, New York: Mentor, 1966.

Estudios lascasianos: IV centenario de la muerte de Fray Bartolomé de las Casas, 1566–1966. Sevilla: Universidad de Sevilla, 1966.

Fabié, Antonio. *Vida y escritos de Don Fray Bartolomé de las Casas*. 2 vols. Madrid, 1879.

Fay, Brian, et al., eds. *History and Theory: Contemporary Readings*. Oxford: Blackwell, 1998.

Feldherr, Andrew. *Spectacle and Society in Livy's History*. Berkeley: University of California Press, 1998.

Ferguson, Wallace K. *The Renaissance in Historical Thought: Five Centuries of Interpretation.* Cambridge, Mass.: Riverside Press, 1948.

Fernández de Oviedo, Gonzalo. *Historia general y natural de las Indias.* 1959. 5 vols. 2nd ed. Edited with a preliminary study by Juan Pérez de Tudela Buesa. Biblioteca de Autores Españoles. Madrid: Atlas, 1992.

——. *Historia general y natural de las Indias, islas y tierra-firme del mar océano.* 3 vols. Edited with an introduction by Amador de los Ríos. Madrid: Real Academia de la Historia, 1851–55.

——. *Las memorias de Gonzalo Fernández de Oviedo.* 2 vols. Selections from *Quincuágenas.* Edited with an introduction by Juan Bautista Avalle-Arce. North Carolina Studies in the Romance Languages and Literatures. Chapel Hill: University of North Carolina Department of Romance Languages, 1974.

——. *Sumario de la natural historia de las Indias.* Edited by M. de Ballesteros Gabrois. Madrid: Dastin, 2002.

Fernández Santamaría, José A. *Juan Luis Vives: Escepticismo y prudencia en el renacimiento.* Salamanca: Universidad de Salamanca, 1990.

Fischer, María Luisa. "Bernal Díaz del Castillo: La memoria y la representación." *Revista chilena de literatura* 44 (1994): 45–52.

Flavius, Josephus. *Sobre la antigüedad de los Judíos (Contra Apión).* Translated by J. R. Bustos Saiz. Madrid: Alianza, 1987.

Fogelquist, James D. *El Amadís y el género de la historia fingida.* Madrid: Studia Humanitatis, 1982.

Forcione, Alban K. *Cervantes and the Humanist Vision.* Princeton: Princeton University Press, 1982.

——. *Cervantes, Aristotle, and the Persiles.* Princeton: Princeton University Press, 1970.

Fox Morcillo, Sebastián. *De historiae institutione dialogus.* 1557. Edited and translated by Antonio Cortijo Ocaña. Alcalá: Universidad de Alcalá, 2002.

Frankl, Victor. *El antijovio de Gonzalo Jimenez de Quesada y las concepciones de realidad y verdad en la época de la Contrarreforma y del Manierismo.* Madrid: Ediciones Cultura Hispánica, 1963.

Friede, Juan, and Benjamin Keen, eds. *Bartolomé de las Casas in History: Toward an Understanding of the Man and the Work.* DeKalb: Northern Illinois University Press, 1971.

Fuentes, Carlos. *Valiente mundo nuevo: Epica, utopía y mito en la novela hispanoamericana.* Madrid: Mondadori, 1990.

Fueter, Eduard. *Histoire de la historiographie moderne.* Translated by Emile Jeanmarie. Paris: Libraire Félix Alcan, 1914.

Genette, Gérard. *Fiction and Diction.* Translated by Catherine Porter. Ithaca: Cornell University Press, 1993.

——. *Narrative Discourse: An Essay in Method.* Translated by Jane E. Lewin. Ithaca: Cornell University Press, 1980.

Gerbi, Antonello. *Nature in the New World: From Christopher Columbus to Gonzalo Fernández de Oviedo.* Translated by Jeremy Moyle. Pittsburgh: Pittsburgh University Press, 1985.

Gilbert, Felix. *Machiavelli and Guicciardini: Politics and History in Sixteenth-Century Florence.* Princeton: Princeton University Press, 1965.

Gilman, Stephen. "Bernal Díaz del Castillo and *Amadís de Gaula.*" In *Studia Philologica* 2 (Homenaje a Dámaso Alonso), 99–114. Madrid: Gredos, 1961.

Gilmore, Myron P. *Humanists and Jurists: Six Studies in the Renaissance.* Cambridge: Harvard University Press, 1963.

Giménez Fernández, Manuel. "Fray Bartolomé de Las Casas: A Biographical Sketch." In *Bartolomé de Las Casas in History: Toward an Understanding of the Man and His Work,* edited by Juan Friede and Benjamin Keen, 67–125. DeKalb: Northern Illinois University Press, 1971.

Ginzburg, Carlo. *History, Rhetoric, and Proof.* Hanover: University Press of New England / Brandeis University Press, 1999.

Godoy Alcántara, José. "Discurso." In *Discursos leídos en la Academia de la Historia en la recepción pública de Don José Godoy Alcántara el día 30 de enero de 1870.* Madrid: Rivadeneira, 1870.

González Echevarría, Roberto. "Humanismo, retórica y las crónicas de la conquista." In *Historia y ficción en la narrativa hispanoamericana.* Caracas: Monte Avila, 1984.

———. *Myth and Archive: A Theory of Latin American Literature.* 1990. Reprint, Durham: Duke University Press, 1998.

Greenblatt, Stephen. *Marvelous Possessions: The Wonder of the New World.* Chicago: University of Chicago Press, 1991.

Hamburger, Käte. *The Logic of Literature.* 1973. 2nd, rev. ed. Translated by Marilynn J. Rose. Bloomington: Indiana University Press, 1993.

Hampton, Timothy. *Writing from History: The Rhetoric of Exemplarity in Renaissance Literature.* Ithaca: Cornell University Press, 1990.

Hanke, Lewis. *All Mankind Is One.* DeKalb: Northern Illinois University Press, 1974.

———. "Bartolomé de Las Casas, historiador." Preliminary study in *Historia de las Indias,* by Bartolomé de Las Casas, edited by A. Millares Carlo. Mexico City: Fondo de Cultura Económica, 1951.

———. *Bartolomé de Las Casas: Pensador político, historiador, antropólogo.* La Habana: Sociedad de Amigos del País, 1949.

Hay, Denys. *Annalists and Historians: Western Historiography from the VIIIth to the XVIIIth Century.* London: Methuen, 1977.

Henríquez Ureña, Pedro. *Las corrientes literarias en la américa hispánica.* 1945. Reprint, Mexico City: Fondo de Cultura Económica, 1994.

Herbermann et al., eds. *The Catholic Encyclopedia.* New York: Robert Appleton, 1907–12.

Huerga, Alvaro. *Vida y obras.* Vol. 1. *Obras completas de Bartolomé de las Casas.* Madrid: Alianza, 1988.

Ife, B. W. "Alexander in the New World: Fictional Archetype and Narrative History." *Renaissance and Modern Studies* 30 (1986): 35–44.

———. *Reading and Fiction in Golden-Age Spain: A Platonist Critique and Some Picaresque Replies.* Cambridge: Cambridge University Press, 1985.

Iglesia, Ramón. "Las críticas de Bernal Díaz del Castillo a la 'Historia de la conquista de México de Francisco López de Gómara.'" *Revista Tiempo* 10 (1940): 23–38.

———. *Cronistas e historiadores de la Conquista de México: El ciclo de Hernán Cortés.* Mexico City: El Colegio de México, 1942.

———. "Introducción al Estudio de Bernal Díaz del Castillo y de su verdadera historia." *Filosofía y Letras* (Mexico) 1 (1941): 127–40.

Jager, Eric. *The Tempter's Voice: Language and the Fall in Medieval Literature.* Ithaca: Cornell University Press, 1993.

Josefus, Flavius. *Antiquities of the Jews.* In *The Works of Flavius Josephus.* Vol. 1. Translated by William Whiston. London: G. Bell, 1811.

Kayser, Wolfgang. "Origen y crisis de la novela moderna." Translated by A. Fuentes Rojo. *Cultura universitaria* (Caracas) 47 (1955): 23–38.

Keen, Benjamin. *Essays in the Intellectual History of Colonial Latin America.* Boulder: Westview Press, 1998.

———. "Introduction: Approaches to Las Casas, 1535–1970." In *Bartolomé de Las Casas in History: Toward an Understanding of the Man and His Work,* edited by Juan Friede and Benjamin Keen, 3–63. DeKalb: Northern Illinois University Press, 1971.

Knight, Franklin W. "On the Poetry of History." *Colonial Latin American Review* 13, no. 2 (December 2004): 283–87.

Kohut, Karl. "Fernández de Oviedo, historiador y literato: Humanismo, cristianismo e hidalguía." In *Historia y ficción: crónicas de América,* edited by Ysla Campbell. Mexico City: Universidad Autónoma de Ciudad Juárez, 1992.

———. "Retórica, poesía y historiografía en Juan Luis Vives, Sebastián Fox Morcillo y Antonio Lull." *Revista de Literatura* (1990): 345–74.

Koselleck, Reinhart. *Futures Past: On the Semantics of Historical Time.* Translated by Keith Tribe. Cambridge: MIT Press, 1985.

Kristeller, Paul Oskar. *Renaissance Thought: The Classic, Scholastic, and Humanist Strains.* New York: Harper and Row, 1961.

Las Casas, Bartolomé de. *Apologética historia sumaria.* 2 vols. Edited by Edmundo O'Gorman. Mexico City: Universidad Nacional Autónoma de México, 1967.

———. *Brevísima relación de la destrucción de las Indias.* Edited by André Saint-Lu. Madrid: Cátedra, 1991.

———. *De unico vocationis modo.* Spanish and Latin. In *Obras completas,* edited by Paulino Castañeda Delgado and Antonio García del Moral, O.P. Vol. 2. Madrid: Alianza, 1990.

———. *Historia de las Indias.* Edited with prologue, notes, and chronology by André Saint-Lu. 3 vols. Caracas: Ayacucho, 1986.

———. *Historia de las Indias.* Edited by A. Millares Carlo with a preliminary study by Lewis Hanke. Mexico City: Fondo de Cultura Económica, 1951.

———. *History of the Indies.* Translated by Andrée Collard. New York: Harper &; Row, 1971.

———. *Obras completas.* Edited by P. Castañeda Delgado. Madrid: Alianza, 1998.

———. *Obras escogidas de Fray Bartolomé de las Casas: Historia de las Indias.* Edited with a critical study by Juan Pérez de Tudela Bueso. Boletín de Autores Españoles, 95–96. Madrid: Atlas, 1957.

Lausberg, Heinrich. *Handbook of Literary Rhetoric: A Foundation for Literary Study.* Translated by M. T. Bliss et al. Leiden: Brill, 1998.

Lejeune, Philippe. *On Autobiography.* Translated by Katherine M. Leary. Minneapolis: University of Minnesota Press, 1989.

Leonard, Irving. *The Books of the Brave: Being an Account of Books and of Men in the Spanish Conquest and Settlement of the Sixteenth-Century New World*. With an introduction by Rolena Adorno. Berkeley: University of California Press, 1992.

Lerner, Isaías. "La visión humanística de América: Gonzalo Fernández de Oviedo." In *Las Indias (América) en al literatura de siglo de oro*. Proceedings of the International Conference, Pamplona, January 15–18, 1992. Kassel: Reichenberger, 1992.

Lévi-Strauss, Claude. *Tristes Tropiques*. Translated by John Weightman and Doreen Weightman. London: J. Cape, 1973.

Lewis, Robert E. "The Humanist Historiography of Francisco López de Gómara (1511–1559)." Ph.D. diss., University of Texas, Austin, 1983.

———. "Retórica y verdad: Los cargos de Bernal Díaz a López de Gómara." In *De la crónica a la nueva narrativa mexicana*, edited by Merlin H. Forster and Julio Ortega, 37–47. Oaxaca: Oasis, 1986.

Livy. *The Early History of Rome*. Translated by Aubrey de Sélincourt with an introduction by R. M. Ogilvie. Harmondsworth: Penguin, 1971.

Loesberg, Jonathan. "Narratives of Authority: Cortés, Gómara, Díaz." *Prose Studies* 6, no. 3 (1983): 239–63.

López de Gómara, Francisco. *Historia de la conquista de México*. Caracas: Ayacucho, 1979.

Lorenz, Chris. "Historical Knowlege and Historical Reality: A Plea for 'Internal Realism.'" In *History and Theory: Contemporary Readings,* edited by Brian Fay, Philip Pomper, and Richard T. Vann, 342–76. Oxford: Blackwell, 1998.

Losada, Ángel. *Fray Bartolomé de las Casas a la luz de la moderna crítica histórica*. Madrid: Tecnos, 1970.

———. "Introducción." In *Demócrates segundo: De las justas causas de la guerra*, by Juan Ginés de Sepúlveda. Madrid: Consejo Superior de Investigaciones Científicas, 1951.

Mackenthun, Gesa. *Metaphors of Dispossession: American Beginnings and the Translation of Empire, 1492–1637*. Norman: University of Oklahoma Press, 1997.

Marcus, Raymond. "La conquête de Cholula: Conflit d'interprétations," *Ibero-Amerikanisches Archiv N.F.* 3, no. 2 (1977): 193–213.

———. "Las Casas: A Selective Bibliography." In *Bartolomé de Las Casas in History: Toward an Understanding of the Man and His Work,* edited by Juan Friede and Benjamin Keen, 603–16. DeKalb: Northern Illinois University Press, 1971.

———. "Las Casas in Literature." In *Bartolomé de Las Casas in History: Toward an Understanding of the Man and His Work,* edited by Juan Friede and Benjamin Keen, 581–600. DeKalb: Northern Illinois University Press, 1971.

Markus, R. A. *Saeculum: History and Society in the Theology of St. Augustine*. Rev. ed. Cambridge: Cambridge University Press, 1970.

Martí, Antonio. *La preceptiva retórica española en el siglo de oro*. Madrid: Gredos, 1972.

Martínez Bonati, Félix. *La ficción narrativa (su lógica y ontología)*. Murcia: Universidad de Murcia, 1992.

———. *Fictive Discourse and the Structures of Literature: A Phenomenological Approach*. Translated by Philip W. Silver with the author's collaboration. Ithaca: Cornell University Press, 1981. Originally published as *La estructura de la obra literaria*. Barcelona: Seix Barral, 1960.

Martyr d'Anghera, Peter. *De orbe novo: The Eight Decades of Peter Martyr D'Anghera.* Translated and with an introduction and notes by Francis Augustus MacNutt. 1912. 2 vols. Reprint, New York: Burt Franklin, 1970.

Mazzarino, Santos. *The End of the Ancient World.* Translated by G. Holmes. New York: Knopf, 1966.

Menéndez y Pelayo, Marcelino. *Historia de las ideas estéticas en España.* Vol 1. Madrid: Tello, 1909.

———. *Orígenes de la novela.* In *Obras completas.* Vol. 13. Madrid: Consejo Superior de Investigaciones Científicas, 1943–62.

Menéndez Pidal, Ramón. *El padre Las Casas: Su doble personalidad.* Madrid: Espasa-Calpe, 1963.

Merrim, Stephanie. "The Apprehension of the New in Nature and Culture: Fernández de Oviedo's *Sumario.*" In *1492–1992 Re/discovering Colonial Writing,* edited by R. Jara and N. Spadaccini. Minneapolis: Prisma Institute, 1989.

———. "Ariadne's Thread: Auto-bio-graphy, History, and Cortés' *Segunda Carta-Relación.*" *Dispositio* 11, nos. 28–29 (1986): 57–83.

———. "The Castle of Discourse: Fernández de Oviedo's *Don Claribalte* (1519)." *MLN* 97, no. 2 (1982): 329–46.

———. "The Counter-Discourse of Bartolomé de Las Casas." In *Early Images of the Americas: Transfer and Invention,* edited by J. M. Williams and R. E. Lewis, 149–62. Tucson: University of Arizona Press, 1993.

———. "The First Fifty Years of Hispanic New World Historiography: The Caribbean, Mexico, and Central America." In *Cambridge History of Latin American Literature,* edited by Roberto González Echevarría and Enrique Pupo-Walker. Vol. 1, 58–100. Cambridge: Cambridge University Press, 1996.

———. "'Un mare magno e oculto': Anatomy of Fernández de Oviedo's *Historia general y natural de las Indias.*" *Revista de Estudios Hispánicos* (Río Piedras) 11 (1984): 101–19.

Mignolo, Walter. "Cartas, crónicas y relaciones del descubrimiento y la conquista." In *Historia de la literatura hispanoamericana.* Edited by Luis Iñigo Madrigal. Vol. 1. *Época colonial,* 57–116. Madrid: Cátedra, 1982.

———. *Local Histories/Global Designs: Coloniality, Subaltern Knowledges, and Border Thinking.* Princeton: Princeton University Press, 2000.

———. "El metatexto historiográfico y la historiografía indiana." *MLN* 96, no. 2 (1981): 358–402.

Momigliano, Arnaldo. *The Classical Foundations of Modern Historiography.* Berkeley: University of California Press, 1990.

Montero Díaz, Santiago. "La doctrina de la historia en los tratadistas del siglo de oro." In *De la historia, para entenderla y escribirla,* by Cabrera de Córdoba, edited by Santiago Montero Díaz. Madrid: Instituto de Estudios Políticos, 1948.

Myers, Kathleen A. "History, Truth and Dialogue: Fernández de Oviedo's *Historia General y Natural de las Indias* (Bk. XXXIII, ch. LIV)." *Hispania* 73, no. 3 (1990): 616–25.

———. "Imitación, revisión y amazonas en la *Historia general y natural* de Oviedo." *Revista iberoamericana* 61, nos. 170–71 (1995): 161–73.

———. "The Representation of New World Phenomena: Visual Epistemology and Gonzalo Fernández de Oviedo's Illustrations." In *Early Images of the Americas:*

Transfer and Invention, edited by J. M. Williams and R. E. Lewis, 183–213. Tucson: University of Arizona Press, 1993.

Nebrija, Antonio de. "Prólogo." In *Gramática de la lengua castellana*, edited by Antonio Quilis. Madrid: Editora Nacional, 1980.

Nelson, William. *Fact or Fiction: The Dilemma of the Renaissance Storyteller*. Cambridge: Harvard University Press, 1973.

Newsom, Robert. *A Likely Story: Probability and Play in Fiction*. New Brunswick: Rutgers University Press, 1988.

Niccoli, Ottavia. *Prophecy and People in Renaissance Italy*. Translated by Lydia G. Cochrane. Princeton: Princeton University Press, 1990.

Noreña, Carlos. *Juan Luis Vives and the Emotions*. Carbondale: Southern Illinois University Press, 1989.

———. *A Vives Bibliography*. Lewiston, N.Y.: Edwin Mellen Press, 1990.

O'Gorman, Edmundo. *Cuatro historiadores de Indias*. 2nd ed. Mexico: Editorial Patria, 1989.

———. *The Invention of America*. Bloomington: Indiana University Press, 1961.

———. "Prólogo." In *Sucesos y diálogo de la Nueva España*, by Gonzalo Fernández de Oviedo y Valdés. Edited by Edmundo O'Gorman. Mexico City: Universidad Nacional Autónoma de México, 1946.

Ortega y Gasset, José. "Esquema de las crisis." In *En torno a Galileo*. Madrid: Alianza, 1982.

Otte, Enrique. "Aspiraciones y actividades heterogéneas de Gonzalo Fernández de Oviedo y Valdés, cronista." *Revista de Indias* 18, no. 71 (1958): 9–62.

Pagden, Anthony. *La caída del hombre: El indio americano y los orígenes de la etnología comparativa*. Translated by B. Urrutia Domínguez. Madrid: Alianza, 1988.

———. *European Encounters with the New World*. New Haven: Yale University Press, 1993.

Parish, Helen Rand, and Harold S. Weidman. "The Correct Birthdate of Bartolomé de las Casas." *The Hispanic American Historical Review* 56, no. 3 (1976): 385–403.

Partner, Nancy. "Hayden White: The Form of the Content." *History and Theory* 37, no. 2 (May 1998): 162–72.

Pastor, Beatriz. *The Armature of Conquest: Spanish Accounts of the Discovery of America*. Translated by Lydia L. Hunt. Stanford: Stanford University Press, 1992.

———. *El jardín y el peregrino: El pensamiento utópico en América Latina (1492–1695)*. Mexico City: Universidad Nacional Autónoma de México, 1999.

Pellicer, Rosa, "La organización narrativa de la *Historia verdadera de Bernal Díaz del Castillo*." *Mester* 18, no. 2 (1989): 83–93.

Peña y Cámara, José de la. "Contribuciones documentales y críticas para una biografía de Gonzalo Fernández de Oviedo." *Revista de Indias* 17, nos. 69–70 (1957): 603–705.

Pérez Fernández, Isacio. "Estudio preliminar y análisis crítico." In *Historia de las Indias*, by Bartolomé de Las Casas. 3 vols. Madrid: Alianza, 1994.

Pérez de Guzmán, Fernán. *Generaciones y semblanzas*. Edited by Robert Tate. London: Tamesis, 1965.

Pérez de Tudela Bueso, Juan. "Significado histórico de la vida y escritos del padre Las Casas." Preliminary study in *Obras escogidas de Bartolomé de las Casas: I. Historia de las Indias,* edited by Juan Pérez de Tudela Bueso. Biblioteca de Autores Españoles. Vol. 95. Madrid: Atlas, 1957.

———. "Vida y escritos de Gonzalo Fernández de Oviedo." Preliminary study in *Historia general y natural de las Indias,* by Gonzalo Fernández de Oviedo. Edited by Juan Pérez de Tudela Bueso. Biblioteca de Autores Españoles. Vol. 117, vii–clxxv. Madrid: Atlas, 1959.

Plato. *Republic.* Translated by P. Shorey. In *The Collected Dialogues of Plato.* Edited by E. Hamilton and H. Cairns. Princeton: Princeton University Press, 1963.

Pomata, Gianna, and Nancy G. Siraisi, eds. *Historia: Empiricism and Erudition in Early Modern Europe.* Cambridge: MIT Press, 2005.

Porqueras-Mayo, Alberto. *El prólogo como género literario en el siglo de oro español.* Madrid: Consejo Superior de Investigaciones Científicas, 1957.

Porras Barrenechea, Raúl. "Los cronistas de la Conquista: Molina, Oviedo, Gómara, y Las Casas." *Revista de la Universidad Católica del Perú* 9 (1941): 235–52.

Press, Gerald A. *The Development of the Idea of History in Antiquity.* Montreal: McGill-Queen's University Press, 1982.

Pupo-Walker, Enrique. "Creatividad y paradojas formales en las crónicas mexicanas de los siglos XVI y XVII." In *De la crónica a la nueva narrativa mexicana,* edited by M. H. Forster and Julio Ortega, 29–36. Oaxaca: Oasis, 1986.

———. *La vocación literaria del pensamiento histórico en América: Desarrollo de la prosa de ficción.* Madrid: Gredos, 1982.

Quintilian. *Institutio oratoria.* Translated by H. E. Butler. Vol. 4. Loeb Classical Library. Cambridge: Harvard University Press, 1922.

Rabasa, José. "Historiografía colonial y la episteme occidental moderna. Una aproximación a la etnografía franciscana, Oviedo y Las Casas." In *Historia y ficción: Crónicas de América,* edited by Ysla Campbell. Mexico: Universidad Autónoma de Ciudad Juárez, 1992.

———. *Inventing America: Spanish Historiography and the Formation of Eurocentrism.* Norman: University of Oklahoma Press, 1993.

Rebhorn, Wayne. *The Emperor of Men's Minds: Literature and the Renaissance Discourse of Rhetoric.* Ithaca: Cornell University Press, 1995.

Rhúa, Pedro de. "Cartas del Bachiller Pedro de Rhua." In *Epistolario español.* 1540. Edited by E. de Ochoa. Biblioteca de Autores Españoles. Vol. 13, 229–50. Madrid: Atlas, 1850.

Rigney, Ann. *The Rhetoric of Historical Representation: Three Narrative Histories of the French Revolution.* Cambridge: Cambridge University Press, 1990.

———. "Semantic Slides: History and the Concept of Fiction." In *History-Making: The Intellectual and Social Formation of a Discipline.* Proceedings of an International Conference, Uppsala, September 1994. Edited by Rolf Torstendahl and Irmline Veit-Brause, 31–46. Stockholm: Kungl. Vitterhets Historie och Antikvitets Akademien, 1996.

———. "The Untenanted Places of the Past: Thomas Carlyle and the Varieties of Historical Ignorance." *History and Theory* 35, no. 3 (Oct. 1996): 338–57.

Riley, E. C. *Cervantes' Theory of the Novel.* Delaware: Juan de la Cuesta, 1992.

Rodríguez Prampolini, Ida. *Amadises de América: La hazaña de América como empresa caballeresca.* Mexico: Junta Mexicana de Investigaciones Históricas, 1948.

Rodríguez-Vecchini, Hugo. "Don Quijote y la *Florida* del Inca." *Revista iberoamericana* 48, nos. 120–21 (1982): 587–620.

Rojas, Mario."Tipología del discurso del personaje en el texto narrativo." *Dispositio* 5–6, nos. 15–16 (1980):19–55.

Rose de Fuggle, Sonia. "'Era el gran Montezuma . . .': el retrato en la *Historia verdadera* de Bernal Díaz del Castillo." In *Cultures et sociétés, Andes et Mesoamérique: mélanges en hommage a Pierre Duviols.* Aix-en-Provence: Université de Provence, 1991.

———. "El narrador fidedigno: Problemas de autoacreditación en la obra de Bernal Díaz del Castillo." *Literatura mexicana* 1, no. 2 (1990): 327–48.

Rubluo, Luis. "Estética de la *Historia verdadera* de Bernal Díaz del Castillo." *Cuadernos americanos* 28, no. 166 (1969): 179–200.

Russell, Jeffrey Burton Russell. *Witchcraft in the Middle Ages.* Ithaca: Cornell University Press, 1972.

Sáenz de Santa María, Carmelo. *Introducción crítica a la "Historia verdadera" de Bernal Díaz del Castillo.* Madrid: Consejo Superior de Investigaciones Científicas, 1967.

———. "Primera sección: manuscritos y ediciones" and "Suplemento" to *Historia verdadera de la conquista de la Nueva España,* by Bernal Díaz del Castillo. Madrid: Consejo Superior de Investigaciones Científicas, 1982.

Saint-Lu, André. "Fray Bartolomé de las Casas." In *Historia de la literatura hispanoamericana.* Vol 1. *Epoca colonial,* edited by Luis Iñigo Madrigal, 117–25. Madrid: Catedra, 1982.

———. "Prólogo." In *Historia de las Indias,* by Bartolomé de las Casas, edited by André Saint-Lu. Caracas: Ayacucho, 1986.

Salas, Alberto M. *Tres cronistas de Indias: Pedro Mártir de Anglería, Gonzalo Fernández de Oviedo, Fray Bartolomé de las Casas.* 2nd ed. Mexico: Fondo de Cultura Económica, 1986.

Sánchez Alonso, Benito. *Historia de la historiografía española.* 2nd ed. Vol. 1. Madrid: Consejo Superior de Investigaciones Científicas, 1947.

San José, Jerónimo de. *Genio de la historia.* 1651. Edited by Higinio de Santa Teresa. Reprint, Pamplona: Editorial Gómez, 1957.

Schevill, Rodolfo. "La novela histórica, las crónicas de Indias y los libros de caballerías." *Revista de Indias* (Bogotá) 19 (1943): 173–96.

Sepúlveda, Juan Ginés de. *Demócrates segundo: De las justas causas de la guerra.* Translated with an introduction and notes by A. Losada. Madrid: Consejo Superior de Investigaciones Científicas, 1951.

Silva Tena, María Teresa. "Las Casas, biógrafo de sí mismo." *Historia mexicana* 4, no. 4 (1955): 523–43.

Smalley, Beryl. *Historians in the Middle Ages.* New York: Scribners, 1974.

Smoller, Laura Ackerman. *History, Prophecy and the Stars: The Christian Astrology of Pierre D'Ailly, 1350–1420.* Princeton: Princeton University Press, 1994.

Solís, Antonio de. *Historia de la conquista de México.* 2 vols. Buenos Aires: Emecé Editores, 1944.

Southern, R. W. "Aspects of the European Tradition of Historical Writing: 1. The Classical Tradition from Einhard to Geoffrey of Monmouth." *Transactions of the Royal Historical Society,* 5th ser., 20 (1970): 173–96.

————. "Aspects of the European Tradition of Historical Writing: 2. Hugh of St Victor and the Idea of Historical Development." *Transactions of the Royal Historical Society,* 5th ser., 21 (1971): 159–79.

————. "Aspects of the European Tradition of Historical Writing: 3. History as Prophecy." *Transactions of the Royal Historical Society,* 5th ser., 22 (1972): 159–80.

Struever, Nancy. *The Language of History in the Renaissance: Rhetorical and Historical Consciousness in Florentine Humanism.* Princeton: Princeton University Press, 1970.

Styers, Randall. *Making Magic: Religion, Magic, and Science in the Modern World.* Oxford: Oxford University Press, 2004.

Tanner, Marie. *The Last Descendant of Aeneas.* New Haven: Yale University Press, 1993.

Tate, Robert B. *Ensayos sobre la historiografía peninsular del siglo XV.* Madrid: Gredos, 1970.

Thomas, Henry. *Spanish and Portuguese Romances of Chivalry.* 1920. Reprint, New York: Kraus Reprints, 1969.

Thucydides. *The History of the Peloponnesian War.* Translated by Rex Warner with an introduction and notes by M. I. Finley. London: Penguin, 1972.

Toffanin, Giusseppe. *A History of Humanism.* New York: Las Americas, 1954.

Traister, Barbara Howard. *Heavenly Necromancers: The Magician in English Renaissance Drama.* Columbia: University of Missouri Press, 1984.

Turner, Daymond. *Gonzalo Fernández de Oviedo y Valdés: An Annotated Bibliography.* University of North Carolina Studies in the Romance Languages and Literatures. Chapel Hill: University of North Carolina Press, 1966.

Uría Ríu, Juan. "Nuevos datos y consideraciones sobre el linage asturiano del historiador de las Indias Gonzalo Fernández de Oviedo." *Revista de Indias* 20, nos. 81–82 (1960): 13–29.

Usón Sesé, Mariano. "El concepto de la historia en Luis Vives." *Universidad: Revista de cultura y vida universitaria* (Zaragoza) 3 (1925): 501–35.

Vann, Richard T. "The Reception of Hayden White." *History and Theory* 37, no. 2 (May 1998): 143–61.

Varela, Consuelo. "Introducción." In *Textos y documentos completos* de Cristóbal Colón, edited by Consuelo Varela. 2nd ed. Madrid: Alianza, 1989.

Vásquez Tapia, Josefina Zoraida. "El indio americano y su circunstancia en la obra de Fernández de Oviedo." *Revista de Indias* 17 (1957): 483–519.

Vidal-Naquet, Pierre. "Atlantis and the Nations." *Critical Inquiry* 18 (Winter 1992). Reprinted in *Questions of Evidence: Proof, Practice and Persuasion across the Disciplines,* edited by J. Chandler et al., 325–51. Chicago: University of Chicago Press, 1994.

Vives, Juan Luis. *Arte retórica (De ratione dicendi).* Translated by Ana Isabel Camacho. Barcelona: Anthropos, 1998.

————. *De disciplinis.* In *Opera omnia,* edited by G. Mayans. Vol. 6, 5–437. 1782–86. Reprint, London: Gregg Press, 1964.

————. *De ratione dicendi.* In *Opera omnia,* edited by G. Mayans. Vol. 2, 93–237. 1782–86. Reprint, London: Gregg Press, 1964.

————. *Institutio feminae christianae.* English and Latin. Introduction, critical edition, translation, and notes by C. Fantazzi. 2 vols. Leiden: Brill, 1987.

———. *On Education.* Translated by Foster Watson. Totowa, N.J.: Rowman & Little-field, 1971.

———. *Opera omnia.* 8 vols. Edited by G. Mayans. Valencia, 1782–86. Reprint, London: Gregg Press, 1964.

Wagner, Henry R. "Bernal Díaz del Castillo." *Hispanic American Historical Review* 25, no. 2 (May 1945): 155–90.

———. "The Family of Bernal Díaz del Castillo." *Hispanic American Historical Review* 25, no. 2 (May 1945): 191–98.

———. "Notes on Writings by and about Bernal Díaz del Castillo." *The Hispanic American Historical Review* 25, no. 2 (May 1945): 199–211.

Wardropper, Bruce W. "*Don Quixote:* Story or History?" *Modern Philology* 63, no. 1 (1965): 1–11.

Weinberg, Bernard. *A History of Literary Criticism in the Italian Renaissance.* 2 vols. Chicago: University of Chicago Press, 1961.

Weinrich, Harald. *Estructura y función de los tiempos en el lenguaje.* Translated by Federico Latorre. Madrid: Gredos, 1968.

White, Hayden. *The Content of the Form: Narrative Discourse and Historical Representation.* Baltimore: Johns Hopkins University Press.

———. *Figural Realism: Studies in the Mimesis Effect.* Baltimore: Johns Hopkins University Press, 1999.

———. *The Tropics of Discourse: Essays in Cultural Criticism.* 1978. Reprint, Baltimore: Johns Hopkins University Press, 1987.

Wolfson, Nessa. "Tense-Switching in Narrative." *Language and Style* 14, no. 3 (1981): 226–31.

Yacobi, Tamar. "Fictional Reliability as a Communicative Problem." *Poetics Today* 2, no. 2 (1981): 113–26.

Yates, Frances. *The Art of Memory.* London: Routledge, 1966.

Zagorin, Perez. "Historiography and Postmodernism: Reconsiderations." In *History and Theory: Contemporary Readings,* edited by Brian Fay, Philip Pomper, and Richard T. Vann, 193–205. Oxford: Blackwell, 1998.

———. *Ways of Lying: Dissimulation, Persecution, and Conformity in Early Modern Europe.* Cambridge: Harvard University Press, 1990.

Zamora, Margarita. "Historicity and Literariness: Problems in the Literary Criticism of Spanish American Colonial Texts." *MLN* 102, no. 2 (1987): 334–46.

———. "Language and Authority in the *Comentarios reales.*" *Modern Language Quarterly* 43, no. 3 (1982): 228–41.

———. *Reading Columbus.* Berkeley: University of California Press, 1993.

———. "Transatlantic Humanism and the Rise of the Spanish American Intellectual: The Case of Las Casas." Paper presented at the Sixteenth Annual Medieval, Renaissance, and Baroque Interdisciplinary Symposium, Miami, February 22–24, 2007.

INDEX